JUSTICE

NOMOS
VI

NOMOS VI

JUSTICE

CARL J. FRIEDRICH and
JOHN W. CHAPMAN, Editors

LIEBER-ATHERTON

New York 1974

NOMOS VI: JUSTICE

Carl J. Friedrich and John W. Chapman, editors

Atherton Press, New York, New York

Address all inquiries to:
Lieber-Atherton, Incorporated
1841 Broadway
New York, New York 10023

Library of Congress Catalog Number 63-19057
ISBN 0-88311-030-X

First Reissue. 1974

Manufactured in the United States of America

CONTENTS

CONTRIBUTORS

HUGO A. BEDAU
Philosophy, Reed College

ARNOLD BRECHT
Political Science, New School for Social Research

JOHN W. CHAPMAN
Political Science, University of Pittsburgh

RICHARD H. COX
Political Science, University of Buffalo

JOEL FEINBERG
Philosophy, Princeton University

CHARLES FRIED
Law, Harvard University

CARL J. FRIEDRICH
Political Science, Harvard University

DAVID GRANFIELD
Philosophy, Catholic University

IREDELL JENKINS
Philosophy, University of Alabama

FRANK H. KNIGHT
Economics, The University of Chicago

RICHARD McKEON
Philosophy, The University of Chicago

CLARENCE MORRIS
Law, University of Pennsylvania

RAYMOND POLIN
Philosophy, The Sorbonne

JOHN RAWLS
Philosophy, Massachusetts Institute of Technology

ROBERT C. TUCKER
Political Science, Princeton University

1

ON THE MEANING OF JUSTICE

FRANK H. KNIGHT

The most important statement to be made about the concept of justice is that its meaning has been radically expanded and transformed by the advent of modern liberal, politically equalitarian democracy. As the word shows, justice is a legal term (*jus* meaning "law"), and the various meanings or kinds of law are the subject of this discussion. In primitive and preliberal societies, broadly speaking, justice was defined and constituted by laws which were "given" and held to be unchanging and unchangeable. In consequence, they were known "naturally" by all normal adults, who learned them as they learned the language of the community. Accordingly, laws were "moral" as well as "jural"; there was practically no distinction between the two ideas. Thus they presented no *problems*—an intellectual concept—but only imposed the *duty* to conform to them. And when, through moral failure, a law was violated (accidents and natural causality were, in general, not recognized), there followed the task of administering punishment, the nature and procedures of which were prescribed, with designation of the human agents of performance, by the given law. Since in our medieval background institutions and ideas were essentially primitive, the scholastic writers were in accord with the facts at the time in holding the notion of an unjust law to be self-contradictory. Under these conditions, the laws were "static," being sacred, which in turn was because they had supposedly originated in commandments from supernatural powers, and a deity does not change his mind.[1]

Since the birth of liberal democracy, justice has remained a legal concept, but the laws to which this attribute is ascribed have been divided into moral and jural, and those of the latter class have come to be "made" to an important extent by each political society for itself, not merely found and recognized for enforcement—let alone believed to have been supernaturally revealed through some prophet. Jural laws are made and enforced by the state, a quite modern development, especially as to lawmaking; enforcement as a political function is older, but still not primeval. Thus democracy has assumed the task, enormously more difficult than enforcing a law known to all, of deciding what the law ought to be and making any changes called for. This is more difficult because it involves an intellectual problem. At the same time, the enforcement of existing laws that constantly change—that is, are changed by public action—has also become enormously more diffi-

[1] This is notably so in the Judaeo-Christian tradition, under God as the supernatural lawgiver (cf. Matt. 1:17 and James 1:17). As regards the "positive" law, this view differed from that of the classical Greek philosophers, who distinguished between just or right by nature (*physis*) and by convention (*nomos,* custom). In the later Middle Ages the conception of the law as "divine" was somewhat modified by calling it "natural," but this still meant absolute, and the view is still upheld as basic moral law, chiefly under religious auspices. It is hardly ever applied to the positive law, at least apart from the (moral) obligation of law-abidance or in comparing an actual law with a supposedly better one. Although it is doubtless "natural" for a community to have some law, the only specific measures more natural than others are those actually in force. In Greece (and Rome) there was, of course, some provision for change in the laws—the social order was partly secular. But in the Dark Ages, after the fourth-century conversion to Christianity (so-called—a mystery cult by then under a hierarchical-authoritarian priesthood), Western Europe in particular reverted to extreme primitivism in this regard as in other aspects of culture. Gibbon called the change the triumph of barbarism and religion.

cult. Enforcement is no longer separable from legislation; as done by human beings, application always involves some interpretation, which introduces change, though gradual and even unnoticed. Justice, then, has come to refer to the justice *of* the law itself, not merely to what the existing laws prescribe, while what the law *is* has become a problem with no definite answer. Yet that problem is much simpler than that of justice as the "best" law, the ideals with which actual law is to be brought into closer conformity by legislative action. And at the same time these ideals are constantly changing.

As a result, the concept of justice now covers social idealism in all aspects and all versions and so cannot be defined in positive and specific terms. For, quite certainly, men will never establish a formula describing an ideal society which could serve as the ultimate goal of institutional change. The real task faced is that of social progress, definable only as a *direction* of change (in a complex sense, mostly negative) through alleviating some of the grosser *in*justices that a society can agree upon and find remediable. In short, there is now no such thing as justice "in general"; one can meaningfully discuss only fairly concrete injustices and procedures for their mitigation with existing social machinery or the possible ways of improving the over-all social organization. That means the government, here assumed to be "democratic," as the agency by which a society acts as a unit in making and enforcing laws. The matter of governmental quality is hardly separable from that of the people as members of the society.

The crucial problem is agreement on a social order or a body of law incorporating common ideals and beliefs. The distinctive meaning of democracy is *free* association; but *order* is of the essence of a society and hence a strict necessity. Freedom itself, the primary commitment is, to some extent, a comparative luxury, as are other human values, even if, like justice, they are also necessities in some form and degree. Since man is willy-nilly a social animal, but one endowed with a mind, desires, and opinions, free association implies conscious agreement on and assent to a pattern of relations, a body of rules. Insofar as harmony of attitudes is not reached freely—which means through the intellectual process of discussion—laws must be forcibly imposed, or the society will cease to exist. Laws are always compulsory to some extent because of the unpleasant but unquestionable fact that, with human nature as it is, interests conflict and opinions differ beyond compatibility with the order required and in the face of much spontaneous harmony. Social action must be "intelligent," i.e., correct within limits; it is always affected by *error,* various in kind and amount, and also—actually to a greater extent—by *prejudice* or sheer arbitrariness. But without a minimum of intelligent direction, it is better not to act and to let events take their "natural" course; for, as things are, in nature and human nature, random action is nearly certain to have "bad" results, on the balance. "Intelligent" means based on "knowledge" (warranted belief) and action on "false knowledge" is worse than acting at random. Since action looks to the future, either to bring about or to prevent some change, knowledge must cover both ends and means. And our concern here is with social action, so that intelligence pertains to the group as a unit, achieved by its members' agreement on ends and means.[2]

Besides the knowledge factor, choice presupposes motives, which are feelings, and also a "will." This last is a mysterious capacity to *decide,* to stop thinking as well as to direct it to some extent, and to control feeling. Its reality is directly known as something more than the domination of a stronger motive over a weaker or some composition of forces, as in mechanics. Analysis of conduct treats motives as forces, but should recognize that this view is not exhaustive. Since chance is recognized as a reality in physics, rigorous causality does not apply even there, and force is clearly a metaphysical concept.

A common and more serious confusion is to define freedom to

[2] No philosophic treatment of knowledge and freedom is called for here, but a few points seem worth noting. Action implies choice, which is always free, among the alternatives open and known to the actor. It is illogical to use the word "action," as is commonly done, to refer to inert natural processes. Discussion is not concerned with "metaphysical" freedom, a pseudo-problem. In that meaning, freedom is implied or exemplified in saying anything, doing anything, or thinking when thinking is more than passive awareness (if the last mentioned occurs). Machines do not discuss, argue, or fight. Human freedom is the opposite of coercion, not of determinism, which is denied in asserting freedom. Coercion means the manipulation of one person's alternatives by another free agent; the reasons or results may be good or bad, but machines do not coerce and are not coerced. (This position needs one major qualification for the role of *persuasion* or purely personal influence apart from intellectual or material considerations; this will be considered later.)

include *power*—the ability to do whatever one wishes. Without power to act, freedom is indeed empty, but power and freedom are different dimensions of voluntary action and give rise to very different practical problems, one positive, the other preventive. Freedom itself is negative; one has freedom *from* coercion by others, *to* do what one wishes, and otherwise *can*.

. . . .

Democracy in its modern liberal form, with its new meaning of justice, is a late product of history. (So is human nature as it is known to men; Ortega y Gasset has remarked, paraphrasing Wilhelm Dilthey, "Man has no nature; what he has is—history"—a literary exaggeration, but an important truth.) In consequence, the understanding of a free society and its problems must be approached in historical terms, as well as analytically and functionally. And one must recognize that history has followed evolution, physical and biological, and that the whole sequence has been marked by occasional emergences of new types of reality. The new has mostly been superimposed on what preceded, building a more and more "pluralistic universe" and in particular a highly and irreducibly pluralistic humanity. Democracy has appeared in human social life, which is in turn (presumably) based on animal society of some kind, and so on back through nonsocial but conscious animal life, whose origin may never be explained. Modern democracy is primarily and specifically distinguished from the Greek city-state form that gave rise to the word by the inclusiveness of its citizenship. This now takes in all normal adults in a political unit defined by residence in a given territory. (Resident aliens and citizens dwelling abroad may be ignored.) The essential feature is that the group acts as a unit, facing problems and dealing with them more or less intelligently, i.e., "correctly," through agreement, direct or indirect, on a constitution and laws. The ideal is unanimous agreement, reached by discussion with equal participation.[3] In a broad view, the laws constitute the all-inclusive social problem, the problem of knowledge.

---

[3] Practically speaking, and ultimately, all correctness or objectivity rests on a consensus in a particular community which is marked by a more or less distinctive culture. Thus truth and all values, including justice—in fact, all concepts—are relative to any given society, i.e., one with a locus in space and time, and this would include subcommunity within some larger unit. There is no absolute knowledge, no one answer to any real question. The existence

The nature of earlier (preliberal) societies was very different, though "perfect" democracy is unattainable. Democracy in our meaning came into the world through a "liberal revolution" which, allowing for slow and spasmodic advance toward freedom through the ages, occurred quite recently and suddenly, in historical terms. And its serious problems are largely due to this recency and suddenness and to the sweeping character of the transformation, which amounted to a virtual *Umwertung aller Werte* (inversion of values) from the ideals and convictions previously accepted as beyond question. This means specifically in Western Europe, but it goes back to "primitive" society. (To the principle of the fixity of institutions, the Greek democracies and Rome were exceptional only within limits, chiefly with respect to constitutional changes—largely violent.) Moreover, cogent, if subconscious, reasoning supports the attitude of abhorrence of change. For institutional change, without serious disorder, is hard at best and is possible only within narrow limits. It involves changing habitual ways of thinking and acting, and man is largely a creature of habit. Order is presupposed in the very concept of free (intelligent) association, since to act intelligently one must first know, roughly, what others will do if one does not act and in consequence of any contemplated action. And in human society the major features of the social order must be consciously accepted by the bulk of the members.[4] Freedom is possible only if men at large develop competence to adapt to and make changes

of a real social or group problem or of genuine group action presupposes democratic organization, as just defined.

[4] The qualifications of "rough" prediction and "major" feature of the social order are dictated not only by human mental limitations, but also by practical and ethical principles. Accuracy is impossible, since individuals cannot act on the basis of predicting what others will do; such action will falsify many, at least, of the predictions. Thus, a consensus is indispensable. And, an agreed upon pattern of relations cannot be precise in detail. Thus Kant's "sole" categorical imperative—"Act only on that maxim whereby thou canst . . . will that it should become a universal law"—cannot be followed if strictly interpreted, for it would mean first willing away all effective freedom, use of judgment, and spontaneity. Incidentally, willing any rigorous law for all human beings would reflect boundless conceit and arrogance. Rigorous law would also violate Kant's other formula, that every human being be always treated as an end, never as a means only. The universal moral law must be that everyone shall follow his own judgment—judgment, of course, based on critical reflection, not mere impulse or sentiment. And no injunction can apply to young children or to adults incapable of making responsible decisions.

in established patterns of social conduct without too much disorganization. Change must be orderly to a requisite degree, hence must be made within a framework of existing law; this carries back to laws that were not made but "just grew" and finally to law not felt as imperative but followed automatically. In fact, men do not "voluntarily" agree to the requisite extent, either on continuing without change or on particular changes, and hence human society must always (at least, since the species became human) have somehow provided for "enforcing" the laws. (Again, within limits; rigorous enforcement would exclude all change as well as all freedom.)

Democracy, however, is founded on the principle that a society may change—change itself—"at will." The liberal revolution even made "progress" a duty, in a sense, since freedom must mean freedom to change, and the use of intelligence dictates that every change shall be for the better. The basic ideal is freedom-for-progress and progress-through-freedom. However, the human mind evolved through the ages under very different conditions in response to other needs and learns slowly to adapt to those produced by such a revolutionary change. A conflict arises between the old norm of order and the new ideal of freedom, although order is still a necessity in some form and to a high degree. In making liberty its main commitment, liberalism seriously limits the degree of order that is possible or desired, and—human nature being what it is—the requirement of order sets limits to freedom.[5] Conflicts between values, especially (but not only) freedom and order, set the problem of democratic justice. The citizenry must agree—freely, intelligently—on many compromises, if the democratic ideal is to be realized. The ultimate ideal would be anarchy; unanimous agreement on the laws and the will to obey them would exclude all need for law backed by force. But there is no hope of reaching this state of affairs with real people in the real world. Political reality, present or in prospect, is far from achieving even literal majority decision on specific issues;

[5] This use of words must now be taken largely in reference to the past. Within less than a generation, the import of the term "liberal" has been inverted; from implying freedom, it has come to mean its opposite, state paternalism—though under democratic forms in the sense of ultimate rule by majorities. How far that means freedom or is compatible with it would call for much discussion.

the closest approximation that seems theoretically possible—majority rule—can be highly despotic and unjust. Serious issues are rarely settled by anything like intelligent discussion alone. Much coercion or pressure of various forms is exercised, and no little violence—fighting or police action; between the major political units, or even within a unit, war is commonly a danger and often breaks out. Justice in the abstract can only refer to a "better" social order in nations and the world and is best designated as "social justice," defined, as indicated, in connection with particular issues.

. . . .

Some more specific limitations on the possiblity of justice as freedom with order and progress and other imperative values may now be noted. Perhaps the most sweeping one is that mentioned in the footnote on Kant's categorical imperative: freedom has no meaning of any kind for infants, and it has content for others only insofar as they command the means of acting and wish to act. But the helpless or weak have rights which a social order must protect, by force where necessary, against violation by individuals. In relations among responsible persons, it is not (as often suggested) a limitation on social freedom, but an obvious requirement, that each shall scrupulously respect the freedom of others. However, individual unwillingness to do this may call for much social use of force to preserve mutual freedom.

In practice, serious limitations arise from the fact that a group generally can act only through individual agents. (A very small group may conceivably be an exception.) Large groups typically act through complex series of smaller groups, each under some form of leadership. Group discussion of action deals with deciding what general type of action is desirable as far as being objective, choosing agents, and fixing the main features of procedure. (In place of "discussion," a more descriptive term would usually be "argument," the competitive effort to persuade.) Group action consists mostly of making and enforcing laws, in which all details are delegated to individuals. Thus arise, of course, the three familiar branches of government—the legislature, executive, and judiciary; the personnel are chosen by "politics" and act more or less in accord with public opinion.

Social problems also arise because under modern conditions

even individuals must often act by delegating to agents both the execution of decisions and, in greater or lesser degree, the deciding itself. This cannot be done very intelligently or at all precisely; it involves selecting the agent for both special competence and for trustworthiness. But the arrangement is dictated by the specialization of knowledge and skill—all because of human limitations. Apart from safeguarding against fraud on the part of agents, a task delegated can be only vaguely specified and adherence to it vaguely controlled. An agent has more or less latitude, hence arbitrary power, and must be widely trusted. An example of a relatively unorganized relation is that of a patient and his doctor. Here the agent has power of life or death, and expert advice is needed to tell the principal whether he needs the advice. For intelligent action, the patient would have to know medical science himself, thus canceling most of the need and, in addition, to know, on terms within his means, the technical and moral qualifications of the available candidates. Much, if not most, of the freedom possible in modern society is that of choosing agents to be one's "boss" within some range. When a *group* acts by delegating power, as in economics and especially in politics (where supreme control lies), further complications arise, admitting only vague analysis. In economic relations, where the bulk of the serious problems lie, the worker or property-owner must either choose whose orders he will obey or himself start an enterprise if he has "what it takes" in resources and personal qualities (as the patient may doctor himself if he thinks that the best course). In most organized relations—for cultural or religious ends or for play, as well as "production"—leadership with *power* is required, severely limiting the individual's effective freedom to order his own life and the extent to which ideal justice can be achieved. This is more the case where the problem is agreement in a group of considerable size, especially beyond the range of direct acquaintance. The extreme case is politics, to which people resort, however rationally, to secure justice in small-scale relations.

Under "primitive" and, in general, preliberal conditions, when the laws were static because sacred (not "made"), the enforcing functionaries acted ostensibly as direct agents not of the society but of the supernatural powers who were supposed to have chosen them and ordained the laws; the human authorities "obeyed

God." Somewhat strangely, these functionaries have generally comprised two kinds, distinguishable as priestly and political. Both had sanctity, but the latter, although ruling by divine right, were less narrowly bound by sacred patterns. In part, it was their arbitrary power that was sacred once they were established in power, even by violence or trickery; but the scope of their power was limited by tradition supported by religion, and gross abuse might cause its loss through insurrection. In early society, real "dynamic" leadership prevailed chiefly in activities not fully reducible to routine, such as war and the hunt, especially for large game. There some advance planning is necessary, with improvising of organization and prompt meeting of unforeseen situations. Throughout history, the two institutional systems—church and state in some form—have functioned in uneasy partnership, their relations varying from near (perhaps complete) identity to antagonism and even violent conflict.

. . . .

From a glance at history, one knows that the "original" nature of human society will surely never be known, i.e., exactly what happened in the transition from the instinctive automatism of animal behavior to law felt, in part, as imperative. It is a question whether the sense of "ought" or "must" was first attached to conforming to law ("obeying" it, we illogically say) or to literally obeying commands of leaders, thus recognizing that they also had "authority." (In etymology, *jus* is closely akin to *jubere,* "to command.") The two views combine insofar as law was held to be commandment. The question, then, is how far "acculturation" took the form of mechanistic suggestion and imitation or the form of a power relation—or respect or love between parents and offspring or between the dominant male "head" and a large family or harem. An impersonal compulsion still felt is the anomalous "work" attitude—aversion to useful as well as imposed conduct or that of ends over instrumental activity. The crux of the transition to man surely lay in the replacement of instinct by "culture," i.e., of gene inheritance of behavior patterns by social inheritance through imitation of their elders by the young of the next generation. The instincts were attenuated into vague drives, getting specific form from culture. This can be conceived as purely automatic conditioning, but apparently men developed from beings already having a well-developed mental life and doubtless already socialized on the principle of order-of-dominance.[6]

Culture also functioned in a largely automatic way, but never entirely so (as instinct does not, rigorously). Two mysteries are, first, the vast divergence and erratic character of culture, which can hardly be called evolution, in contrast with the convergence of biological evolution, which produced a practically uniform human species; second, and crucial for culture itself, is the appearance of speech, seemingly as a part of it. This doubtless grew "somehow" out of animal cries, explicable in terms of biological function. Laughing and weeping, also uniquely human, may have formed an intermediate stage or stages. These suggest that speech itself functioned from the first more in the emotional field than in that of instrumental intelligence, especially as promoting biological values. Speech doubtless always served as a medium for transmitting culture, whatever the "utility" of the latter. It could enable vastly more rapid adaptive change than the slow process of chance gene mutation and natural selection, but it mediated the development of a strikingly new mentality, differing from that of earlier animals more on the emotional side than on that of intelligence, and human emotions often oppose biological ends.

The relation of a culture to the people bearing it is much like the relation of a plant species to the soil in which it grows, following its special laws and undergoing mutations. Culture changes are, of course, limited by viability, but the constraint is surprisingly tolerant. Human motives more or less prefer "quality" of life to quantity, especially numerical increase, and the qualities they strive for are a tissue of paradox. Humanization was marked by a vast increase in "intelligence," but the superiority is only in part instrumental to ends outside the mental life itself, let alone biological ends and is largely used to invent new

---

[6] In some animals, a kind of "teaching" of the young appears, notably in birds. This is interesting because the bird class is a side branch of the evolutionary sequence leading to the mammals and man. Birds also show other distinctive resemblances to man, notably imitation of speech, which a man's closer kindred do not do though they have the same vocal apparatus and that of birds is very different. Similar remarks apply to sex and family relations.

ends and pursue them, circumventing original human nature with its biologically useful drives. With advancing civilization, the functional relation between the mental and the bodily life is progressively inverted; the bodily is treated as a means to "experience," which is weirdly diverse in nature.

Language itself is the purest example of culture or custom, particularly in its independence of intentional control. Individuals act in their use of it more or less purposively and intelligently in terms of their interests, and their conduct results in cultural change; but such change is usually slow, unintended, even contrary to their wishes. The genesis of a change may be some virtually random act, which happens to have some appeal and be imitated, starting a new fashion—from a passing fad to a relatively enduring change in custom or mores—possibly to be later embodied in the jural or punitively enforced law. Or, there may be a deliberate leader, who builds up a following because of personal charisma or on more or less rational grounds. Quite certainly, neither law nor leadership was first established through intelligent group discussion (*pace* the social contract). And though democracy has been well defined as "government by discussion," the role of discussion is limited and subtle beyond clear analysis. (The limitations of natural selection need no further emphasis.) The ideal of justice as direction of historical change by intelligent discussion, finding good and effective means to good ends, has operated within very narrow limits; the laws must express mass attitudes, and men in general are averse to such activity. Capricious and dogmatic, they learn to appeal to force of some kind to secure agreement and cooperation, which at least subconsciously they recognize as important; but they tend to mean that "others" should agree and cooperate with "me." Thus, innate contentiousness and the urge to use power possessed to secure more power become further major obstacles to the intelligent quest for ideal justice. One of the most—perhaps *the* most—important form of power is that of *persuasion,* mentioned earlier. Persuasion is commonly treated as the opposite of coercion, but is clearly a form or method of the latter, and ethically not a notably high form since it is rooted in deception. (Like other forms of coercion, it may be good or bad by intention and in consequences, but history copiously illustrates the principle that power corrupts.) Confounding persuasion with convincing or informing underlies this fallacy.

A final limitation on defining the concept of justice for a free society demands notice. It lies in the lack of the knowledge required for agreement on valid means and ends. The ends present by far the greater difficulty. ("Means" is commonly used for procedure, ways of using means in the literal sense, and for democratic action only procedure is practically in question; the means are the people themselves, or their capacities, including external "property" under individual control.) What a free society does is to make and enforce laws, prescribing ends and procedures for the conduct of its members in their relations with one another. This, to repeat, is done chiefly by selecting and commissioning agents for the concrete performance. Law*making* was the great innovation of the liberal revolution, following the birth of modern science. But legislating intelligently calls for thinking of a type categorically different from that required for science. Scientific thinking functions instrumentally as the basis of technology, the use of concrete means to produce a concrete result, by an individual or a group already agreed on the constitution and law by which it acts as a unit. The social end includes "efficiency," but the harder part is the matter of ideals, or values. These serve as a basis for comparative appraisal of material ends, where agreement is felt to be necessary, but more especially in regulating social relations and developing human character. The task is not instrumental, but *critical,* and resists analysis in detail. Values are commonly classified under three heads—the good, the beautiful, and the true. This division is unsatisfactory, even illogical, since the kinds are far from homogeneous and a definition of any one will cover much of both the others.

On this tripartite division, a few observations may be allowed, with no pretense of philosophic treatment. All knowledge is of "truth," but truth is very different in kind and source depending on the subject matter, on what it is "about." The most solid knowledge men possess is science, dealing as it does with empirical, sense-observed facts and relations. Each one's knowledge of his own mental content we pass over, merely observing that it is not empirical in the meaning stated. More important and more subtle, is knowledge of other people's minds; this comes from two sources: interpretation of empirically observed behavior and communication, chiefly through speech. Both are uncertain, and the two often disagree. The latter is more important, though sometimes "actions speak louder than words." Valid empirical knowledge also depends on communication for its verification, and the corpus of human knowledge has been built through history as an element in each culture and world culture. Increasingly in modern times, individuals have come to make distinctive contributions. Communication of sense observations and formal inferences is much more reliable than that of other matters and reveals a common object-basis, the "external world." Ends as mental content consist of desires and values, which are also desired but have an additional quality of objectivity. Both have universal features, but vary widely in detail. Everyone cherishes goodness, beauty, and truth, but examples differ and conflict. Liberal society assumes that there need not be close agreement on aesthetic taste; by definition, there must be on truth, and social order requires some consensus on moral values, hence reconciliation of conflicting desires. Truth about nature—scientific facts and laws—is desired for its own sake and as an instrument in guiding conduct; it is a value, a factor in the "good life," as is truth about aesthetics and moral norms. These species of truth overlap widely, often indistinguishably, as exemplified by the concepts of good manners and decency. Aesthetic values are peculiar in not depending on supernatural sanctions, as have morals and truth—but prior to science, truth was a moral category, unbelief or doubt a sin. The sanctity of custom has been largely destroyed by the advent of science and social freedom, both of which imply change. Taste—the taste that *is* discussed, not that described in the proverb to the contrary—is the broadest of the categories, extending to all areas of judgment. To work together, people must have a general knowledge of others' tastes, but the free-market economic order makes it unnecessary for them to agree in order to multiply efficiency through specialization and cooperation (except on laws, of course, which are needed to protect or limit freedom). Such further analysis as can be given here is best approached through a survey of the chief meanings and kinds of law.

. . . .

The concept of law has two main divisions, the descriptive and the imperative. Both have already been tacitly considered; in the realm of nature only descriptive laws apply, but both kinds are relevant to mental life and conduct, although the notion of justice pertains only to imperatives. The class of imperatives must again be divided into two main subclasses, and one of these further subdivided, yielding concepts that form a serial order. At one extreme are the jural laws, which are rather definitely formulated for enforcement by inflicting penalties for violation. All other imperatives form the moral class, meaning that they are upheld by moral forces in contrast to material penalties. A wide range of species is included without clear dividing lines. Moral laws in a narrow sense differ negatively from the jural, which also state duties, in being enjoined only by conscience and sanctioned by the feeling of guilt. This separates them also from numerous proprieties supported rather by embarrassment, though this grades into shame, guilt, and remorse. Examples are "correct" speech, dress, etiquette. As noted, these hover between esthetic and moral norms, decency falling into the latter realm and even into that of jural law. All the types or grades are also upheld from outside the individual by various attitudes of other persons variously expressed (i.e., social forces). Especially noteworthy are ridicule, scolding, and even expression of sympathy. Moral laws, including the jural as an upper stratum, are (or were) sanctioned in the literal sense by religion, and faith, which took the place of knowledge, was a duty, heresy being a capital crime. In extreme cases, informal sanctions are overeffective, causing dread of digression and mortification at making a slip or *faux-pas.* Humor is a paradoxical value, being usually more-or-less cruel or obscene or both; "dirty" words are a curious case, as there are "clean" words with identical meanings.

The words justice and injustice are regularly used only in certain cases of social approval or condemnation, but *may* be employed for nearly any. Mere fashion may exert as strong a compulsion as objectively serious matters, and fashion affects virtually all areas of human concern, from science and religion down to passing fads in speech or dress: language itself is only an extreme case. Fashion combines the opposite cravings to be like others and to be different, to follow and to lead; people dislike too close or too widespread copying. There is commonly no discoverable reason for changes, notably in language, the primary social institution; they embody no biological advantage—change itself is rather bad—and reflect no human purpose to effect them. As noted, the term "evolution" hardly applies, and "progress" not at all. In many fields, agreement is necessary—first of all, logically speaking, on the boundary of the area. How this is achieved is usually a mystery; rational discussion rarely plays an important role. Agreement is typically more important than the specific practice established. In such a case as driving on the right or left, agreement is all that matters, and this is almost true of language. But stable patterns are necessary because, to repeat, intelligent conduct requires knowledge of what others will do. Where preferences or opinions clash, where there is no appeal to sense observation and rules of logic, and where experiment is precluded, it is notoriously difficult to discuss or find premises on which to base argument. Knowledge of values is a totally different problem from natural science, in which phenomena can be definitely classified and measured or at least form such classes that "laws of chance" can be applied.

In the sciences of nonhuman nature, communication simultaneously establishes the objectivity of the subject matter and its own validity. Knowledge takes the form of descriptive laws, the other main type, and these are interpreted in terms of such forces as causality. In the human realm, behavior is conduct and expresses motives of two forms—wishes and value judgments. Here communication gives direct information, which differs from the implications of sense-observed behavior and proves that neither source of information can be relied on as completely accurate. The difficulty stems from the fact that men are only in part mechanisms that react automatically; in addition, they have active interests as well as awareness of the world, each other, and themselves. They differ categorically even from the highest nonhuman animals, which clearly "know" in some sense or "feel" what to do and in general do what is good for them without asking and answering questions or thinking, which depends on culture and symbolic communication. In acquiring culture (i.e., replacing instinct) and developing their minds, men have lost this natural knowledge. They confront manifold uncertainty and, more strangely, have come to believe much that they really know is false and absurd, often prompting destructive action. In their mental life, men are romantic and sentimental; truth is not a predominant interest; many kinds of fiction, poetry, and humor are more interesting than facts; and the appeal of truth itself depends little on its utility, especially in the biological meaning of the term.[7]

We now turn to brief consideration of the descriptive laws. They are not called just or unjust, but must be noticed because not far back in time they run together with the imperative type.

---

[7] Truth is akin to justice, and the word is a reminder that the semantics of our subject is a topic of interest and of some importance for history and understanding. The original meaning of "truth" was fidelity," not "verity" (cf. German *Treue*), and belief is cognate with "love," "leave," etc. The import of all such concepts was emotional, not cognitive (as laughing and weeping are probably older than language). The languages of today hardly have words for "positive" facts and causes except as such meanings have been superposed —mostly in recent time—on earlier ones reflecting the anthropomorphic or animistic and moralistic world view of "primitive" men. "Fact" means a deed. Here we do have two words, but ambiguity is more common, because we speak of a "true" friend as well as a "true" statement. More confusion results from the vagueness of the terms "cause," "because," and "why." We use "reason" for a natural cause, "end" for purpose, and "action" for inert process. And examples could be multiplied. We dislike to admit ignorance of what we perceive and what we interpret into the primary data; modern science affords grounds better than Plato and the idealists dreamed of for viewing mental phenomena as more real than physical. The mind-body relation doubtless has no intelligible explanation.

Many vagaries affect the words "justice," "law," and their kin. In different degrees and in different contexts, "just" and "legal" are either synonymous or contrasting, and "just" has a wide variety of meanings often equivalent to both senses of "true." "Fair" takes its place in connection with sports and games, both for accordance with rules and for appraising them, but it is a value judgment resisting definition. The English word "law," though phonetically similar to the Latin *lex* (referring to a particular law), is unrelated to it; *lex* comes from *legere,* "to read," and "law" is akin to "lay" and "lie," with the idea of fixity (a clearer notion in the German *Gesetz*).

The much discussed word "right" is by etymology a legal term meaning "regular" and carrying either moral or legal import. The corresponding French *droit* and German *Recht* are more ambiguous. The relation of "right" to *rex,* a (personal) ruler, brings up that between law as custom, a fashion with authority, and law as command. Justice may mean "desert," often deserved recompense, imputed without reference to a corresponding obligation. The world does not owe anyone anything, and the idea of what society owes merely raises the whole problem of justice and law. (Punitive justice is a very different, hardly related, problem.) Hume and Mill reduced justice to utility. In *On Liberty,* Mill gives five meanings of injustice; the list contains confusions, but not ones to be criticized here.

What had been done in the past was the original content of what should or must be done now. The first felt imperative was undoubtedly to follow the beaten path and not to wander from or interfere with the regular course of activity. Human limitations and subservience to habit assure that what is must always be the main content of what ought to be—despite all discontent and complaining. In the beginning (of humanity) this compulsion doubtless developed as our ancestors awoke to the awareness that such patterns as descriptive laws did exist, but they "could" break them. And various reasons for doing so no doubt appeared about as early.[8] But "follow nature" is still preached as a rule of conduct —one rather typical for lack of meaning. The strong tendency for freedom to cause divergence and disorganization (assuming human nature somewhat as we know it) could have led natural selection to produce the mentality that made established custom imperative, sacred, and unalterable. But most historical "why's" are answered only by hypotheses that raise equally insoluble problems.[9]

. . . .

---

[8] Among such motives were, no doubt, an innate desire for novelty especially *rivalry,* inherited in germ from animal ancestors but checked in them by serial dominance. Later rationalization has ennobled the love of freedom—in fact, largely the craving for power—and greatly reduced the roles of tradition and authoritative leadership. The sense of obligation may have arisen in the conflict of fight-versus-flight, the latter "selfish" impulse opposed by a "duty" to defend the young, the herd, the domicile, or the territory. Courage is suggested by the etymology of the word "virtue," but this also suggests moral control over sex relations, which must have developed as instinct and the order-of-dominance system ceased to afford sufficient control.

[9] The argument about natural science as mechanistic and the inapplicability of critical judgments (approval–disapproval versus liking–disliking) in relation to it needs qualification for the position of at least the higher animals. Their mentality is shown in many ways, in particular as they become companions and friends, virtually adopted members of families, or antagonists of man. And civilized law allows them rights and gives them protection. Their role as beasts of burden is ambiguous, and their role as material for scientific investigation arouses qualms.

People not only like and dislike things, esthetically, but regularly *personify* natural objects, even abstractions and "the universe," and they impute praise or blame, entreat and curse. All this is doubtless a survival of primitive anthropomorphism, for which it is no compensation to reduce man himself to physical terms. Man is above all the talking animal, and it may be noted that most formally declarative statements are figurative in some way and degree.

Not much need be said about descriptive laws, after noting the complex and paradoxical relation between this class and that of the imperative, in relation to human nature and conduct. The relation is one of categorical difference in principle but wide overlap in concrete experience, making it impossible to draw a sharp distinction. To the modern scientifically sophisticated mind, explanation or understanding of phenomena tends to mean finding and applying laws in the sense of "uniformities of coexistence and sequence," in the positivistic or Comptean phrase. In preliberal thought, the opposite was the case; explanation ran in terms of motives; the English word "why" was originally an instrumental case of the relative pronoun, and this clearly survives in the French *pourquoi,* the German *Warum,* and in other modern languages. Molière ridiculed scientific explanation by having his doctor explain that opium induces sleep because it possesses a dormitive virtue. That is all that science ever does, though our usage would replace "virtue" with "quality" or "nature." Only this kind of explanation makes sense in connection with inert natural phenomena, where we do not impute purpose.[10]

In human phenomena it is impossible to deny that "behavior" is in part explained by conscious motives, making it "conduct," but also largely conforming to descriptive "positive" laws, both at the physical and mental levels, thought and feeling, and even value judgments. But there is a residue of choice which involves

[10] Just where the line between purposive and nonpurposive phenomena is to be drawn is a disputed point, particularly with respect to life phenomena. We do seem involuntarily to impute purpose here, even where we do not impute consciousness. Mechanists in biology and philosophy use such purposive concepts as function, adaptation, and struggle for existence, when they are not trying to prove a contrary theory. And idealists find purpose in the cosmic process as a whole. The difficulty here is that nature's "purposes," seem to be "cross purposes," notably in biology. A crucial case is the spider's web—highly purposive from the standpoint of the spider, the opposite from that of the fly. And the most striking examples of apparently ingenious adaptation are found in parasitic and predatory species.

It seems worth noting that no "explanation" can be given for consciousness, either in terms of physics and chemistry or of biological function. We cannot deny that it is functional, in the animals that manifest it as well as in ourselves, but no one can say how or why. This fact has led some thinkers, principally the behaviorists, to deny its existence even in man, even in themselves, in the face of the fact that the denial itself is a consciously purposive act. Of course, language allows such self-contradictions to be asserted in grammatical sentences.

"will." People do have some degree of real *freedom*—implying complete unpredictability—which is practically obvious and universally recognized. The scientist in particular, although seeking explanation in terms of positive laws and tending to carry this into human phenomena, cannot scientifically explain his own distinctive activity. To do that would be on a par with—or go beyond—lifting oneself by one's own bootstraps; it would involve saying that one is not saying anything or thinking that one does not think, the ultimate in self-contradiction.

It now seems strange that historically it took human minds—the "best" minds—so long to distinguish at all explicitly between the two classes of laws. They were completely confused in much eighteenth-century philosophizing. Now, of course, the contrast between what is and what ought to be is much stressed; in fact, too much to the neglect or blurring of the distinction between what is wished for and what ought to be, the connection in which problems of conduct and social relations arise. But the difference between desiring and objectively valuing is vague. Values have a degree and kind of objectivity, or factuality, finally akin to that of perceived objects, which must be recognized if human society and human life are to exist, though its basis is very different. But only through common recognition of common and paramount values can the conflicting desires of different persons be reconciled, and peace and order maintained. And, on the other side, the ideal of personal freedom gives some quality of "rightness" to individual desires. This is limited first by the duty of everyone to respect in others the freedom that he claims for himself and much further by social values that are not reducible to individual desires and which often conflict with these and are judged more important.

The distinctive trait that man vaunts in himself is superior intelligence. (He calls his species Homo sapiens, man the wise, or knowing and understanding.) But the vogue of science has led to taking a fatally narrow view of intelligence, restricting it to the role of enabling people to satisfy their wants indiscriminately, disregarding the major issue of the reasonableness or legitimacy and compatibility of the wants themselves. The original nature of intelligence may have been biologically functional, the promotion of survival and increase. It *may* have been; we do not and cannot know, and there are grounds for believing that it has always served other ends and operated in ways that do not fit the instrumentalist theory at all. In any case, the role of the *scientific* intelligence is instrumental to the discovery of descriptive laws, which enable the human being to act intelligently in the sense of predicting the consequences of acts and so directing conduct to an intended result. It does not tell whether any such result is good or bad; it reveals alternatives but does not compare them for desirability. That must be done by a different kind of intelligence, the critical faculty, and choice itself falls to a still different capacity, the will. (It is also true, as noted before, that scientific knowledge is both desired for its own sake and recognized as an objective value.)

It may be noted that descriptive laws take two forms and predict in different ways. (The close relation of the two need not be developed here.) The familiar scientific laws predict hypothetically: if *A* occurs or is observed, the occurrence or existence of *B* is indicated. Ideally, they state a quantitative functional relation between measured amounts of *A* and *B*. Based on uniformities of sequence or association observed in the past, they are extremely useful in enabling men to bring about or prevent future events in nature or to infer facts not momentarily observable. In human relations, common-sense knowledge of this form is useful within limits, but for reasons already given, that is not very far; efforts to improve on ordinary experience by systematic investigation have not achieved much success.[11]

The other subspecies is that of historical laws, which use, in addition, the different procedure of prediction by projecting a time-series of events which have exhibited a *trend* of change. The ideal historical science is found in the field of nature in astronomy, which predicts accurately what *will* happen, not merely conditional events. The method, extrapolation, is also employed in the laboratory sciences, in connection with temporal and other series, and that of uniformity of association is used in historical studies. Every science is in this way more or less different from others. Biological concepts and methods differ widely from those of

[11] This should have been foreseen. The idea that the procedure by which men predict and control inert nature, with which they have a one-sided relation of knowing and using, should also enable them to predict and control themselves and each other shows lack of insight or of will-to-truth, though it is widely preached.

2

JUSTICE: THE JUST POLITICAL ACT

CARL J. FRIEDRICH

What is justice? One of the perennial questions of political and legal philosophy, it has produced many a normative or stipulative reply. In this essay, an attempt is made to answer a more specific question: what aspect of political situations do men usually refer to when they say that the acts involved in it are just? [1] Before taking up this question, we shall briefly indicate which questions about justice we do not propose to take up and why. After delineating the answer to the selected question, we hope to show the ways in which it illuminates the problems of authority and legitimacy. Finally, we shall deal with the reasoning component and the link of the just to the true.

The famous triad *Honeste vivere, neminem laedere, suum*

[1] For an elaboration and the systematic context, see Carl J. Friedrich, *Man and His Government* (1963), especially chapters 12–16.

cuique tribuere is not only the broad formula of natural law on which the Corpus Juris Civilis is supposed to rest, but also the ground on which philosophers, notably Leibniz and Kant, have built their theories of justice. These propositions have been treated as intuitively known and universally accepted; their formulation is so general that it is as difficult to dispute such a claim as to prove it. Jurists, whether accepting or rejecting them, have tended to the view that it is difficult to specify definite legal norms as derived from these propositions. These are much discussed problems, but we shall not try to deal with them.

This approach undoubtedly expresses an elemental view of justice in general. But we are here not concerned with justice in general nor with what has been looked for as the essence of justice, but rather with the function of justice in the political community. What particular act or complex of acts and/or events, recurrent in all politics, what concrete political experience is meant when people speak of justice and injustice? This is the empirical question to which our analysis is addressed. It is not pretended that this question is the only one which might be raised with regard to justice, but that it is a possible one and an important one, at that.[2]

Nor do we propose to deal with the issues David Hume raised when he discussed justice in utilitarian terms. His views have recently had a resurgence in the writings of certain language philosophers.[3] Like Hume's, these treatments seem to be premised on the proposition (unproved) that "all virtuous actions derive

---

[2] Ch. Perelman, in *De la Justice* (1945), develops an interesting distinction between a just act and a just rule, the latter being said to be just when it is not arbitrary in the sense of being in keeping with a system of norms from which it derives. This distinction, whatever its value for other purposes, is not germane to our question, since, politically speaking, rule-making is a particular kind of political act; arbitrary acts, as well as arbitrary rules, are unjust.

[3] Notably J.D. Mabbott and John Rawls; see J.D. Mabbott, "Moral Rules," *Proc. of the British Academy,* 39 (1953); and J. Rawls, "Two Concepts of Rules," *Philosophical Review,* 64 (1956), 3ff. See also Hart (1962), and Nowell-Smith, *Ethics* (1954), pp. 263ff. and 271ff. See also the interesting summaries on "national" conceptions by Eugenio Garin, Luis Recasens Siches, Gregory Vlastos, Ch. Perelman, and W.G. Becker, in *Revue internationale de philosophie,* No. 41 (1957), with an introduction by Richard McKeon on "The Meanings of Justice and the Relations among Traditions of Thought," 253–257.

their merit only from virtuous motives" [4] and that, therefore, just actions can be just only as a result of "artifice" or conventions. "It (this convention) is only a general sense of common interests" related to the notion of mutuality which makes a man behave toward his neighbor as he wishes the neighbor to behave toward him, especially regarding property. Hume's ingenuous argument is necessitated by his dubious assumption—a secularized version of Christian ethics. For, although there can be no question that motivations play their role in ethics, and hence that particular acts may be considered just because "utility pleases," as Hume puts it, the justice of acts and rules is a less subjective datum. The question of whether the decision of a judge is just or unjust does not depend on whether he made it motivated by Hume's general sentiment *or,* rather, because he, being very ambitious, saw it as a chance to secure advancement *or* because, being of a particular religious persuasion, he entertained certain prejudices. The justice of his decision depends on its possessing a certain objective relation to the setting in which it occurs, presently to be more explicitly specified. At least, that is the political theorist's view of it, as he observes political behavior and seeks to generalize from it. Justice expresses a political relation of persons and things and as such has a function in political situations.

Of the three constituents of the triad, Roman law singled out the third for special emphasis; indeed, the *Corpus Juris* begins with identifying it with justice after explicating the *suum* as meaning *jus.* But it discusses justice as a quality of human beings, or rather of their will, and adds the specification that it must be a constant and perpetual will. In short, it refers to justice as a subjective quality. Again, we are not here concerned with such excellence, that is, with justice as a virtue, a commendable trait of human beings. It is well known that the great philosophers of classical antiquity, especially Plato and Aristotle, were very much preoccupied with this aspect of the matter, their core question being, "Who is a just man?" In terms of the present analysis, it is not difficult to answer this question once our primary question has been resolved; the just man is the man who behaves justly, who takes just action, who acts justly. Whether such behavior is, in turn, the result of a certain character, a disposition of the

[4] Hume *Treatise* 3.2.1.

"soul," as Plato was inclined to argue, is a question for the psychologist and perhaps the metaphysician, for it seeks to *explain why* people act justly, rather than to *describe what* it is that they do, when they are said to be so acting. It will be shown that there may also be strictly political explanations for a man's acting justly, but these explanations may be said to be extrinsic, as contrasted with the intrinsic explanations of psychology and metaphysics (as well as religion).

Since the ancients, it has been recognized that justice is closely related to goodness. Plato, in drawing his famous and questionable analogy between the individual human being and the political community, asserted that a just political community was one in which a lasting order prevailed. In such an order the wise ruled, the "spirited," or the energetic carried out the rulers' orders and defended the community, and the moderate attended to the various economic and related chores. The Good in the fullest sense was thus realized. Justice served goodness by ordering human relations in a stable hierarchy. This is not the place in which to restate once more Plato's doctrine of ideas which provides the rational (philosophical) underpinning for such an elitist structure. The Platonic position is cited because it contains a specific political doctrine of justice as the ideally right ordering of the political community. Even he who shares neither Plato's political outlook nor his metaphysical convictions can recognize that his view implies the proposition that justice has something to do with whether the actions of men in communities are in conformity with the values and beliefs shared by the members. But if justice were to be defined merely in terms of such conformity with communal values and beliefs, it would become indistinguishable from goodness. Some distinctive trait of the particular kind of goodness of actions which is justice must be identified (and, of course, has been identified). It is implicit in the Aristotelian doctrine which relates justice to equality.

We are now at the point where the basic position may be stated explicitly, for the doctrine relating justice to equality may be put more broadly by stressing the comparison involved in equality judgments. An action—and hence likewise a rule, a judgment, or a decision—may be said to be just when it involves a comparative evaluation of the persons affected by the action and when that comparison accords with the values and beliefs of the political community. This is the point of Aristotle's *isotes,* which is politically relevant and which can be summed up in the statement that equals should be treated equally. For the alleged equality can become a standard only when the values and beliefs relevant to a determination of equality are concretely stated. The recurrent political situation, which can be observed wherever human beings live in political communities, is that actions are praised when they appear to be based on a comparative evaluation of the several persons affected that is in keeping with the prevailing values and beliefs and that other actions are condemned when they do not appear so based.

Such a tie-in with prevalent values seems to be at variance with the notion of impartiality which is customarily associated with justice. The proverbial blindness of justice refers to this aspect of just acts and just rules—it is said not to differentiate among persons. Actually, as we have just seen, such differentiation is typically part of a just act. It is just *because* it differentiates. Aristotle's distinction between proportional and numerical equality was meant to cope with that difficulty, and we can say, with Orwell's big brother pig, "We are all equal, but some are more equal than others." The role of impartiality is analogous: only an impartiality molded and determined by the value preferences of the political community is considered truly impartial. To put it paradoxically, only a partiality to the prevalent values will appear truly impartial. To let women and children use the fire exit first appears just; the guard seeing to it appears impartial in insisting on such partiality. Such partiality appears just because it conforms to the values and beliefs prevalent in a given community. What the requirement of not being partial asks of the just act is that it should not *deviate,* by yielding to particular interest, from what the prevalent values and beliefs call for in comparative evaluation of persons and their situations. It is then a matter of disinterest rather than impartiality? No, for the same objections can be raised against disinterest. All that can really be derived from the general principle of comparative evaluation is the absence of arbitrariness, for arbitrariness is clearly incompatible with adherence to prevalent beliefs in making the evaluation. It has, therefore, always played a role in discussions on justice.

Related to this avoidance of the arbitrary is the avoidance of the impossible. The structure of the relation is somewhat different, however. An act that attempts the impossible when done by a person by himself may be considered stupid rather than unjust, or even noble under certain conditions. It becomes unjust if it were a demand, order, or other norm requiring those to whom it applies to do the impossible. *Ultra posse nemo obligatur* is an ancient rule expressing such inherent injustice. Again, we can say that it derives directly from the very nature of comparative evaluation in terms of prevalent values and beliefs. The difficulty with this derivative principle stems from the uncertainties surrounding what is impossible, especially in the political sphere. Patent impossibility is rarely involved in these situations, so that what seems unjust to one may seem quite just to another. It is existentially unjust only when the impossibility can be supported by reasoned elaboration in terms of the prevalent values and beliefs.

The avoidance of the arbitrary and the impossible reinforces the comparative evaluation: something is just when it is adequate. Discrimination and classification do not appear as deviations from a presupposed general equality, but as reasonable differentiations against which the proponent of equality has to argue. In modern philosophy, the problem has often been reversed, especially in America, because of the value claim of equality. It then becomes the task of political theorizing to explain such deviations. One might attempt to explain all such value-determined deviations from an absolute numerical equality of treatment by interpreting them as based on three grounds: agreement, special contribution, and special need. There can be no question that all three of these involve particular and communally determined value judgments, providing qualifications of one sort or another. It does not seem very satisfactory, however, from a political standpoint, to erect an unreal standard—absolute numerical equality—as the norm and then to treat all real situations involving justice as deviations from it. Actually, the three grounds identified here possess relevance even within our more general conceptual framework, for, from time to time, there may be deviations from the communally determined comparative evaluation of persons and situations. These are indeed based on one of the three grounds. But it is evident that each provides only a limited leeway, because agreements (contracts) become invalid if they deviate too markedly, special contributions will themselves be evaluated in terms of prevalent values and beliefs, and the same holds true of special needs. Thus the above-mentioned just action at a fire exit might be justly altered if an old man in a wheelchair appears (special need) or a fireman wants to pass (special contribution). The prevalent values cannot be avoided in determining what is just.

Before we enter a fuller exploration of the links between justice and other basic political phenomena, it seems desirable to reinforce the preceding analysis by considering injustice as a disvalue related to other disvalues and disbeliefs. It is a remarkable fact that men's feelings are more sharply aroused by an act of injustice than by one of justice. Whatever may be the psychological reasons for this fact—and they are many—the existential ground on which it rests is the threat to the beliefs and values cherished by a person and the consequent anxiety induced in him. An unjust act causes a man anguish because it not only challenges a particular belief and value, but, owing to the interrelation of such beliefs and values, it challenges the community as a system of shared values and beliefs. Conflicts over justice are embittered by explicitly experienced injustice. One claims that it is unjust to take his property, another that it is unjust that his children are not being properly educated; one argues the injustice of having to continue a marriage without love, another that it is unjust to leave children without a home. Such arguments can, with difficulty, be fitted into the generalizations in terms of justice; it is more evident that they involve comparisons. In any case, they show that justice relates actions to the entire value and belief system by insisting that they be based on valid comparisons of the persons involved and of their several competing value claims.

Such value claims and their comparisons are, both because of the *number* of values and beliefs and the degree of intensity with which they are felt, not absolutes, but they possess degrees of strength. Hence all analyses of just political acts proceed not in terms of a radical dichotomy of *either* just *or* unjust, but rather in terms of *more or less* just. It is the degree of relatedness to values which determines the relative justice of an act and, hence, also of a person as political actor. Such degrees of justness may be, though they usually will not be, quantifiable. Here is an important field for more detailed inquiry. Because of the built-in contradictions of value aggregates which exist in actual political communities and which defy systematic clarification, recurrent attempts have been made to relate justice to the inner convictions of individual persons, to that disposition of the soul mentioned at the outset, but by so doing, we remove the just from the political perspective. The most just act is the act which is compatible with the largest number of values and beliefs, allowance also being made for their intensity. Thus it would be more just to let the man in the wheelchair pass and less just (and in that sense, unjust) to allow some of the women and children nearest the exit to precede him. As a result, controversies about justice may frequently be reduced in sharpness and bitterness by seeing them as alternative ways of effecting a distinctive part of the value aggregate of the community.

The requirement of prevalence of the values and beliefs involved in the comparison raises the question of what such prevalence does, in fact, exist. That question calls for an exploration of authority and legitimacy. Justice, in the political perspective, is therefore inseparable from both authority and legitimacy. Conformity with values and beliefs prevailing in a political community raises issues which are beyond unequivocal demonstration; assertions concerning it will, therefore, turn on two questions: does the person who asserts such conformity speak with authority, and does he occupy the position or office which enables him to speak legitimately? Conversely, the authority of an actor, a rule-maker, or a ruler will contribute to the justice of the acts and rules. Authority is associated with communications having the potentiality for reasoned elaboration, and the bearers of such authority presumably possess the capacity to actualize this potentiality. One of the most important kinds of reasoned elaboration is that which elaborates in terms of the common values and beliefs shared by a political community. Since the comparative evaluation of persons affected by a given action—such as a rule or a decision to be made—turns on values, obviously it is held to be just when the judgments on which the evaluation is based are in accord with the value judgments of those who consider it just, and unjust when the opposite. The bald statement that political authority *is,* or *ought to be,* just power provides a shorthand expression for the fact that authority provides the bridge, that is, the link between power and justice. Actually, a given person may possess the capacity for reasoned elaboration in terms of one set of values, for example, Christian, and not in terms of another, for example, Masai. Therefore, Nteranke can say to his English lawyer friend that "he might have presented the case with more knowledge of what a Masai feels. 'Our language is very different. Our life is also completely different. A translation into English words is not enough. Our traditions, our feeling also must be translated. . . . Your law is not our law. . . . To us cattle are just as important as people. That is an absolute fact.' "[5]

The linking of authority with justice has been traditional in Catholic political thought. It is based, however, on the notion that only a particular kind of reasoning, namely that which is in accord with Christian theology, provides authority of a genuine kind. It involves a dramatic re-evaluation of the concept of justice, as found in Cicero and derived from Plato and Aristotle. This re-evaluation is explicitly set forth by Saint Augustine in those passages in which he disputes Cicero's conception of a republic as founded on justice. Recalling that justice means to give to everyone what is his (due), Augustine states that, since in the Roman Republic "demons," rather than the true God, were worshiped it is evident that God did not receive what was due him. Therefore, unless one were to refuse the name of republic to Rome, which seems inconvenient, it is better to reject the Ciceronian definition and to substitute another. The great bishop suggests that we might "say that a people is a gathering of reasonable beings bound together by common agreement as to the objects of their affection, and that a republic is composed of such a people." We have only to observe what a people cherish in order to discover its character and the kind of political order which suits it. In modern words, a political community rests on common values and beliefs. But there exists a true *civitas,* the city of God, in which justice in the full sense is realized, and its representative on this earth, the church, is the nearest approximation to it, whereas, *regna* and *respublicae,* kingdoms and republics, serve to maintain peace and

[5] Richard Llewellyn, *A Man in a Mirror* (1961), pp. 25–28.

order. The church makes use of this peace, whereas the heavenly city "calls citizens out of all nations, and gathers together a society of pilgrims of all languages, not scrupling about diversities of manners, laws and institutions whereby earthly peace is secured and maintained." But within this *civitas* authority is hierarchical, and that means justice is determined accordingly, in part directly by the priesthood, in part indirectly by secular powers. The overarching requirement of doctrinal authority calls for an evaluation of the activities of the latter by the former. This conclusion was not stated by Saint Augustine; it was, however, implicit in his outlook and, reinforced by Platonic notions, was further evolved in the course of the Middle Ages.

This view becomes generally valid if it is recognized that different beliefs may produce different authorities and that it is the function of authority to ensure that comparative evaluations of situations and persons are made by those possessing the capacity for reasoned evaluation, such as judges, teachers, and, more recently, experts and specialists. The appearance of the last mentioned has caused some very serious difficulties, as a number of trials and retrials have made evident. For, if, in criminal law, it is thought that an illness, especially a mental illness, constitutes a valid difference and may justify nonapplication of the law, then the determination of whether a given individual belongs to this special category of persons becomes of vital importance. The authority of a psychiatrist is obviously linked with his professional training and standing. Even if a court or jury, let alone the general public, can follow his views only in part, they will be accepted as authoritative because of his capacity for reasoned elaboration of the comparative evaluation he has offered.

Does such a position oblige us to accept value relativism and hence a relativistic conception of justice? By no means, for the values themselves do not lie beyond reasoning and reasoned elaboration, as is evident from the case of the medical expert. Actually, the argument over values is going on all over the world. Although the starting points may be as far apart as the Christian and the Masai, the search for justice will lead to an elaboration if the human beings cherishing these values are thrown into community. Indeed, it is the essence of politics, in a way, to argue about justice, that is, to argue about who may be compared with whom for what treatment. Modern parties are organizations fighting or arguing over justice. Justice is not static but highly dynamic, since it seeks to relate the evolving values of the community to what is done on its behalf, whether in rule-making, settling disputes, or any other activity. Even in those ages when men thought that the only task was to find the rules, they were actually fighting over them, as we can readily see in studying the legal controversies of the European Middle Ages. Justice is never given; it is always a task to be achieved. Its incomplete realization does not result from the complexity of the criteria, but from their fluidity. In fact, fluidity is not the right word either, for it is the steady evolution and devolution of values which cause the difficulty. Since this evolution occurs in time and the evaluation also takes time, the standpoint of the original evaluator and the subsequent one who claims that the original one was unjust may differ by the value differential that has occurred in the intervening period. Perfect justice could only be achieved in the completely stable community, as Plato fully realized. And since he did not wish to give up seeking perfect justice, he had to try to make the political community perfectly stable. In the process, the freedom of most of the community's members had to be surrendered, with the result that the values involved in the comparisons which rendered actions just turned into disvalues.

The Platonic dead end brings us back to the problem of legitimacy in its relation to justice. It has often been said that legitimate government is just government. Stated in such base form and viewed in the light of our conception of justice, this proposition is an overstatement. (It can, of course, be meant simply as a definition of justice, in which case it would mean that a just ruler is a legitimate one and a just man one who is legitimately doing whatever he is doing.) But it contains a kernel of truth. For if justice relates communal values and beliefs to actions by providing comparisons between persons and their situations thus enabling the actor to treat equals equally, then the extent of the success in so doing will help convince those affected by the action that the ruler or other actor is a rightful ruler or actor. In view of the very specific meaning which equality has acquired in modern political parlance, it is better to speak here not of equality, but of adequacy. When Aristotle, in his famous analysis of justice in terms of the mean (*mesótes*), undertook to show that justice is related to equality, he really had in mind the arguments of the various parties in the Greek city-states over what was adequate treatment in terms of believed-in values. The suggestion that a proportional equality must be admitted as an alternative to numerical equality was a skillful attempt at devaluing the argument in favor of equality in the modern sense of eliminating inequalities unrelated to or unsupported by the prevalent value judgments of the community. Proportional equality is inequality for which an argument, a reasoned elaboration, can be provided.

It is the value system in its positive content which typically establishes the adequacy of the comparison on which the inequality of treatment is based. If a man is punished justly, the comparison is not only or even primarily with other men likewise punished, though this is an important factor in the judgment. It is also usually a matter of "making the punishment fit the crime." This "fittingness" calls for comparison of the man before and after. Today, whipping a man publicly for stealing would seem unjust, even if it were done generally and to all thieves. It did not seem unjust to a community which valued property more and human life and dignity less.

This argument, insisting on adequacy and comparability of evaluations involved in decisions and actions, is peculiarly relevant in considering the relation between legitimacy and justice. All legitimacy being, as we said, a believed-in right to act or, more especially, to rule, it presupposes inequality (or proportional equality). It calls for a judgment which says such and such person possesses the unusual qualities required for ruling us. If he does not, his rule is illegitimate. Such a judgment may be based on several very different kinds of values: descent, merit and capacity, and election (the confidence of those ruled), the last being perhaps the most important. They can, as is well known, occur in combination: only a man of certain descent (American-born) and capacity (literate) who has been duly elected may thus be a legitimate ruler. Such a brief hint serves to bring out that legitimacy is a result of a communal judgment similar to that which the actor who acts justly makes: a comparative evaluation of a particular sort and thrust. Thus we conclude that legitimate government is not just government, but is government based on the just action of those who establish and maintain it.

At this point in our analysis, it becomes important to consider a position which Aristotle first developed when he distinguished between distributive (*dianemētikon*) and amending or corrective (*diorthōtikon*) justice. The distributive just "is concerned with the distribution of honor, wealth and such other goods as may be shared by members of the community," more especially, therefore, power and rule.[6] The peculiar field of such distributive justice is, therefore, public office. What distinguishes the democrat from the more or less aristocratic or plutocratic partisan is that he bases his political decisions, especially his decision as to who is entitled to rule, on the conviction that each man is equal to every other man in the ability to decide correctly who should rule him. He does not, except when he carries these views to their radical extreme, assert that all men are equally capable of ruling. In fact, he argues that the difference between men in this respect is so great that the selection of rulers cannot be left to such accidents as heredity or the acquisition of wealth involve.

The aristocratic notion of legitimacy is based on the belief that the capacity to rule is hereditary and on the disbelief in the capacity of most men to make a sensible choice between different candidates for public office. The same disbelief animates the plutocratic idea of legitimacy, but it argues positively that the acquisition and possession of wealth provide the basis for sound rulership. Omitting other types of legitimacy, we might say in sum that these three familiar types of legitimacy show how the idea of justice, of comparative evaluation for differential treatment, intrudes itself into the argument about legitimacy. It is a special sort of distributive justice; though rulership is a burden as well as a prize—let alone a reward—comparative evaluation is at work in determining the ground for legitimate rule.

Thus, a relation between legitimacy and justice is apparent: a

---

[6] *Nicomachean Ethics,* 1130bff. *Diorthōtikon* is incorrectly rendered as "commutative"—a term used by Thomas Aquinas. In the view here favored, rule is "stabilized and institutionalized power." Cf. Friedrich, *op. cit.,* Chapter 10.

just act is required to produce the legitimate ruler, whereas the legitimacy of the ruler helps render his actions just by providing them with an authority which bare or brute power does not possess. This important double link between legitimacy and justice and the parallel link between authority and justice are at the present manifested in the emergence of the new nations. The demand for an independent government or political order is based on the relation of justice, authority, and legitimacy. The colonial power lacked authority and legitimacy to an increasing extent as the values embodied in and expressed by its decisions and actions, which were not those of the subject peoples, were subjected to critical evaluation by them. Lacking such legitimacy and authority they are deemed unjust. The argument turns on the fact that a new community whose value judgments transcend those of the former rulers is emerging. But here it might be interjected that such rule was always unjust. To support that argument, recourse is usually made to belief in the equality of all men. It is patent that the men who set up colonial empires did not entertain such a belief, even though they may have professed the Christian faith. This faith is far from unequivocal on the matter of rule, and the equality which it insists on is that in the face of divinity, for "we are all miserable sinners." There exists another line of reasoning leading to the conclusion that such rule is always unjust. This argument depends on a nonrelativistic conception of justice that requires further exploration now in another direction.

Since all justice presupposes comparison and evaluation, it is intimately linked to reasoning, as our demonstration of its link with authority has already indicated. The ancient symbolism of justice, blindfolded and cold, is indicative of this rational component of justice. It is most apparent in the work of courts. The judge is supposed to have good reasons for his decision. These reasons are intended to relate the decision to previous decisions and the rules involved in them. Hence his work can be stated in terms of syllogisms. Yet, basically, his work is not different from that of others who share in the government of the community. They, too, have to engage in extensive ratiocination. The life of the law certainly is shot through with logic, though equally surely it is not to be equated with logic. Judge Holmes's celebrated dictum may seem to deny this, but he would have been the first to recognize that it was a false dichotomy, for the life of law is reasoning on experience.

The tie between justice and reasoning suggests another tie, equally important and not always sufficiently emphasized—the tie between justice and truth. An act, a decision can only be said to be just if it is based on objectively true thought, on correct information. To put this proposition in reverse may make its cogency more evident. Whenever it can be shown that an act, whether of rule-making, settling of disputes, or any other, was based on untrue information, whether because of lies or misunderstandings, the resulting act will seem unjust if the untrue assumptions were crucial for arriving at the decision to act in that way. That the data be not untrue is a necessary premise of the comparative evaluation; it would not hold if the facts were not so. In terms of our earlier analysis, the comparison is falsified and thus a discrimination is applied which would not be found if the falsehood has been absent (or the reverse, of course). Because this requirement of truth is so very apparent, "the necessity of stating it explicitly and inquiring into it is often overlooked," says Arnold Brecht. In fact, the proposition linking justice with truth raises for justice the entire range of problems which truth conjures up. Obviously, they cannot be explored here. But two points need brief discussion. One is that truth is always an open question. Truth is not given us, except as a task to be pursued. Because of its dependence on truth, justice is likewise an open question. It also can never be certain in any absolute sense. That is one reason why justice calls for tempering by mercy. It is not merely the element of discrimination which it contains but the uncertainty surrounding any "facts." The role of truth accounts for the importance of authority in rendering acts just; through reasoned elaboration authority can fill the gaps in the knowledge of truth. A comparable role is played by legitimacy, when the right to decide accomplishes what reason could not.

The other point is that truth is, in the political realm, often impolitic. The famous "secrets of rule," the *arcana imperii* on which the sixteenth and seventeenth centuries built their arguments in favor of "reason of state," often suggest that important information remain undisclosed. Chesterton, in *The Man Who*

Knew Too Much, told a number of stories in each of which the rendering of justice was made extremely difficult if not impossible because of some secret of empire that could not be revealed. The administration of criminal justice is full of such situations, and criminal law has developed definite rules for dealing with a variety of such situations. Here is one of the points at which the divergence of law and justice is patent; law requires that it be made public. And one reason why clemency is at times indicated is that the rule of law which is public does not meet the concrete situation which contains undisclosed aspects that have to be kept secret.

Circumstances such as these have at times misled thinkers into maintaining that truth is not a necessary condition of justice. What they recite are the cases that make a jury (and the judge) deny that a certain fact existed, because the defectiveness of the legal rule is such as would otherwise produce an unjust result. Actually, such cases prove, on the contrary, the paramount importance of the link to truth. Those seeking a just decision in such an instance are actually questioning the rule, not the circumstances of the situation. What has been called "situation sense," a sense for the situation *as it actually exists,* provides the truthful guide to the just decision, as against the truth-distorting implication of the defective rule. How justice is linked to truth in such cases may well be hidden from the casual onlooker or even the interested outsider. This is the circumstance which relates such a phenomenon to the "secrets of rule."

The rational aspect of justice, derivative from the comparative evaluation of persons and situations on which justice is built, has often been made the basis for arguing against anything like the "feeling for justice" or *Rechtsgefuehl.* Although it is true that such arguments have often taken the form of circular reasoning—where they presuppose the justice to which the feeling is related—it is nonetheless important to take account of the fact that some such feeling universally exists among men. We have already referred to the anxiety which is part of a sense of injustice and have suggested that it is linked to the felt threat to the entire system of values which justice ties to particular acts by providing the appropriate comparative evaluation of persons and situations. In that sense one could perhaps speak of an *Unrechtsgefuehl,* or sense of injustice. This threat to the values of a community involves, as we said, the political order of the community as such. Obviously, then, the rational component of justice and the feeling associated with it are not opposed to each other, but are themselves part of the total syndrome of justice. A feeling that an injustice has been done is a feeling that something counterrational has occurred. If untruth becomes legitimate and authoritative, the foundations of authority and legitimacy are shaken and threatened with destruction. This set of reflections is the obverse of that which Hume would have founded society on, which is a sense of the value of the communal bond.

It is, therefore, in a sense true that "the just is the straight, the unbendable," is that which is oriented toward the same point. But only within the limits of allowable comparisons. Beyond it, this very "straightness," when it violates the sense of justice, is characteristic rather of the law in its conflict with justice, not of justice itself. It is undoubtedly the function of justice to serve as a standard for evaluating the law. The word jus-tice embodies the *jus,* that is, *droit,* right, *dike,* and so on, and such words as *dikaiosyne* and *Ge-recht-igkeit* carry the aboriginal implication of ancient right (believed-in values) as against positively established law (statute). Justice, in the legal perspective, can be understood only if it is taken to be the right solution, be it act or rule, toward which the law is oriented as an approximation. Such an approximate realization is a dynamic process which takes place in time; it is dominated by forces struggling with each other for their effectualization within the general framework of the political order. But the underlying assumption of all such processes is the notion that political acts *ought to be* just in the sense in which we have interpreted justice. Justice in this sense introduces the dynamic element into the legal order and continues to transform it in accordance with emerging groups and the values which they cherish and insist on.

This dynamizing function of justice in the legal sphere, its specific political function, may be made more explicit by a further reflection on the Aristotelian notion of justice as equality. If one starts from the premise that men ought to be equal to each other, that they should, for example, be "equal before the law," the question of equality becomes political, for it now becomes important who determines the relevant comparisons by which such equality is assessed, more specifically, who makes the just law. Such answers as were given by Rousseau in his doctrine of the general will evade the real issue. The development of modern politics in the West has given a fairly unequivocal, conventional answer: it is the majority of the people who decide about laws and their application to persons as classified into categories of equals.

Such a reference of the problem of justice to a majority decision does not solve it, but transposes it to another level of discourse, which is the politics of a constitutional democracy. Only if it can be asserted that in every free community there exists a sufficient number of conscientious and responsible persons seeking to find not only a compromise between conflicting interests but also a higher synthesis transcending the particular interests (and an accommodation of divergent values, beliefs, and convictions) can the problem of justice be solved in the sense that a continuing concretization of the general task of successfully comparing persons in terms of believed-in values can be achieved. That this is not always merely a matter of finding the diagonal in a parallelogram of forces between rival interests should be patent, though certain schools of thought in both jurisprudence and political theory have argued the opposite position. Although theirs was a useful corrective to the overstress laid on values transcending the interests of separate elements in the political community, the so-called public interest or common good, it constituted an exaggeration. For, although many laws are nothing more than such compromises of particular interests (and as such just), there are others which embody common interests and which usually involve passionate arguments concerning justice. For example, the laws regulating military service or the governmental service in general can scarcely be said to be compromises between rival interests. What holds for laws holds equally for judicial decisions and other acts, of course. In all such cases, the common concern for the well-functioning of the political order is taken to be a first step toward the achievement of justice. Plato and Aristotle were right in stressing this aspect of the matter. Where they went astray was in believing that all or even most laws and other political acts belonged in this category and in not recognizing that much of it is a matter of particular interests and their adjustment to each other. Nor was Plato right in thinking that just decisions on general rules were a task for the wise alone, to be arrived at without consultation with the members of the community at large. Aristotle had a sounder appreciation of this process and at one point explicitly stated that the many are often better judges than the few, not individually, but collectively. "Not the thoughts of the clever or wise, but the talk of the people create the law. . . . Thus a genuine, necessary right will be called for and implored (*beschworen*), until it becomes law." Thus, one modern thinker supports the view that "justice must forever be realized anew." This requirement of renovation does not, however, imply a particular authority, such as the people, unless it is realized that the continuous transformation of values and beliefs occurs in the community at large in response to new experience, whereas the tensions and crises engendered thereby call for a continuous adjustment of particular interests to each other, as well as the redefinition of the common interest or interests. That common interest is first and foremost an interest in the maintenance and good functioning of the political order itself.

Let me conclude the argument by a rather poignant illustration of general import. A major political act the justice of which has been disputed through the ages is war. The argument over *justum bellum* shows very well how in the common man's view a just war is either a war fought for survival or one fought for an ideal (transcendent value). It is evident that wars may be compared and evaluated in terms of the values of very different and potentially hostile political communities and consequently appear just or unjust to either party. If, on the other hand, peace is posited as the paramount value, as happens in Kant, for example, the notion of a just war appears absurd. The world community might well incline toward such a view and seems increasingly to do so. But this change is not unrelated to technological developments that appear to render the attainment of the goals formerly sought by war actually unprocurable by that means. By these developments war, except in self-defense, ceases to remain an arguable just act, because of the principle which excludes from justice those acts based on a will to achieve the impossible.

. . . .

By way of summary and conclusion, the following might be said. After excluding some of the great traditional issues surrounding the just as a quality of acts, rules, and persons—especially whether justice is a relative or absolute value, or what it is in and of itself, specifically what kind of excellence or virtue it is in persons—we concentrated on that aspect of political situations and acts which is very widely observable as inherent in most of them: the comparative evaluation of persons according to the prevailing values of a political community. This, we showed, is the kernel of Aristotle's doctrine of equality in relation to justice; in its original form it is misleading because it suggests that the essence of equality is inequality.

That some values are prevalent and that persons will be differentiated according to such values seem indisputable. Such comparisons can only be in accord with the prevailing values if the facts on which they are based are not untrue, if the relation between facts and values is not arbitrary, and if the norms derived from such comparisons are not asking the impossible. The criteria *not untrue, not arbitrary,* and *not impossible* are, in other words, derivatives of the inherent meaning of the quality of just as defined. A political act is just, therefore, if it is based on a balanced evaluation of the persons it affects, comparing (and classifying) them on the ground of values prevalent in the political community concerned. We finally showed that such a view of justice as a quality of political acts (including rules) mediates the tension between power and authority and provides a deeper understanding of the legitimacy of rulers and their acts. By contrast, justice when defined in terms of the highest good—as has been done by philosophers, political and legal, from Plato to the present day—constitutes a specific application of the general principle of comparative evaluation; it resembles in its specificity the selection of some particular religious and national value system. Such a stipulative definition of justice is not excluded by our analysis but should be seen as the act of personal preference which, in most instances, it is. Only a reasoned elaboration of such a preference in terms of the demonstrable practical consequences for any given political order constitutes scientific knowledge. That such demonstrations are possible only the analysis of actual political orders can show; the demonstrated link between justice, authority, and legitimacy is an indication of the more fruitful lines of inquiry.

3

JUSTICE AND EQUALITY

RICHARD MCKEON

It is difficult to separate facts from judgments in the history of political institutions and political actions, for *judgments made* are facts conditioning the other facts of human action and *facts recorded* are results of judgments determining the performance of actions and of judgments organizing the record. This ambivalence of fact and judgment in political action is reflected in the development of political theory and in the uses of history in the interpretation of present circumstances and problems. The problems of justice which men face today and for which theories are instruments of understanding and of action are in important respects without precedent, yet discussion of these problems elaborates basic distinctions which provide the continuity of changing conceptions and applications of "justice." All the terms which are used to relate or to separate the novel and the traditional in "justice"—such as "equality," "freedom," "values," or "knowledge"—have a similar ambivalence which contributes plausibility to statements both of radical novelty and of persistent tradition. Throughout the discussion and pursuit of "justice," one of the marks of justice has been "equality." The history of both processes, of understanding and of achieving justice, has shown two long-run tendencies—increase in the number of those who are considered "equal" and diversification of what is sought as "equal." Variety or innovation has been found in extensions of justice to more people and to different activities. But those extensions have constituted a history of "justice" because they have encountered and explored the basic distinctions discovered in theories and applications of justice.

This ambivalence is neither an obstacle to progress nor an impediment to clarity; on the contrary, it is one of the preconditions of rational development in political action and inquiry. Political situations change and problems arise from changed conditions and circumstances. Yet the new problems fall under a finite number of issues, what the Roman rhetoricians called *status* or *constitutiones,* encountered in human associations and communities. It is at once true both that "justice" and "equality" have taken on entirely new meanings in our times and also that the fundamental issues raised in these new meanings and interpretations have been encountered in earlier politics. The framers of the American constitution met to construct institutions which they were convinced had not been possible before, equipped as they were with detailed notes of preceding theories and practices. The problems of justice in the twentieth century extend beyond the speculations and imaginations of the eighteenth century, but Madison would have found guidance in his notebooks to the issues which they raise. To ignore the persisting basic issues is to ignore the meanings of "equality" when it is used to characterize justice; screened from the meanings developed in the treatment of problems of justice, one may easily conclude that equality means inequality or that men are in fact not equal.[1] To ignore the changing circum-

---

[1] Thus, J.B.S. Haldane demonstrates in overwhelming detail in *The Inequality of Man* (1932) that the advance of science has shown that man is unequal in respects in which political theorists and philosophers had always granted his inequalities when they examined the grounds and conditions of political equality.

stances is to ignore the varieties of "equality" which influence judgments of actions and policies of cooperation; screened from the circumstances which raise problems of justice, one may easily neglect newly developed inequalities in the pursuit of well-known adjacent equalities. What is involved is not an opposition between innovation and tradition, but a fruitful interplay between change and structure which is the pattern of progress. This interplay of innovation and tradition is clarified in the case of the use of "equality" to define "justice" by distinguishing two factors in the definition: 1) the novelties introduced by new conditions which often remove an earlier basic opposition and 2) the continuities of persistent issues which often introduce unanticipated basic oppositions.

I

The history of the changes in conceptions of justice and equality under the influence of conditioning circumstances may be schematized in the succession of controversies concerning the bases of the just political act. At each stage the controversial oppositions of the previous stage seem to disappear as a new set of controversial oppositions arises. The key terms of the earlier discussion are usually continued, but the contrarieties are harmonized into accord, as part of the vocabulary of the new contrarieties. Thus in ancient Greece, which put together much of the terminology in which we express ourselves about justice and political acts, two controversies were prominent in the determination of political principles—justice, in the state and in the individual, is either natural or it is conventional, and justice, in action and in judgment, is either the exercise of power or the application of knowledge. Principles were found *either* in nature *or* in social compact, *either* in right which establishes authority *or* in might which makes right. The political philosophers who influenced constitutional theory in the seventeenth and eighteenth centuries used radically divergent philosophical analyses, yet Hobbes, Spinoza, Locke, Rousseau, and their contemporaries agreed in combining natural law with social compact, and in making theories of sovereignty contextures of knowledge and power. The writers of *The Federalist* papers were convinced both that the new republic was possible because of recent advances in political science and that the new constitution should institutionalize the plurality and oppositions of factions. The members of the constitutional convention in Philadelphia raised no serious objection to the rule of the majority, but they were greatly concerned about the threat of the tyranny of the majority and of the predominant power of the large states. A new set of controversial oppositions grew up in the interpretations and consequences of the French Revolution—an opposition of "revolution" to tradition which found early classic expression in Burke and Paine and an opposition of political and economic justice which ran from Babeuf through the variegation of economic and socialistic theorists of the nineteenth century who explored the economic foundations of constitutions and the economic forms of expropriation and alienation.

Recent political and legal theory has exhibited recrudescences of the opposition of nature and convention, of knowledge and power, and of reason and feeling, in the discussion of natural law, of power politics, and in the guise of emotive or persuasive theories of law. Yet in the context of present problems they are clearly unreal dichotomies which retain an element of apparent relevance from earlier controversies. We have been pushed by circumstances into a set of new problems. The nature of those problems has become apparent in the measures and policies that we have devised to treat them, but little attention has been given to the modifications which they have introduced into the meanings of the terms in which we discuss them or to the need for further modification and specification. The present transition in political thinking may be clarified by examining it against the background of the earlier transitions.

Political theory is concerned with the associations of men, in particular with the most inclusive association which is called "political." The successive stages of political theory have been selections of perspectives or orientations adapted to the problems which circumstances brought to the center of attention. Their formal sequence in Western theories has left a trace in etymologies and applications of words which Greek thinkers used in early theories and which assumed central importance in later theories. The first theories were political (*politike*) since they were concerned with the city (*polis*). The determination of justice and law, and therefore of "equalities" and "rights," was the proper function of the city. The meaning of "democracy" that was explored most fully was "political democracy." Even in the early theories, however, it was recognized that cities are distinguished by constitutions (*politeia*) which are structures of offices, functions, and powers, that is, structures of interacting equalities based on justice and law, powers and rights. The elaboration of ideas concerning "constitutional democracy" was facilitated by bringing natural law into relation with social compact and by introducing rational structures in the oppositions of power. Finally, we have come to recognize that early political and constitutional theories included considerations of problems which are social rather than political, and the problems of democracy which we face suggest that "social democracy" is a precondition of political and constitutional democracy. It is not irrelevant to our problems to recall that two words for "community" and "association" were used in the development of political and constitutional ideas which influenced the early meanings of "society"—community or communication in the possession of things in common (*koinonia, koinonema*) and association or alliance in war (*summachia*). The communities and associations of men in a state and of states with states present problems of democracy which introduce new complexities into political and constitutional democracy.

There would be some grounds for arguing that the history of the theory and pursuit of justice is divided into three periods, that men first conceived of justice and equality within the institutions and laws of states, later thought of rights (*jus*) and equalities which condition the constitution of states and the institution of laws, and finally discovered the dependence of political and constitutional rights on the right and equality which condition the justice according to which states are established and the justice according to which they operate. But such a division separates long episodes of human action within which exploratory actions and speculative inquiries anticipate and prepare transitions. The bills of human rights and the constitutions, unwritten and written, marked a transition from theoretic consideration to practical application in institutions of the equality of men and their right to frame governments, which was made possible in the seventeenth and eighteenth centuries by long discussion of justice and rights and long experience with political and judicial institutions. The problems of sovereignty, authority, and legitimacy which came to the fore in facing these new problems prepared for the emergence of the self-governing nations instituted in large numbers after the second world war, but did not provide for the new turns of problems presented by their aspiration for justice and equality. The "common good" and the "public interest" had in the interim been enlarged to include treatment of problems of economic and social justice and treatment of forms of human rights and aspirations to equality which had been unexamined or ineffective ingredients in earlier theories and situations.

The preparations antecedent to the major shifts which separate these three periods are integral parts of the large movements. The problems of justice during the first period were problems of the relation of ruler to ruled, and it would seem plausible that, with the institution of self-governing democratic republics in which the ruled were recognized as sovereign rulers, these problems should be superseded by new ones. John Stuart Mill characterizes this transition by saying that a time came in the progress of human affairs, "when men ceased to think it a necessity of nature that their governors should be an independent power, opposed in interest to themselves." [2] Yet long before in the history of political theory, at least as early as Aristotle, the distinction between ruler and ruled was not thought to be an ultimate political reality. When Aristotle sought the definition of a "state," he found it necessary first to examine the nature of "constitution" or "government" (*politeia*), which he found possible, in turn, only after examining "citizen" (*polites*), which he defined as one who shares in the administration of justice and in offices. He granted that this definition is best adapted to the citizens of a democracy, but from it he formed a definition which includes citizens of other states; the state is then a body of citizens sufficiently numerous for self-sufficiency (*autarkeia*) of life.[3] The element of self-rule in the establishment of states intrudes at many points in Greek political and legal theory. When Aristotle divides the true forms of gov-

---

[2] *On Liberty,* Chap. I, "Introductory."

[3] *Politics* iii. 1. 1274^b32–1275^b21.

ernment, which are ordered to the common interest, from the perversions, which are directed to some private interest, the true form balancing the perversion called "democracy" is given the name "constitution" or "polity" (*politeia*), since the citizens at large administer the state for the common interest.[4] Self-mastery is one of the virtues of the state and the individual for Plato,[5] and the social compact elaborated by the Sophists and Epicureans is an expression of the consent of the governed. But the center of interest was political theory and justice in the internal and external operations of states, and they were studied in the variety of offices and powers in 158 constitutions by Aristotle, in the degradations from the perfect state traced by Plato, or in the cultural histories in which Protagoras or Lucretius related progress in the arts to the development of justice. The transition from the long discussion of rights and constitutions to the actual establishment of institutions to protect rights and of constitutions to define the powers which make and administer laws marks an important change in theory as well as practice, notwithstanding anticipations and lags in the language used to express both processes.

The problems of justice during the second period were problems of the relation of the individual and society. There is a tendency, as Mill points out, to think of the "tyranny of the majority" as operating like other tyrannies chiefly through the acts of public authorities, but the sources of inequality extend beyond the operation of politics and the law to the tyranny of prevailing opinion and feeling. The problems of the inclusive political community and of the relation of ruler and ruled had taken their place in the social context of opinions and feelings which determine the character and operation of the political community. The resolution of "constitutional" problems sets the principles for the treatment of "political" and legal problems. Mill hoped to find the resolution of problems of freedom and equality in two maxims which distinguish actions for which the individual is accountable to society from actions for which he is accountable only to himself. In the course of the nineteenth century other foundations or antecedents of political and legal justice were translated from theoretic discussion to programs for

[4] *Ibid.* 7. 1279^{a}37–39.
[5] *Republic* iv. 430E–431D; *Gorgias,* 491D.

action. They were based on economic and social equality or justice rather than on rights of expression and association or on extension of franchise. Economic and social justice had been advanced within the framework of political constitutions by interpretation of the due process of law and of the exercise of police power, and increase in economic and social equality had affected the writing, amending, and interpreting of constitutions. A crucial issue of priority arose from the interplay between these two processes and set the opposition between "parliamentary democracy" which argues for the priority of civil and political rights and "mass democracy" which argues for the priority of economic and social equality. This and other ambiguous issues of the recent past suggest that circumstances have carried us to the point at which the "social" equalities underlying "constitutional" and "political" equalities must be examined as conditioning principles to make explicit the respects in which the relation of "individual" and "society" has been found to be an interdependence or coincidence, rather than an opposition or antithesis, similar to the relation evolved between "ruler" and "ruled."

The problems of justice in the third period, on which we have started, are neither problems of the rule of the majority nor of the tyranny of the majority, nor are they problems of possible oppositions between use and abuse of popular power. They are primarily problems of the manipulation of the majority and of its opinions affecting both its rule and its being ruled, both its tyrannizing and its being dominated. Problems of the tyranny of prevailing opinion and popular rule have taken a new form as a result of the development of mass media of communication which unsettle some of our assumptions and anticipations, including our firm convictions concerning the nature of the individual and of society. The problems of the relation of the individual and society have become problems of the relation of the private to the public. All actions—the actions of individuals and the actions of communities—have public consequences as well as private consequences: individuals and societies are at any moment the products or the accumulations of such consequences. All unified agents—individuals or communities—are structures or proportions of parts ordered by a ruling principle: rulers and ruled are at any moment the discernible determinants of the characteristic actions which result from the applications of the ratios of interrelation. The principles of social justice lay the foundations for the just relations of man to man and therefore for just political relations which are ordered by constitutional justice, much as the principles of constitutional justice lay the foundations for the formation and modification of constitutions and therefore for political justice within constitutions. Problems of the rule of the majority and problems of protection from the tyranny of the majority and of prevailing opinion are subservient to primary problems of how men are influenced and how opinions are manipulated. Problems of protection of property and problems of protection from excessive concentrations and unjust alienations of property are posterior to primary problems of the use of property in the pursuit of values and in the satisfaction of needs. Our statements of issues are ambiguous because we frame them still in terms of precepts of imputation or calculations of accountability, relative to intentions and the good or to consequences and the useful. Distinctions between intentions and consequences, duties and inclinations, the good and the useful have had a long period of fruitful application and tantalizing controversy, but they have been merged in the morality of responsibilities and values in which our actions are set. The history of emerging circumstances and opportunities has faced us with problems of justice and equality for which we have not devised adequate formulations, and there is some hope that the persistent issues may provide guidance in making the required new formulations.

II

However the history of justice and equality is traced, it is a history of kinds of equality at each stage and of changing meanings and applications of equality from stage to stage. The continuities which make it a history are found in persistent basic questions, and the novelties which form its sequence as history are introduced by new conditions which define the scope and application of the basic issues. The three stages in the version of the history of "justice" sketched above are marked by historical circumstances that throw emphasis in turn on Justice, Rights, and Right—*Justitia, Jura,* and *Jus.* In the first stage justice is sought within and between established political states, and problems of justice center on the establishment in institutions, and the examination in theories, of devices to protect the exercise of rights and to secure the rectification of injuries. In the second stage the rights of men are sought in establishing constitutions and participating in governments and in defining and protecting regions of freedom from governmental interference. In the third stage right is sought in societies and in the society of societies; according to it men have a hand in determining their own destiny and selecting their values, and justice is found in equality of opportunity and of consideration. Like basic issues among kinds of equality arise in characteristic forms at each of these stages.

The equality of justice was never set forth as an equality of persons and natural abilities. It was always proportionate equality established between persons and things or circumstances. The basic ratio is between person and person, and that ratio, which might be established as a ratio of ability, knowledge, or virtue in the utopian state, is measured in all actual communities by two interrelated ratios—the ratio of honor, wealth, or other external assets at the disposition of the community and the ratio of law, custom, and opinion by which the community is ruled. Approximation to justice in any particular case and progress toward justice in the associations of men reflect the degree in which external marks of recognition are more or less reliable indications of "equal" qualities pertinent to the association and the degree in which the conditions of association are determined by "equalities" in the members. This complex interplay of proportions in the equality which defines justice was examined subtly and in detail by Greek poets, orators, historians, and philosophers, and distinctions relevant to it were embedded in the language of political theory which they constructed. They wrote about "equality," but they also constructed a large number of compound terms in which the prefix "equal" is specified in its application. There was no one preeminent kind of equality, and there was no one dominant theory of equality. Tragedies, litigations, revolutions, and philosophical controversies were based on clashes or alleged clashes of rights and justices. The history of later circumstances permitted the continued recognition of kinds of equality and justice in meanings adjusted to the changed conditions, and the oppositions of policy and purpose sometimes expressed themselves in the same theory and sometimes gave their opposition opposed theoretic foundations.

Aristotle's exploration of this thicket of interrelated aspects of just action is well adapted to serve as the beginning point of an examination of the continuing structure of issues because he was committed to seeking literal distinctions and to expressing himself in univocal terms. The distinctions he makes are found differently expressed in other theories, and alternative formulations modified the interpretation of Aristotle's statements or were substituted for them in the developing history of theoretic influences. Aristotle makes one of the ratios the basis for the distinction between justice as one of the moral virtues of individual men and justice as the bond of men in states. Political justice is thought to consist in equality, but men's conceptions of equality are imperfect, and they do not express the whole idea.[6] There are, therefore, as many kinds of justice and equality as there are constitutions. Despite this variability justice is the principle of order in political communities, since the administration of justice determines what is just.[7] Political rule (*politike*) is a government of free and equal men.[8] The mark of citizenship and the end of the state may be sought in ability, virtue, or knowledge, but the natural tendency is to seek them in external marks like birth, wealth, power, or freedom. A city ought to be composed of equals and similars, and these are generally the middle classes.[9] The only stable principle of government is equality according to proportion and for every man to possess what is his own.[10]

Ethics and politics are parts of the same science, and distinctions discovered in the operation of political justice are related to differentiations in actions proceeding from moral justice in individual men. The two kinds of moral justice which Aristotle distinguished have different definitions. The use of the same word "justice" in these two meanings is, therefore, an equivocation.[11] "Justice" differs from "virtue" in essence and definition, for virtue

---

[6] *Politics* iii. 9. 1280^{a}7–12.
[7] *Ibid.* i. 2. 1253^{a}37–38.
[8] *Ibid.* i. 7. 1255^{b}20.
[9] *Ibid.* iv. 11. 1295^{b}25–27.
[10] *Ibid.* v. 7. 1307^{a}26–27.
[11] *Nicomachean Ethics* v. 1. 1129^{a}26–^{b}1.

is the habit or state of an individual, and justice is virtue relative to other men. Nonetheless, one kind of justice is the lawful (*nominon*), for laws aim at the common advantage, and justice in this sense is the whole of virtue: the community and its laws lay the foundations of all the values and virtues of its members. The second kind of justice is the equal (*ison*), for among the "goods" sought by man, those related to prosperity and adversity—honors, wealth, security—are peculiarly dependent on other men and they are sought whether or not they are "good" for those who would achieve them; justice in this sense is a part of virtue and a part of the lawful. The unjust man corresponding to the first kind of justice is unlawful; the second kind of unjust man is a man who seeks to get too much or more than his share (*pleonektes*).[12] Particular justice, the just as equal, is divided into distributive and rectificatory justice. Distributive justice divides wealth, honor, and other possessions of the community among those who share in the functions or the constitution of the community. It sets up a geometric proportion in which differences of men and their functions are taken into account, and the measure of merit varies in different forms of government or constitutions. Rectificatory justice equalizes injustices or injuries done in the transactions between man and man, both voluntary transactions (like selling, buying, lending at interest, pledging, lending without interest, depositing, letting for hire) and involuntary transactions, both furtive (like theft, adultery, poisoning, procuring, enticement of a slave, assassination) and violent (like assault, imprisonment, murder, robbery with violence, maiming, abusive language, contumelious treatment). It sets up an arithmetic proportion which measures injury and reparation but holds men constant and equal.

The conception and operation of justice is seen to have a normative basis in which justice is closely associated with virtue; it takes on particular forms in particular constitutions which are based on partial conceptions of justice but which determine what

---

[12] The antisocial disposition to seek to "have more" was the subject of meticulous scrutiny by Plato and many other Greek writers. Its continuing influence is apparent from the place it occupies in John Stuart Mill's list of "dispositions" leading to acts injurious to others. See *On Liberty*, Chap. IV, "Of the Limits to the Authority of Society over the Individual"—"the desire to engross more than one's share of advantages (the *pleonechia* of the Greeks)."

is just in the state so that the just coincides with the good only in a good state; for the most part, finally, the determination of merit in actual states takes the form of recognizing external signs like wealth, position, birth, and power. Aristotle distinguishes these three levels in the operation of law. He argues that the majority of the acts commanded by law are those which are prescribed from the point of view of virtue taken as a whole, "for the law bids us practice every virtue and forbids us to practice any vice." [13] They are prescribed by law with a view to the common good. However, few states undertake the education of the individual as such to make him without qualification a good man. Finally, most of the administrative and judicial functions of governments, applying the law and adjudicating disputes, fall under particular justice which deals directly with "goods" sometimes indirectly connected with the "good" and the "common good," and sometimes at variance with them. In later theories and discussions, law is treated primarily in terms of particular justice. Distributive and rectificatory justice have provided the framework and the instrumentalities not only for all the problems adjudicated in courts but also for problems treated by legislators and administrators, with only occasional references—rhetorical, investigatory, admonitory, or projective—to justice or the good. Politics and the law treat of external relations between men. Such relations are marked and established by external considerations and they initiate actions which have material consequences.

Equality in the relations of men to each other in acquiring and retaining "goods" is a device to relate those processes to a "common good," and the search for equalities moves from political equality in established states, to constitutional equality in the establishment of states, to social equality in the relations of men among which political relations is one species. Distributive justice in the conditions of a well-ordered and peaceful state takes its structure from the constitutions which establish the distribution and functions of offices and the manner in which they are filled. If one seeks distributive justice prior to the constitution in the way in which it serves as the structure for the establishment of constitutions, it is found in the rights and equalities of men which were early identified in the theoretic language of

[13] *Ibid.* 2. 1130^{b}20–24.

politics—equality of rights (*isopoliteia*), equality of privilege, honor, or value (*isotimia,* or *isotimema*—the contrary of *pleonechia*), and equal right to vote (*isopsephia*). Rectificatory justice in a similarly stable and orderly state is made operative by the execution of the decisions of courts, civil and criminal. The amendment of constitutions and the establishment of new constitutions, however, are designed to rectify injustices in the law or its execution, and the rights and equalities on which this rectificatory justice is based were likewise identified—equality under the law (*isonomia*), which may become a synonym of good order (*eunomia*), and equality in sharing (*isomoiria*). The pursuit of such equalities in the establishment of frameworks for political equalities is involved in questions of economic, social, and cultural equality.

The revolutions of the eighteenth century, like earlier revolutions, were insurrections of dissatisfied groups against established governments. Aristotle constructed a theory of such revolutions in the fifth book of his *Politics.* The revolutions of the twentieth century—of Sun Yat-sen, of Gandhi, of Lenin, and of numerous deviants from these three models—engaged in long ideological, educational, propaganda campaigns to prepare or form or render acceptable or admirable the dissident group, and the strategy of that campaign merged with the strategy of the campaign against the established government. The pattern according to which a dissatisfied people were led by a decent respect for the opinions of mankind to explain their revolt was radically changed to a pattern according to which the opinions of mankind and the relations among peoples are used to stimulate aspirations which unite groups and peoples in disaffection. Revolutions to rectify social inequalities serve as substitutes, preparations, or pretexts for insurrections to rectify political inequalities; and social inequalities within states are easily analogized to inequalities of peoples in the society of nations. The persistent issues which have taken on new meanings in these new circumstances may therefore be seen either in the movements to secure rights and equalities within states or in the movements of states to secure rights among states. A consideration of the equalities of the citizens of a newly established self-governing nation and of the equalities of the nation they constitute will disclose a general pattern applicable to the interpretation of other problems of just action in society and in the society of nations.

Former colonial peoples are convinced that they have suffered injustices. They seek rectificatory justice, and in the present climate of opinion in the relations of peoples their claim to this form of equality has, for a variety of reasons, been recognized most readily. In an established and well-ordered state rectificatory justice is equality before the law, civil and criminal. In the modification and establishment of constitutions and states, it is good order and equality of sharing, which has moved from equality in redress of injuries to equality of opportunities. The justice of equality of sharing is recognized in programs of economic assistance and in programs of technical and cultural cooperation designed to remove inequalities in provision of food, clothing, shelter, medical care, education, employment, and security. Equality in satisfying minimum material needs is a first step toward equality in sharing the progress made possible by advances in knowledge and technology and by increasing accessibility of the arts and cultural values. Equality of sharing is the means of securing freedom from want.

Newly self-governing people seek equality of justice as well as equality of means of satisfying needs. Rectificatory justice in established and well-ordered states depends on the law. In the modification of constitutions rectificatory justice is rectified by improvement of the law. In the society which is the context of political change rectificatory justice depends on relating the acquiring of goods to the securing of the common good. Rectificatory justice broadens in a world context to a justice common to mankind, in which the justice of one people is comparable to the justice of other peoples. The plurality and arbitrariness of particular justices are related in the justice of equal law, which in its equality is good law. The preservation of the particular justices adapted to the desires and preferences of different peoples is made possible by a common justice elaborated rationally. Equality of law or of good law is the means of securing freedom from fear.

In an established and well-ordered state, distributive justice appears in the equalities set up among the ratios of functions in the community to the rewards and privileges accorded those who exercise them. Changes in constitutions involve changes in those equal ratios of service and reward; the distributive justice governing changes in distributive justice is equality of vote, simple or proportional. In the larger social context in which equality of voting becomes an issue, the franchise is a specific form of a more general equality of participation in making decisions which affect one's life and destiny. In the larger society what is sought is equality of the part one has in basic decisions affecting one's own actions and common actions with the parts other people have in particular and common decisions. Equality of vote is the means of securing freedom from subjection.

Newly self-governing peoples seek equality of estimation as well as equality of vote. Distributive justice in established and well-ordered states discriminates roles in the community and assigns prestige and rewards according to contribution. In the modification of constitutions distributive justice is redistributed by the exercise of equality of rights. In the society which is in the context of political change equality of rights is manifested in equality of esteem and dignity. A newly self-governing people assumes its place among nations at the same moment that it becomes a nation. As a people it has its own conception of values and accomplishment, which we call a culture, and a desire not only to preserve its culture but to make use of the conception of justice embodied in it to judge the operations of other nations and of the world community of which it is part. The plurality of conceptions of justice which must operate in the determination of joint action which is just in the equality of law cannot be based on a "toleration" of differences; it is possible and effective in the degree that the conceptions of others are understood and their values held in high esteem. Distributive justice among peoples is felt as a sense of accomplishment by the various peoples, and for each people it is the conviction that they and those like them are getting somewhere according to their own conception of where they want to get. Equality of honor, estimation, or privilege is the means of securing freedom from discrimination.

The continuity of the issues of justice and equality and the radical changes they undergo in changed circumstances is apparent in the reception of aspirations to equality in the modern world. They are accepted as reasonable extensions of earlier achievements of human rights; they are opposed as mutually contradictory and destructive of rights and values. We recognize the claim that equality in the satisfaction of basic needs is justice, and we raise no question concerning equality under an impartial rule of law as justice. But the combination of the two in social justice is new, and the results of the combination are difficult to understand and difficult to put into action: the rights of the eighteenth century—the freedoms of worship, speech, and assembly—required political institutions to protect individual action; the rights of the twentieth century—the freedom from want, fear, and discrimination—require social education to form new communities of feeling and cooperative action to achieve new ends. Similarly we recognize that equality of participation in common decisions is justice, and we raise no question concerning equality of man in dignity and in accomplishment as justice. But the combination of the two seems to involve an obvious contradiction, since the premature participation in decisions may provide no ground for a sense of getting somewhere in the accomplishment of values.

As in the case of past transitions, the issues of our new situation are new issues and the language developed to discuss previous issues no longer sets forth contrarieties relevant to the situation. Nature and compact, reason and power evolved from use to formulate antithetically opposed positions to use as supplementary parts of a single position, and we continue today to find it useful to make periodic announcements of recrudescences of natural law or arbitrary convention, power politics or rational models. Similarly, all institutions may be designated, for support or attack, examples of tradition or of revolution, and economic rights have political bases no less obviously than political rights have economic bases. There is some hope that these ambiguities in which different or even contrary terms may be applied to the same person or institution (a phenomenon familiar to ancient semanticists) might be clarified if we turned our attention to the just act by which the just principle and the just agent is recognized. The apparent contradictions among equalities become in such analysis promising possibilities of action, and the dependence of individual rights on common actions found in recently formulated rights is seen as a definitory trait of just actions. Individual and society are interdependent and the actions of both have private and public aspects; whatever the outcome of the dispute between the ethics of duties and the ethics of inclinations, all just acts are judged both by the intentions from which they derive and by the consequences in which they eventuate.

In the analysis and performance of just acts, the multiplicity and interplay of kinds of equality is an instrumentality of progress, not a defect of analysis. The "mixed constitution" advanced justice by a balance of powers; the "mixed society" has begun to open up approaches to justice by a balance of desires and preferences. In the absence of universal and rational agreement concerning ends, progress to a predefined end is not equality but despotism; conversely, the interaction of ends is not haphazard and relativistic when equality enters into the determination of ends. The function of reason in human actions is not to lay down a master plan for imposition on all as the common interest, nor is its function to design a strategy for execution by some to secure private interests. Justice is the adjustment by rational means of the use of reason to secure material goods to the use of reason to establish a common treatment of men in the community. Justice is the adjustment by rational means of the use of one's own reason in making decisions to the use of common reason and consensus to analyze truths and to achieve goods. It would be easier to arrive at ends if we were clear about them from the start, but that lack of clarity is advantageous since preconceptions concerning ends are reexamined in the course of pursuing them, and they are related to changing conditions and divergent aspirations. In this interplay equalities contribute to progress, and they define freedom. They set the persistent issues of justice, and they clarify the emergent problems which remove the antitheses found in earlier problems and present new oppositions for fresh analysis and formulation.

4

THE ULTIMATE STANDARD OF JUSTICE

ARNOLD BRECHT

In declaring any act, condition, or judgment "just" or "unjust," we generally apply some measure, standard, yardstick, or norm. Leaving aside for the moment any question as to whether the norm is correctly applied to any given case, there remains the fundamental issue whether, and in what sense, the norm (measure, standard, etc.) itself is or is not "just," or, what is the same thing, whether the norm (measure, etc.) that regulates or measures "justice" is valid.

When we try to apply scientific methods of thinking to this question of validity, even where our interpretation of what is "scientific" is unfailingly strict, we are by no means so limited. We can enter a wedge or two. We may disclose all the observable *facts* of the case, we may clarify the *meaning* (or the conceivable alternative meanings) of the question, and we may also give *conditional answers* of the following type: "*If* we apply the traditional views of our own country (or civilization) or of some other country, *then* the norm is, or is not, valid." [1]

This type of scientific argument comes to an end, however, when references to specific traditions, cultures, opinions—traditional or other—are not accepted as final and insistence is put on providing an answer to the question whether the specific traditions or opinions referred to are themselves "just" or "unjust," or—what amounts to the same thing—whether the standards of justice set by them are "right" or "valid."

Again, it is hardly controversial that this *is* the remaining issue on which lawyers, philosophers, and social scientists are divided, and divided within their own groups, as well. But neither is it a matter of controversy that, even on this irritating question, significant scientific contributions can be made by investigating the *consequences* of the various views, the *risks* involved in their espousal and activation, the *common elements* underlying all or several of them, and the biological, sociological, historical, or *biographical factors* that have led people to hold the opinions they do. The examination of consequences and risks in particular presents an almost inexhaustible area for relevant scientific work.[2]

Even after this, however, there may remain, and often do remain, irreconcilable opinions held in good faith on the validity of the ultimate standards or norms of justice, and the controversies cannot be resolved in an intersubjectively compelling manner. "When Thou hast done, Thou has not done," to quote Donne. Individually and in groups we may still feel able to take

---

[1] See Carl J. Friedrich's contribution to this volume and the section on "Traditional Justice" in my *Political Theory—The Foundations of 20th Century Political Thought* (1959).

[2] See *Political Theory,* pp. 96ff. and Chapter xii. As "common elements" I have attempted to verify (Chapters x and xi): truth—or at least veracity—in the statement of facts and in the profession of value preferences; generality of the norm; absence of arbitrariness in interference with equality and liberty; respect for the necessities of nature. In the course of the discussion, which I did not attend, Karl Llewellyn is said to have questioned the universal nature of the interrelation between justice and truth because judges and juries often distort the facts intentionally in order to avoid a sentence that appears to them unjust. This illustration, however, serves to confirm rather than to contradict the postulate, since judges and juries are here supposed to use the trick of distorting the facts merely for the purpose of leading to victory their *true* views of what justice requires in the face of the *true* facts of the case. See my remarks on the "white lie," *ibid.,* pp. 413ff. and 570.

a definite stand, supporting our views by religious or philosophical reasons or with reference to "intuition." But we cannot resolve such differences in terms of *scientia transmissibilis* (knowledge that can be transmitted qua knowledge).[3]

This is the sound core of *"scientific* value relativism," which, of course, remains sound only if it limits its confession of impotence strictly to the "scientific" (i.e., *scientia transmissibilis*), sphere, not overlooking or belittling the scientific contributions that are possible on "consequences," "risks," and the like, and carefully avoiding any pretenses that religious and philosophical arguments also be limited in the same manner. Any type of value relativism that is meant as a compelling doctrine to limit not only scientific work but religious and philosophical contributions as well must be rejected as inconclusive. This warning also applies to those who would transplant their scientific mode of thinking indiscriminately to the juridical area, as we shall see presently.

Scientific value relativism has, indeed, led most of its protagonists to deny the possibility of any statements, either scientific or juridical, on the "justice" of positive law and, in particular, on the limits to be set to the latter's validity on grounds of its injustice. It is my purpose here to point to the fundamental difference between the two questions: 1) whether some norm is or is not *juridically* valid at a specific time and place; and 2) whether the norm or its opposite is *scientifically* valid regardless of time and place. My thesis, almost too simple to be offered, but unfortunately much in need of enunciation, is that the answer to the question of which orders are or are not *legally* binding at a specific time and place does not depend on a previous answer to the question of what is true or valid everywhere and at any time or what is true or valid in an other than legal (juridical) sense.

More concretely, whether some legislative act or decree, although issued in line with formal requirements, may be, or should be, denied legal validity on the ground that it is in conflict with some norm or principle of justice regarded as being of a "higher" order does not necessarily depend on the scientific verification of the proposition that there *is* a higher order. It may suffice to state

---

[3] For details, see *Political Theory,* especially pp. 271–281. Dewey's recommendation to concentrate on the concrete case fails to resolve the difficulty; *ibid.,* pp. 266ff.

that at some time and place commands given in violation of those principles that are considered higher are not regarded as juridically valid or binding, especially for courts and administrators.

The types of commands that ought, or ought not, to be regarded as juridically valid is primarily a political question concerning the desirable form of government and not—or at least not necessarily—one of science.

Kelsen has rightly pressed the point that the habit of deriving answers to questions of legal validity from a nation's constitution —written or unwritten—logically presupposes the acceptance of a basic norm that declares the constitution the supreme law and ultimate source of legal validity. This is equivalent to saying (as indicated above) that science can make conditional statements of the type "*If* legal validity is determined by a nation's constitution, *then* such and such commands are, or are not, legally valid." Logically correct as these observations are, there is nothing in them to compel us either to accept any basic norm or hypothetical condition at all or to accept them precisely in Kelsen's rigid and total formulation. We may, instead, accept a basic norm of a substantially different content, which would say that commands based on constitutional authority are valid unless they infringe on certain basic human interests that are considered "inalienable" on any grounds whatever—religious, philosophical, scientific or pseudo-scientific, historical, popular will, fear of abuse of power, or any other.

The confusion of juridical validity with scientific validity has in some instances—especially in decisions concerning the validity of cruel governmental decree-laws—led to harsh practical alternatives depending on whether natural-law doctrines were or were not considered scientifically valid. It then appeared as though the denial of scientific validity to the doctrines of natural law compelled recognition of the legal validity of the most barbarous governmental commands, provided only that they had been issued in accord with constitutional procedure. But this mode of argument is the outcome of poor thinking. Even one who refuses to accept the doctrines of natural law as genuine science need not therefore regard the barbarous commands of a reckless legislator or dictator as legally valid.

The resolve to deny legal (juridical) validity to certain types of governmental measures is not limited to scientific grounds. Just as questions concerning what types of commands should positively be considered legally valid—i.e., binding on courts, administrators, and people at large—are primarily not for science to decide but for the discretionary human political will, particularly that of constitution-makers, so the negative determination that certain types of governmental commands should *not* be considered legally valid is primarily not a matter for science but for human political design. The determination to set limits to the legal validity of governmental measures may be inspired or guided by presumedly "scientific" grounds or by religious convictions, but it may just as well be propelled simply by preferences for a certain style of living. This determination may be satisfied with checks and balances and bills of rights formally included in the text of a written constitution, or—especially where no written constitution or bill of rights exists or where the bill of rights has been suspended under emergency clauses—it may go beyond the meek submission to legislative techniques. All this is not a matter for science but for the political or juridical will.

Nor is it the function of science to say who is entitled or able to make this political decision on the limits set to the validity of governmental orders—whether that must be done only in the formal process of making or altering a written constitution, or, if the courts can do it on deeper authority, whether popular opinion, the doctrines of churches, or the ideals and maxims of a resistance movement or long tradition should decide. Science can, of course, attempt to find out what forces have actually been considered legitimate in determining legal validity and its limits at a certain time and place, and it can investigate the consequences and risks involved in the various views; but it has no authority whatever to determine itself the rules of legal validity.

At this point I feel urged to add a few words to underline the significance of this distinction between the legal and the scientific validity of norms. I hold that on purely scientific grounds we cannot even establish the validity of the most fundamental of our modern humanitarian principles, namely, that in certain basic aspects the life and the liberty of all human beings—regardless of their obvious differences and regardless, too, of our different subjective relations to them in terms of friendship or enmity and the like—should be treated with equal respect. We may indeed feel entitled to assume as a universally accepted principle—and even demonstrate—that in matters of justice whatever is equal ought to be treated equally. But such an assumption or demonstration will not enable us to state that *all* human beings *are* equal or essentially equal; on the contrary, we cannot deny that they are very unequal in many ways. Although scholars have established scientifically to a remarkable extent that differences in intellectual, artistic, and moral qualities are not tied to external distinctions such as color, bone structure, and the like, we cannot by purely scientific means establish that within each race, and among all races, the life and liberty of all persons, notwithstanding obvious differences in intellectual, artistic, and moral qualities, ought to be equally respected.

It is an apparently undying popular fallacy that all men ought to be treated equally on the ground that all are in the same predicament when born, having had no choice whether they wanted to be born at all and what parentage and conditions of life would be theirs. If this were a conclusive argument, it would prove far too much, since all animals share this plight with us. But, to argue the case for equality in secular terms of natural law, one is compelled to fall back, in the second line of defense, on the time-honored reference to reason as the distinguishing criterion of man. And this reference, in turn, proves too little, since men have reason in such different measures that *without religious additions to the argument* it would not be possible to infer from the fact that every man has *some* reason that all ought to be treated equally. Science alone is unable to provide this maxim. Science alone cannot even refute the proposition that feeble-minded children, the lazy, the sick, the members of hostile or potentially hostile tribes, and indeed even healthy and friendly people if there are too many of them to be fed, may be done away with. It can only warn of possible errors, abuses of power, other risks and consequences, and the like.

In other words, our great principle of human equality—that maxim according to which we grant certain basic rights even to sick and inferior people, to strangers and enemies—is *not a scientific principle.* It cannot be established by purely scientific means. It has its historical basis in the *religious* doctrine of the equality of all men before God and in respect for the fact that every man is equal to every other man in his ability to choose between good and evil. From this religious origin it has come to its present eminent status by a long, long process of historical evolution. If we would prefer putting the same principle on a nonreligious and nonhistorical foundation, we are free to do so by reference to the creative idealism of individuals or groups determined to see a world built on peace and sympathy rather than on war and hatred. But on scientific grounds alone the principle cannot be conclusively founded.[4]

This is by no means bad. On the contrary, it is very wholesome, particularly so if looked at from the angle of one concerned with ethics. Only after fully recognizing that our humanitarian ideals in their most important aspects cannot be extracted from nature solely by scientific means, only then are we mature enough to comprehend our personal responsibility, individually or in groups, in choosing our ultimate standards of measurement, our ultimate norms. (The term "responsibility" is used here in its broadest sense to include not only moral responsibility but any share in the causation of events irrespective of moral evaluation; this may be called "causal" responsibility.) No longer then can we take the easy way of "waiting for science to find out what is true." Education of the self and of others then seeks its ultimate orientation not in science but in our own responsibility and in the firm resolve to take it seriously.

Our shrinking stature grows. Whether believers, doubters, or atheists, we acknowledge the significance of our religious heritage, whose influence on the formation of our culture and humanitarian ideals we all share; no longer do we try to deny or minimize this influence by offering or accepting pseudo-scientific substitutes. Our responsibility, and our resolve to live up to it, becomes an essential part of our way of life. What fundamental attitude to take toward the claim of all men to a share in human freedom and happiness and what limits to set to the legal validity of government measures that disregard this claim, we do not decide by scientific standards (whether agnostic, pseudognostic, or enigmatic in this area), but by religious or philosophical convictions or our creative moral and political will.

[4] This and the following are adapted from my German contribution "Die Tröstungen der strengen Wissenschaft" zu *Politische Ordnung und menschliche Existenz—Festgabe für Eric Voegelin* (1962).

5

JUSTICE AND PERSONAL DESERT

JOEL FEINBERG

What is it to deserve something? This guileless question can hardly fail to trouble the reflective person who ponders it. Yet, until its peculiar perplexities are resolved, a full understanding of the nature of justice is impossible, for surely the concepts of justice and desert are closely connected. This essay has as its ulterior purpose the illumination of that connection; its direct aim is analysis of the concept of personal desert.

The phrase "personal desert" is no pleonasm. Many kinds of things other than persons are commonly said to be deserving. Art objects deserve admiration; problems deserve careful consideration; bills of legislation deserve to be passed. Although such statements are not wholly unrelated to questions about justice, they are less central than statements about the deserts of persons and will not be considered here. Nor shall we consider statements construing natural events as deserts, such as: "The villain crushed in the landslide got what he deserved." Persons are in this manner often held to deserve things other than treatment at the hands of their fellows; but this essay will be concerned only with personal desert of other-personal bestowals.

On those rare occasions when personal-desert statements are discussed by philosophers, they are often held to stand in some close logical connection to rules, or they are explicated in terms of rights and obligations; [1] and, when philosophers themselves make judgments about personal deserts, the deserved modes of treatment they have in mind are almost invariably punishment and rewards.[2] The following schematic analysis will suggest, on the contrary, that desert is a "natural" moral notion (that is, one which is not logically tied to institutions, practices, and rules); that it represents only a part, and not necessarily the most important part, of the domain of justice;[3] and that reward and punishment are only two among the several irreducibly distinct modes of treatment persons are said to deserve. The first section of the essay considers some generic aspects of desert, particularly its relations to rules and to the rule-connected concept of qualification and the relation between desert statements and reasons. Then, since further analysis of personal desert depends on what mode of treatment is said to be deserved, the second section carries the analysis further by considering some of the generic modes of deserved treatment. The final section discusses the relation between desert and social utility and also some of the unfortunate consequences of treating personal desert as a kind of "moral entitlement."

---

[1] For two apparent examples in recent literature, see S.I. Benn and R.S. Peters, *Social Principles and the Democratic State* (1959): "'Desert' is a normative word; its use presupposes a rule . . ." (p. 137); and D.D. Raphael, *Moral Judgment* (1955): "Our conclusion then is that the concept of desert . . . is a way of speaking of the presence or absence of an obligation in special circumstances" (p. 77).

[2] For example, John Hospers, in his recently published *Human Conduct, An Introduction to the Problems of Ethics* (1961), considers the topic "justice and desert" under two headings, "reward" (pp. 433–451) and "punishment" (pp. 451–468); and Austin Duncan-Jones, who devotes an entire chapter to "desert" in his sensitive discussion of Butler, *Butler's Moral Philosophy* (1952), discusses the concept exclusively in connection with punishment.

[3] For the contrasting view, see Hospers, *op. cit.*: "Justice is getting what one deserves; what could be simpler?" (p. 433).

I

DESERT PROPRIETY

To say that a person deserves something is to say that there is a certain sort of propriety in his having it. But this is also true of the statements that he is eligible for, qualified for, or entitled to something; that he has a claim on it or a right to it; or simply that he ought to have it. Our first task, then, is to characterize the particular kind of propriety distinctive of desert. This may be most effectively done by contrast.

Consider first what it means to be "eligible" for something. According to *Webster's*, a person is eligible when he is "fitted or qualified to be chosen," when he is "legally or morally suitable." Eligibility is a kind of minimal qualification, a state of not being disqualified. We discover whether a person is eligible for some office or employment, prize, or reward by determining whether he satisfies certain eligibility conditions as specified by a rule or regulation. For example, to be eligible for varsity athletics, one needs a medical certificate, at least a C average, and at least sophomore standing; to be eligible for the presidency of the United States, one must be thirty-five or older and a "natural-born" citizen.

Eligibility is one kind of qualification: satisfaction of some important preliminary necessary condition. Another kind of qualification, equally rule-connected, is satisfaction of a sufficient condition for, say, an office or prize. So, for example, in this sense a man qualifies for the presidency of the United States by winning a majority of the electoral votes or for first place in the hundred-yard dash by crossing the finish line before his competitors. Anyone who qualifies in this strong sense can claim the office or the prize as his *right;* according to the rules he is entitled to it.

I think it clear that qualification in neither of these senses is the same as desert. There are millions of persons eligible to be president who do not deserve to be, and it is often plausible and always intelligible to say that the man in fact elected president did not deserve to be. To deserve something, one must be qualified in still a third sense; one must satisfy certain conditions of worthiness which are written down in no legal or official regulation. To be "truly qualified" for the presidency, for example, a person must be intelligent, honest, and fair-minded; he must have a program which is really good for the country and the tact and guile to make it effective. Any candidate who satisfies these and similar conditions to a degree greater than his rivals deserves to be president. But these conditions are not requirements specified by some rule in the sense of authoritative, public, sanctioned regulation or in the sense of "canon," or in the sense of "rule of procedure." At best, they are the conditions "required" by the private standards or principles of a sensitive voter.[4]

In respect to modes of treatment which persons can deserve, then, we can distinguish three kinds of conditions. There are those whose satisfaction confers eligibility ("eligibility conditions"); those whose satisfaction confers entitlement ("qualification conditions"); and those conditions not specified in any regulatory or procedural rules, whose satisfaction confers worthiness or desert ("desert bases").

DESERT BASES

If a person is deserving of some sort of treatment he must, necessarily, be so *in virtue of* some characteristic or prior activity. It is because no one can deserve anything unless there is some basis or ostensible occasion for the desert that judgments of desert carry with them a commitment to the giving of reasons. One cannot say, for example, that Jones deserves gratitude although he has done "nothing in particular." If a person says that Jones deserves gratitude, then he must be prepared to answer the question, "For what?" Of course, he may not know the basis of Jones's desert, but, if he denies that there is any basis, then he has forfeited his right to the desert terminology. He can still say that we *ought* to treat Jones well for "no reason in particular" or simply "for the sake of being nice," but it is absurd to say that Jones *deserves* good treatment for no reason in particular. Desert without a basis is simply not desert.

But not any old basis will do. A characteristic of mine cannot be a basis for a desert of yours unless it somehow reveals or reflects some characteristic of yours. In general, the facts which constitute

[4] For a useful survey of six senses of the word "rule," see Kurt Baier, *The Moral Point of View* (1958), pp. 123–127.

the basis of a subject's desert must be facts about that subject.[5] If a student deserves a high grade in a course, for example, his desert must be in virtue of some fact about *him*—his earlier performances, say, or his present abilities. Perhaps his teacher *ought* to give him a high grade because it will break his neurotic mother's heart if he does not; but this fact, though it can be a reason for the teacher's action, cannot be the basis of the student's desert.[6]

There are two ways in which a desert judgment can be infelicitous. On the one hand, it can either lack a basis altogether or else have a logically inappropriate one; on the other hand it may simply be false or incorrect. Put another way, it may either lack an appropriate "basal reason," [7] or the basal reason may not be a justifying reason. The claim that a person deserves to be beaten up "just for the hell of it" lacks any basal reason; in fact, a basis is explicitly denied. The claim that a mother's mental health is the basis of a student's desert has a logically inappropriate basal reason. Both of these claims egregiously misuse the word "deserve." Not only do they lack good reasons (justifying ones), but they lack the right kind of reason, and are as offensive to logic as to morals.[8] On the other hand, the frequent contention that

---

[5] This appears to hold true of such nonpersonal subjects as art objects, problems, and bills of legislation as well as of persons.

[6] The basis of desert may be a complex relational fact, but in that case the subject must be a party to the relation. The basis of desert cannot be wholly outside the subject. To suppose otherwise is probably to confuse a basis for desert with any sufficient condition for it. It may follow, for example, from the fact that God wills that a person be punished that he deserves to be punished. Reference to God's will then is a reason purporting to justify a desert claim; but it does nothing whatever to identify the basis of the alleged desert. God's will could be a *ratio cognoscendi* of some person's desert, but not its *ratio essendi*.

[7] I borrow this useful term from George Pitcher, "On Approval," *Philosophical Review* (April 1958).

[8] For a number of inadvertent examples of "logically inappropriate" reasons for desert judgments, the reader might well consult Hospers, *op. cit.*, pp. 440–442. He discusses there the question of just wages and salaries, which he regards as "rewards." He then seriously considers need as a criterion for the just distribution of income, as if anyone could seriously consider rewarding (as opposed to compensating) anyone for his needs! The author considers achievement, effort, ability, and need as proposed criteria of desert and then writes: "Thus far, all our criteria have had to do with the worker or what he can produce. Further suggestions, however, may come from another quarter: *criteria may be found having nothing to do with the worker* but with the

ability per se is a desert basis for reward commits neither of these mistakes. It cites the right kind of reason for desert, namely, a fact about the person; but, in my opinion, it is not a good reason. This, however, is a notoriously controversial question involving the conflict of rival value systems and not easily settled.

A logically inappropriate basis for a person's deserving some mode of treatment may, of course, be a relevant and even a conclusive reason in support of the judgment that he ought to be given that mode of treatment. Ought judgments sometimes have a certain finality about them; we say that S ought to get X "all things considered" or "in the final judgment." On the other hand, they often have a quite different force. When we have not had time to survey all the relevant reasons, when we are unable to strike a balance, or simply when we are generalizing about classes of cases, we are likely to use the word "ought" in a *ceteris paribus* or *pro tanto* sense. We say that an S ought to get X "other things being equal" or insofar as some one kind of reason among many has bearing on the situation. That a subject deserves X entails that he ought to get X in the *pro tanto* sense of "ought," but not in the "all-things-considered" or "on-balance" sense. That is simply another way of saying that a person's desert of X is always a reason for giving X to him, but not always a conclusive reason, that considerations irrelevant to his desert can have overriding cogency in establishing how he ought to be treated on balance.

We have yet to give a complete account of the requisite character of desert-bases. It is necessary that a person's desert have a basis and that the basis consist in some fact about himself, but neither of these conditions is sufficient. They do not exclude, for example, need as a desert basis for reward or ignorance as a desert basis for punishment. Both seem inappropriate, and yet they are, after all, facts about the deserving subject. It is impossible, however, to list the necessary and sufficient conditions for personal desert in the abstract, for the bases of desert vary with the mode of deserved treatment. Here we have had to content ourselves

---

society in which he lives" (my italics). Hospers then considers "the open market," "public need," and "public desire for the product of one's labor" as alleged bases of a worker's desert. These considerations, of course, are quite pertinent to the question of what a worker ought to be paid (all things considered), but they are wholly irrelevant to the question of his desert.

with a few important generic properties of desert which do not vary from context to context.

II

A philosophical analysis of the concept of desert can go no further without paying separate attention to each of the major kinds of treatment which persons can be said to deserve. For, if we consider the schema "S deserves X in virtue of P," where S is a person, X a mode of treatment, and P some fact about S, it is clear that the values of P (the various desert bases) are determined in part by the nature of the various X's in question. What makes a man deserving of a high grade in a mathematics course, for instance, is not identical to that which makes him deserving of unemployment compensation.

What are the various kinds of treatment that persons deserve from other persons? They are varied, but they have at least one thing in common: they are generally "affective" in character, i.e., favored or disfavored, pursued or avoided, pleasant or unpleasant. The deserved thing must be something generally regarded with favor or disfavor, even if, in some particular case, it is regarded with indifference by a person said to deserve it. If we were all perfect stoics, if no event were ever more or less pleasing to us than any other, then there would be no use for the concept of desert.

The varieties of deserved treatment are many, and they are heterogeneous to a degree not usually appreciated. For the sake of convenience and with no claim to taxonomic precision or completeness, I have divided them into five major classes or general determinables and then grouped these under two generic headings. The five major groupings are as follows:

1. Awards of prizes
2. Assignments of grades
3. Rewards and punishments
4. Praise, blame, and other informal responses
5. Reparation, liability, and other modes of compensation

I have not included positions of honor and economic benefits on this basic list because they are usually subsumed under one or another or some combination of the other headings. The problem of subsuming offices and honorable positions I have reserved for the end of this section.

The two generic headings are (1) forms of treatment which define contexts in which desert is a "polar" concept and (2) those which do not. In respect to polar desert, one can be said to deserve good or to deserve ill—reward or punishment, praise or blame, and so on. Polar desert is central to what has traditionally been called the concept of retributive justice. Nonpolar desert, on the other hand, has a different sort of symmetry. When it is a prize, an honorable office, or a grade that is in question, we do not divide persons into those who deserve good and those who deserve ill, but rather into those who deserve and those who do not. Nonpolar desert is central to what philosophers have traditionally called the concept of distributive justice. Let us consider nonpolar contexts first and begin with the awarding of prizes.

PRIZES

When prizes are awarded to the victors in individual and group games, races, and tournaments; in essay, cooking, or corn-husking contests; spelling bees; and the like, they consist either of independently valuable objects or of medals, distinctions, or titles. In any case, they are taken to be tangible expressions of admiration, of "recognition" of talent, as means of honoring the victor. Only one competitor wins (barring ties); the others must lose or there can be no "distinction" to the prize. If everyone qualifies for the prize, then no one has won it, for the aim of the competition is to separate the best from the others.

Although the concept of desert seems at home in this context, there appears to be no use for the concept of ill desert, or, at any rate, ill desert and no desert come to the same thing. Either a contestant deserves the prize or he does not; there is no further alternative of deserving ill, no analogue of punishment. Moreover, since desert is here distinguished from mere worthiness,[9]

[9] It is only in respect to competitive prizes that we commonly distinguish desert and worthiness; elsewhere, they are usually synonymous. Two or more men might deserve punishment for the same crime or reward for the same achievement, and the same is true of grades, praise and blame, and compensation. To be worthy of and to deserve, in these contexts, seem to amount to

there are no degrees of desert. If the prize rightly went to Green, we can say that Jones came closer to deserving it than Smith, but not that he deserved it more than Smith, for neither deserved it.

Among the various rules which govern games, tournaments, and contests are those which specify the basis of the competition (throwing the javelin, baking a cake, writing an essay) and the condition to be satisfied by the winner. The latter, which can be called "victory conditions," represent the form taken by qualification conditions in competitive contexts. They vary from those which allow the victor to be determined with mathematical precision (as in broad-jumping, spelling bees, and races) to those that leave wide scope for interpretation and judgment, as in essay contests or cake-baking competitions. The basis of the competition is always some sort of skill. If that were not the case, then, like lotteries and raffles, the activity might still be a kind of game, but not a competitive one.

The general distinction between desert bases and qualification conditions applies clearly to competitive situations. The desert basis is always pre-eminent possession of the skill singled out as a basis of competition, whereas the qualifying condition is satisfaction of the victory condition specified by the rules. The distinction is often obscured, however, by our tendency in competitive situations to use the word "desert" in two ways—not only in its customary sense of "worthiness," but also for "qualification." Even when this happens, though, our important distinction is reintroduced in new language: deserving a prize is distinguished from deserving to win a prize. In a contest of skill in which the winner can be determined by exact measurement, e.g., a high-jumping contest, there can be no question of who deserves the prize (qualification). It is deserved by the contestant who has demonstrably satisfied the condition of victory, in this case by jumping in the prescribed way the highest distance off the ground. There might still be controversy, however, over who deserved to win. To be sure, the victor deserved the prize, but who deserved to be victor? Perhaps the man who truly deserved to win did not

---

the same thing. But, in certain competitive situations, there may be many worthy of the same prize but only one who deserves it, namely, the most worthy. When worthiness and desert are distinguished in this way, worthiness is to desert very much as eligibility is to the strong sense of qualification.

in fact win because he pulled up lame, because he tore his shoe, or suffered some other unforeseeable stroke of bad luck. In a contest of skill, the man who deserves to win is the man who is most skilled, but (because of luck) he is not in every case the man who does win.[10]

In a contest of skill whose rules specify a condition of victory which cannot be determined with precision but which is at least in part a matter of judgment—e.g., a beauty pageant or an essay contest—there can be controversy both over who deserves the prize (i.e., who satisfied the imprecise victory condition) and who deserved to win (i.e., who is the most skilled at the basis of competition). If the prize is awarded to a person who does not deserve it (i.e., did not qualify for it), then it is either because the judge is venal or because he erred in applying the victory criteria to the facts. On the other hand, there are several possible grounds for maintaining that the person who deserves the prize is not the person who deserved to win it. The latter may have had bad luck or an off day, or the victory condition written into the rules might itself have been ill chosen, not truly gauging excellence at the skill which is the ostensible basis for the competition.[11]

In a game of chance, finally—for example, a lottery or a game of roulette—controversy can arise only over who deserves the prize, and even here it would turn only on relatively trivial matters of fact, for the satisfaction of the victory conditions specified by the rules of such games is usually determinable with precision. In a game of chance, one cannot speak of who "really deserved to win"—i.e., who has the most skill at that sort of thing—for, *ex hypothesi,* no skill is involved. Here we would all gain in clarity if we resolved to use only the legalistic language of qualification and entitlement and not speak of desert at all.

GRADES

The nonpolar concept of desert finds application not only in formalized competitive situations but also in contexts call-

[10] Hence the sense in which the ritual utterance "May the better man win" is not merely a pious, optative tautology.

[11] Perhaps the girl who "really deserved" to win the Miss America contest failed because the rules gaves too much importance to the bathing suit ratings and too little to poise and talent

ing for assessment of skill or quality generally. Following J.O. Urmson,[12] I will call such contexts "grading situations." The point of grading, unlike that of awarding prizes, is not to express any particular attitude toward its object, but simply to make as accurate as possible an appraisal of the degree to which it possesses some skill or quality. The desert basis of a grade is the actual possession to the appropriate degree of the quality assessed.

There are various formal procedures for grading qualities, each involving its own criteria of qualification conditions for each grade. In the case of most human qualities which we try to grade by formal criteria (of course, there are many which we could not hope to grade that way) and especially skills and abilities, the formal grading procedure takes the form of a test. Performance on the test then establishes qualification in the sense of entitlement for some grade in a manner dictated by rules.

It is not essental to a grading situation that the concept of desert have a positive–negative symmetry, and for that reason I have characterized the concept when applied in such contexts as "nonpolar"; but, of course, a relatively crude system of grading can utilize a polar concept of desert. If we are concerned to divide our apples into only two groups, those which are edible and those which are not, for example, we can speak of all the apples in the unsorted pile as deserving either the good or the bad grade. Most grading situations, however, involve a much greater range of alternatives. Some systems for grading students, for example, allow the use of each of the first one hundred positive integers as grading labels. Here, there is a whole continuum of deserts; in other situations, there are triads or quintets of marks deserved, and rarely are there only two possibilities—"high" or "low," "good" or "bad," "passing" or "failing."

The situation, however, is rather more complicated than this. Human interests themselves have an essential polarity; desires are either satisfied or to some extent frustrated, ambitions fulfilled or to some degree disappointed. And since persons take an interest in how they and their fellows are graded, they tend, by their interests, to convert grading systems into systems of reward and punishment. Whatever grade an ambitious student gets, he takes it as

[12] "On Grading," in A.G.N. Flew, ed., *Logic and Language (Second Series)* (1953).

a reassuring compliment or a slap on the wrist, for, relative to his ambition, it is usually something welcome or unwelcome. What especially complicates discussions of human grading is that the grades are used by the graders themselves or by others for other purposes—filling positions, granting licenses and privileges, etc.—and that these further purposes are well known to those who are to be graded. But to avoid confusion we should remember that a grade as such is simply a way of ranking something—an apple or a man—in respect to some quality or skill, an appraisal which may be put to some future use or may simply be put on the record for no other purpose than to register the truth.

REWARDS AND PUNISHMENTS

We come now to contexts in which the concept of desert is essentially and necessarily polar. These are situations which are such that, if there is any desert at all, it must be either a good or a bad desert. The word "prize," which fits only a nonpolar concept of desert, has no antonym; neither do the grading expressions "73" or "B minus." But the responses which persons are said to deserve in polar contexts come in neat contrasting pairs—reward and punishment, compensation and liability, charge and credit, praise and blame—one word in each pair standing for a mode of response presumably pleasant or unwelcome. The similarity here to the nonpolar contexts of competition and grading is only partial and contingent. Failure to win a prize or a grade of C minus might be unpleasant and unwelcome, but unpleasantness is not in the same way an essential part of their *raisons d'être;* suffering is an accidental and unintended consequence of competitions and gradings, not what those undertakings are for. The point of a competition is to single out a winner, not to penalize the losers; the point of a grade is to accurately appraise achievement, not (simply) to please or hurt. It is an essential and intended element of punishment, however, that the victim be made to suffer, and of liability that he be made to pay; these are not mere regrettable derivatives of the undertakings but rather their *terminus ad quem.*

Henry Sidgwick shrewdly observed that reward is "gratitude universalized" and that punishment is "resentment universalized."[13] There is little doubt that the services and deprivations which we call "rewards" and "punishments" are conventional means of expressing gratitude and resentment, for these attitudes are prototypically those involved in the "urge to reward" and the "urge to punish." Consider typical occasions for the expression of these "urges." A whole town is endangered by a plague, and one heroically diligent scientist working against long odds perfects a serum which saves the day. Is not the feeling which prompts the normal urge to reward this man precisely gratitude and the need to give it expression? And, when vigilantes and lynch mobs organize to punish a murderer, are not they propelled by their resentment of what has been done? Of course, it is not up to me to feel grateful for a benefit done one stranger by another; and, according to *Webster's,* resentment, too, is largely confined to responses to personal injury and affront. That is why Sidgwick defined punishment and reward as resentment and gratitude "universalized." Originating in private feelings and reactions, they become social devices for sharing imaginatively in the resentments and gratitude of all victims and beneficiaries.

Important as Sidgwick's insight is, it is not the whole truth about the "expressive functions" of reward and punishment. Gratitude and resentment are important, probably the most common, and almost certainly the original attitudes expressed by reward and punishment; but they are no longer the only ones. In fact they are probably not even necessary ones. If an entire community, for example, adopted the cold-blooded Kantian attitude toward punishment, approving of it only because it vindicates the moral law and eschewing altogether any personal resentment toward criminals, the result would no doubt still be recognizable as punishment, although in no sense could it be said to "express" public resentment. And the father who rewards his small son with a quarter for bringing home a good report card is hardly expressing his gratitude; after all, *he* was not the beneficiary of some service.[14]

---

[13] *The Methods of Ethics,* Book III, Chapter 5.

[14] Moreover, as reward and punishment become attached to highly specialized statutes defining technical "offenses" and "services," they tend to become highly impersonal. Parking tickets and bounties for wildcat skins have neither their origin nor their function in the venting of personal feelings; their job

Rewards are, then, as Sidgwick realized, conventionally recognized means of expressing gratitude for services rendered; but they are also, as Sidgwick did not realize, means of expressing recognition, appreciation, or approval of merit or excellence. Similarly, punishment is a standard vehicle for the expression of resentment of injury received and also (but perhaps much less commonly) for the expression of recognition and disapproval of evil.[15] The word "recognition" deserves a brief comment. When the father paid his son a quarter, he acknowledged his son's achievement without necessarily feeling joy, gratitude, or any other attitude. His reward was tangible and public evidence of his acknowledgment; it testified to his recognition. Note that "testimonial dinners" are so called because they manifest the public recognition of the achievements of the recipient; they "testify" to his virtues.[16] On some theories, at least, punishment, *mutatis mutandis,* does the same sort of thing.

---

is simply to help oil the social machinery or, to switch the metaphor, to keep the social traffic moving.

[15] In the difference between resentment and disapproval lies the basis of that between (angry) vengeance and (righteous) retribution. Both vindictive and retributive punishment can be distinguished from mere penalties or "regulative sanctions," however, in that they can plausibly be taken to express public or authoritative attitudes of some kind or other.

That the expression of either resentment or some form of reprobation is an essential ingredient in what is called "punishment" is widely acknowledged by legal writers, but it has been largely ignored in recent philosophical discussions, even those purporting to give explicit definitions of punishment. One legal writer is quoted in Prof. Henry M. Hart's "The Aims of the Criminal Law," *Law and Contemporary Problems* 23 (1958), 401, as follows: "It is the expression of the community's hatred, fear, or contempt for the convict which alone characterizes physical hardship as punishment." Professor Hart adds his own definition of punishment as (in part) "a formal and solemn pronouncement of the moral condemnation of the whole community. . . ." Lord Denning, in the *Report of the Royal Commission on Capital Punishment,* speaks of punishment as "the emphatic denunciation by the community of a crime." Among the minority of philosophers in recent decades who have made reprobative expressiveness essential to punishment are E. F. Carritt, who wrote that "the essential thing in punishment . . . is not pain, but the expression of censure, which is necessarily painful" [*The Theory of Morals* (1928), p. 111]; and Morris R. Cohen, who wrote in *Reason and Law* (1950) that "we may look upon punishment as a form of communal expression. . . . By and large such expression of disapproval is deterrent. But deterrence here is secondary. Expression is primary."

[16] Cf. A.C. Ewing: "It is not merely that we think the good ought to be happy but that we think they ought to be recognized or manifested as good, and the most impressive form of recognition is by bestowal of the means to happiness." *The Morality of Punishment* (1929), p. 128.

The responsive attitudes typically expressed by reward and punishment—gratitude, appreciation, approval, "recognition," resentment, disapproval, condemnation—and indeed all the attitudes and responses expressed by deserved modes of treatment have an important characteristic in common. It is essential to all that they have a kind of phenomenological target, that they be felt in virtue of something. All of these states of mind or attitudes contain as introspectible elements their own ostensible occasions. To resent someone, for example, is not merely to dislike him, but to have a negative feeling toward him in virtue of something he has done, and what follows the "in virtue of" is as much a part of the feeling as is its unfriendly or aggressive character.

These attitudes are not mere automatic responses to stimuli but are self-conscious responses to desert bases, not mere "reactions to," but "requitals for." If a person asks, "What for?" in reply to a declaration that the speaker resents him (or is grateful to him), he means not, "For what purpose?" These feelings are not the sorts of things that can have purposes. Rather he means, "In return for what injury [or service]?" So interpreted, the question is always pertinent. These attitudes, then, have ostensible desert logically built in. We do not use such words as "resent" and "grateful" unless there is an ostensible desert basis of the logically appropriate sort for our feeling. We can be fond of a person for no apparent reason, but we cannot be grateful "for nothing at all"; we can feel hostility for no apparent reason, but we cannot resent someone for "no reason at all." Bradley, in a famous line, wrote that punishment without desert is not punishment.[17] This seems to me to be wrong; but it is clear, I think, that resentment without an ostensible desert basis is not resentment. The point that emerges is that the attitudes in question are all felt as deserved; they cannot be freely or gratuitously bestowed or deliberately entertained "in the public interest" or "for utilitarian reasons" without any further basis. And the impossibility is not merely psychological. We can, after all, artificially induce baseless anger; but if we could do the same with resentment, it would not be resentment. We would have to call it something else.

Legal punishment and official rewards are tied up in rules and regulations, offices and functions, duties and prerogatives; they are

[17] "Punishment is punishment only where it is deserved." *Ethical Studies* (2nd ed.; 1927), pp. 26–27.

formalized and institutionalized to an extent not even suggested by a mere concern with the attitudes they typically express. Punishment, after all, consists of such treatment as forcible seizure of property, incarceration, and whipping—never the mere feeling of resentment; and reward is the tangible expression of gratitude or recognition—never its mere harboring. Moreover, punishment is a prerogative reserved for those with the requisite authority and then only under certain strict conditions specified by law or, in the cases of families and private organizations, by what might be called "house rules." Reward and punishment, then, like other modes of deserved treatment, have qualification conditions as well as desert bases, and these are specified by rules and regulations and confer rights and duties.

Probably because private rewards, unlike "private punishments," are harmless and even benign in their social consequences, governments rarely administer programs of reward on a large scale. Most government grants are either utilitarian inducements and subsidies or compensations. Rewards are, however, given by a large variety of private individuals and groups for a large variety of (basal) reasons, so there is no easy generalizing about their qualifying conditions. These are usually determined by criteria of excellence reflecting the values of the conferring groups, or, when they are directly analogous to punishments, they are reserved for acts of daring or self-sacrificing heroism. A person can be entitled to a reward that he does not deserve, or deserving of a reward he has not qualified for. An informer who, from the basest motives, betrays his brother, is entitled to the advertised reward, but he surely does not deserve it. The wife who sacrifices all to nurse her hopelessly invalid husband through endless tortuous years until death deserves a reward, but unless she qualifies under some set of institutional rules she may not be entitled to one. She may not even be eligible for one.

It is much easier to generalize about punishment, or at least legal punishment. Its universal qualification condition is expressible in two words, namely "legal guilt." What legal guilt is, in turn, is a far more complex matter, defined by thick and ponderous rule books. It is consequent on conviction after a fair trial according to due process, which in turn is defined by an elaborate code of procedural rules.

Of all those modes of official treatment for which a person might qualify under some institutional rules, only punishment seems resistant to the language of rights; for, unless we are philosophers in the idealist tradition, we do not as a rule say of a criminal who is "qualified" for punishment that he is entitled to it or that he has a claim or a right to it. It is tempting, if only in the interest of symmetry and conceptual tidiness, to hold that a convicted criminal has a perfect legal right to his punishment, whether he wants it or not, in quite the same sense as that in which a person who qualifies for an advertised reward has a right to it whether he wants it or not. Perhaps the difference is simply this: a renounced right ceases, sooner or later, to be a right, and the criminal's "right" to be punished is well nigh certain to be renounced.

PRAISE AND BLAME

When we come to informal responses which have the nature of requitals but are not tied to institutional rules, the distinction between desert bases and qualification conditions collapses. It takes no special authority to praise or blame, and anyone can admire or deplore. These modes of treatment are not restricted to such special officials as judges, referees, instructors, and welfare administrators, operating under public rules specifying invariant conditions. Consequently, praise and blame, admiration and contempt, applause and jeering, and so on, though manifestly responses persons are sometimes worthy of, are never treatments people are qualified for. Just as the winners in lotteries are entitled to their prizes but cannot be said to deserve them, so persons sometimes deserve praise or blame but are never entitled to them.

COMPENSATION, REPARATION, AND LIABILITY

Still another mode of treatment which persons are often said to deserve is compensation for loss or injury. We say that persons deserve compensation for harm wrongly inflicted by others, in which case it is called "redress of injury," "amends," or "reparation" and functions not only to repair the damage but also to "restore the moral equilibrium" as would an apology or expression of remorse. Reparation "sets things straight" or "gives satisfaction." But not all injuries are tortiously inflicted. Some are the results of risks voluntarily incurred in the service of others, some are unavoidable accidents, and others are the inevitably iniquitous consequences of the specialization of labor in a technologically complex society. I will reserve the term "reparation" for redress of injury and speak of "compensation" for losses which are no one's fault.

Desert of reparation for wrongful injury is, I believe, a polar concept, despite the grammatical awkwardness in speaking of its other "pole." If reparation is to be received by a victim, it would seem that it must be given by a wrongdoer; and it seems to follow that, if one person deserves to take, another deserves to give. But, of course, we do not talk that way. We no more say of a tortfeasor that he deserves to make reparation than we say of a warden that he deserves to punish. What we do say is that the wrongdoer deserves to be held liable for the harm he has caused; he deserves to be forced to compensate his innocent (or relatively innocent) victim. The other pole of deserved reparation is deserved liability.

Compensation for harm which is no assignable person's fault is, however, a different matter. The unemployed may deserve compensation for their loss, but it is not necessarily true that there is someone who deserves to be held liable for it. Workers in especially unpleasant, onerous, or hazardous jobs may deserve compensatory bonuses, but we would probably not express this by saying that their employers or any other assignable individuals deserve to have liability imposed on them. In short, where compensation is not the redressing of injury and hence where it lacks the character of the mandatory repayment of a debt, there desert is nonpolar. Either the innocent suffering deserve aid and succor or they do not, and that is the end of the matter. When the moral equilibrium is not unbalanced, there is no compensatory analogue of deserved punishment.

When a person suffers a loss, it may be the fault of another person or it may not be, and, as we have seen, the nature of desert differs in the two cases. There is, however, a third possibility. The loss or injury may be his own fault. In that case, though he may well be entitled to help, we would be loathe to say that he deserved it, for we do not as a rule compensate people for their folly or indolence, and even when we do it is not because we think they deserve it. Herein is the difference between helping a person out of a jam simply through charitable beneficence and giving him aid he deserves.

If reward is the tangible expression of one or more of a small range of such appropriate attitudes as gratitude, recognition, or approval, what can proffered help be said to express? Again, I think that it depends on whether it is reparation of injury by a culpable party or simply compensation for unforeseeable bad luck that we are talking about. Reparation can express sympathy, benevolence, and concern, but, in addition, it is always the acknowledgment of a past wrong, a "repayment of a debt," and hence, like an apology, the redressing of the moral balance or the restoring of the *status quo ante culpum.* In the case of mere compensation, it is none of these extra things. In either case, however, the proffered help implies the recognition of a loss for which the victim himself cannot be held wholly to blame. Thus, compensation, though it is often a conventional expression of sympathy, can never express mere pity. There is nothing pitiable about a person who deserves help.

As in the case of all the other modes of treatment here discussed, so, too, in respect to compensation and reparation there can be desert without qualification, and vice versa. A man may be technically entitled to unemployment compensation, for example, because his situation satisfies the qualifying condition of a badly drawn rule, when in fact he does not "really" deserve it; on the other hand, deserving victims of economic blight may have "exhausted their benefits" under the law and thus fail to qualify.

OFFICES AND POSITIONS OF HONOR

I have listed what seem to be the major headings, the *summa genera,* under which the various treatments persons deserve can be grouped. This is an important start in classifying the types of deserved treatment generally, but it raises some nasty problems of subsumption. Under which heading, for example, should we subsume those high offices and positions of honor and responsibility which Sidgwick called "functions and instruments"? Are presidencies, chairmanships, generalships, professorships, papacies, and the like prizes awarded to winners in rule-governed competitions? Sidgwick thought it natural to so regard them, especially when (in his elegant words) they "are interesting and delightful in themselves, or such as are normally and properly attended with dignity and splendor of life, fame, material comfort, and freedom from sordid cares." [18] Other writers, of whom A.C. Ewing is perhaps the most prominent,[19] find it more natural to regard positions of honor as rewards, means by which gratitude or at least recognition of past achievement, service, or contribution are expressed.

Still others prefer to downgrade these aspects of honorable offices and regard them instead as positions of trust and responsibility to be filled in accordance with the criteria of present ability and future promise (what Sidgwick called "fitness" for the job and rather inaccurately characterized as a utilitarian consideration), rather than desert in either of its more familiar senses. "We certainly think it reasonable," Sidgwick admits, "that instruments should be given to those who can use them best, and functions allotted to those who are most competent to perform them: but these may not be those who have rendered most services in the past. . . . Thus the notions of desert and fitness appear at least occasionally conflicting. . . ." [20] Fitness and desert, however, are not quite so opposed as Sidgwick maintained. Consider the situation in which officials make careful appraisals of the relevant abilities and potentialities of each candidate for a job, that is, assign a grade to the fitness of each, and then use that grade as a desert basis. There is surely no logical oddness in the statement: "In virtue of his special fitness, Jones deserves the job." And, if the position is a competitive one, a prize to be awarded to the

---

[18] *Op. cit.*, p. 254.

[19] This is a strong inference from his remarkably broad tentative definition of "reward" and from his interpretation of wages and salaries as rewards. See *The Morality of Punishment, op. cit.*, p. 130: ". . . our whole social system is built upon a scheme of rewards in the shape of salaries and wages"; and then, in a footnote: ". . . if . . . reward is defined as the bestowal of some good for a service rendered, they clearly come under this heading."

[20] Sidgwick, *loc. cit.*

winner, then fitness very likely is the basis of the competition to be demonstrated by performance on some test and, a fortiori, is at home with, rather than in conflict with, desert. Sidgwick has seen the distinction between regarding a "function" as a reward (for past services) and as a prize (for present fitness), but he has misconstrued it as a distinction between fitness and desert, as a result of pre-empting the concept of desert for rewards and therefore considering only past service as a desert basis.[21]

How we select our criteria of desert, then, for such modes of treatment as selection or appointment to coveted positions, depends on how we conceive those positions—whether we regard them as prizes, rewards, or compensations, for example. To make the matter even more complicated, many positions of honor are properly subsumable under two or more of our major rubrics at once. Consider, for example, a C.P. Snow-like contest between two leading candidates for the mastership of a Cambridge college. Candidate A is, on the whole, more fit for the function (considered simply as a function). He is a better administrator, a tireless worker, a clever money-raiser, and has a cooler head. In view of this superior fitness, his partisans claim that he deserves the position, conceiving it as a sort of prize. Candidate B is a rather older man, past his peak in all respects, but on the basis of his past scholarly achievement much more distinguished than A and also better liked. His partisans argue that his distinction deserves recognition and that only the mastership would be a suitable reward. One man deserves the job when it is conceived as a prize, the other deserves it in its aspect as a reward. The

---

[21] It is tempting to argue that selection to fill an office, as such, is neither a reward nor a prize, but a "generic mode of treatment" in its own right, that its desert basis is Sidgwick's "fitness" and its qualification conditions sometimes tests, sometimes selection criteria of other kinds. Then it could be argued that it is only when offices (or functions) are *also* "positions of honor," highly coveted sources of pleasure to their occupants, that the problem of subsumption and conflicting desert bases arises. On such a view, a position of honor considered *only* in its aspect as "office" or "function" has as its desert basis fitness, but insofar as it is also a coveted source of pleasure, it can be considered also a prize and a reward, in which cases competitive skill and past contribution are relevant desert bases.

The temptation to adopt this view, however, should be resisted. An office considered simply "as such" can have nothing to do with desert and hence *no* desert basis, for, unless it is something pleasant or painful, welcomed or dreaded, the concept of desert can have no intelligible application to it.

problem is not desert against advantage, justice against utility, but desert against desert.

The problem can be even more complicated. Partisans of Candidate A, though admitting that Candidate B's scholarly achievements deserve recognition, might counter that Candidate A has worked much harder for the well-being of the college and especially has won gifts and endowments for it, making possible increases in salary for each fellow; hence his past services deserve gratitude, of which the mastership would be a suitable expression. One candidate deserves reward as an expression of recognition, the other deserves reward as an expression of gratitude. And it can get still worse. B, through bad luck, had been passed over twenty years earlier, though everyone now agrees that he deserved the job then more than did his rival. Some of his supporters argue that only his election now can redress that injury, that he deserves reparation. But partisans of A point out that A has injured his health and suffered private pecuniary losses in his efforts to bring more contributions to the college and that therefore he deserves the compensation represented by the mastership. And so it goes—desert of prize against desert of reward, gratitude against recognition, compensation against reparation.

This familiar story should be sufficient to lay to rest the philosophical myths that desert is a single factor to be weighed against other "utilitarian" considerations in ethical decision-making and that it represents uniquely the claim of justice. It is high time that this simplistic account, an offspring of another period's quarrels between intuitionists and teleologists, retributionists and utilitarians, is rejected once and for all. The claims of justice are hardly exhausted in the vacuous principle that everyone ought, *ceteris paribus,* to get what he deserves. Suppose that we decide that, "all things considered," Candidate A deserves the mastership (assuming that *that* makes sense), and then we discover that Candidate B is *entitled* to the mastership (it was formally promised to him twenty years earlier; or a long-forgotten rule makes mandatory the selection of an entomologist for every other mastership, and he is the only entomologist in the college); surely we would not describe this conflict of reasons as a conflict between justice and utility. Rather, it is a conflict between desert and entitlement, between one claim of justice and another. Moreover, it seems plainly false that in *every* such ethical conflict desert has the stronger claim, that persons *always* ought, on balance, to get what they deserve.

Finally, suppose that, as they are trying to choose between A's desert and B's entitlement, the fellows receive a telegram from a Texas oil tycoon offering to make a $1,000,000 gift to the college with no (further) strings attached, but only if they elect A. Now, at last, *there* is a genuine utilitarian consideration to be thrown into the balance with like considerations of profit and gain.

III

Having presented this analysis of the concept of desert, I shall conclude by briefly indicating three kinds of errors it might forestall.

NAÏVE UTILITARIANISM

A utilitarian, I suppose, is anyone who is greatly impressed by the social utility of good things and in one way or another, reduces the goodness to, or identifies it with, the utility. There is no doubt that the modes of treatment discussed in this essay have considerable social utility. The awarding of prizes directly promotes cultivation of the skills which constitute bases of competition and indirectly stimulates such socially valuable conditions as physical fitness, keenness, and competitive ardor. Assigning grades of various sorts to persons increases predictability, order, and control and permits efficient allocation of men and resources. Hope of reward creates incentive to worthy deeds, and the threat of punishment deters wrongdoing. Awards of reparation ease private resentments and promote domestic tranquility. Compensation distributes losses and handicaps more broadly and induces workers to take disagreeable but necessary jobs. So far, so good; utilitarianism has its points. It is in error only when it misconstrues the relevance of social utility.

First of all, utility is not a desert basis for any deserved mode of treatment. It follows from our analysis of desert statements that to say that "S deserves X because giving it to him would be in the public interest" is simply to misuse the word "deserves."

Second, utilitarian qualification conditions, though not conceptually absurd, would in most cases be self-defeating. A utilitarian grading criterion, for example, would be a grading criterion but it could not very well do the job of a good grading criterion, namely, to allow as accurate as possible an appraisal of some skill or quality. If we are concerned to appraise a student's knowledge of mathematics, a "math exam" would surely be more useful for the purpose than a direct appeal to "utility." A utilitarianism which interprets utility as either a universal desert basis or a universal qualifying condition then, is more than "naïve"; it is either absurd or self-defeating.

What is the relevance of social utility to "modes of deserved treatment"? Let us start from the beginning and work up to it. Men, or at least "reasonable men," naturally entertain certain responsive attitudes toward various actions, qualities, and achievements. They recognize and admire; they assess objectively; they are grateful and appreciative, resentful and disapproving; they feel remorse, sympathy, and concern. None of this, so far, has anything to do with utility. Now each of these responsive attitudes has its own appropriate kind of target. We do not "naturally" feel grateful for what we take to be injury or remorse for someone else's behavior; these are logically incongruous targets. But, even when the object of the attitude is logically appropriate, it may still lack a certain kind of propriety. Glee, for example, is an inappropriate response to another's suffering, and, if some humanitarian philosophers are right, no kind of *Schadenfreude* is ever a fitting response to another's ill fortune. I am not sure how, if at all, these judgments of moral appropriateness are to be verified; but I suspect that they resemble certain aesthetic judgments—for example that crimson and orange are clashing colors—more than they resemble judicial pronouncements—for example, that a certain person is to be punished for a crime or that a certain runner is to be awarded the prize for the hundred-yard dash.

If this is so, then the kind of propriety characteristic of personal desert is not only to be contrasted, as it was above, with qualification under a rule or regulation; it is also to be likened or even identified with a kind of "fittingness" between one person's actions or qualities and another person's responsive attitudes. This suggests, in turn, that responsive attitudes are the basic things persons deserve and that "modes of treatment" are deserved only in a derivative way, insofar perhaps as they are the natural or conventional means of expressing the morally fitting attitudes. So punishment, for example, might be deserved by the criminal only because it is the customary way of expressing the resentment or reprobation he "has coming."

So long as we stay on the level of responsive attitudes, there is still no place for utilitarian considerations. For example, the fact that some person has done us a favor is a reason for his desert of our gratitude whether or not there is any utility in it. Gratitude is a "fitting" response to service. But now we come to the question of giving vent to our feelings, translating our appraisals into grades, impressing our recognition on deserving persons, and so on. We could simply do it directly, with no further rigamarole, as we do when we praise and blame, for example, or we could harbor our attitudes unexpressed; but, instead, we often establish imposing institutions, formulate elaborate regulations, appoint referees and appraisers, judges and administrators and require that persons prove their deserts by qualifying for them in trials and tests and competitions.

Here, at last, is where utilitarian considerations come in, and they have a double role. They give a reason (in addition to natural inclination) for expressing and acknowledging our attitudes and appraisals in public and conventional ways. We could, after all, merely harbor our resentments of the wrongdoer, but that would neither unload our aggressions nor deter crime; we could simply feel sympathy toward the unemployed, but that would not prevent food riots. Second, in requiring people to satisfy qualifying conditions specified by public regulations and administered by impartial officials, we have the system which, in respect to many kinds of activity, is probably the most reliable guide to the deserts themselves. We could allow all the responsive attitudes free expression (like praise and blame) without requiring their objects to publicly qualify; but, by and large, that would be hit or miss. Desert is not always readily manifest, and when it is not, the "deserved modes of treatment" would be like shots in the dark. Qualification conditions specified by the rules of competitions, tests, trials, and the like, then, are often necessary to minimize injustice. And, though this is not strictly a "utilitarian consideration," it yields one immediately: we are all better off—happier, more secure—for living in a society where threat of injustice is minimized.

INFLATED DESERT THEORY

If utilitarian theories are apt to misconstrue the relevance of utility, antiutilitarian theories are apt to inflate the role of desert. One of the aims of the various institutional practices we have considered is to guarantee that persons get what they deserve with a minimum of injustice. But to make this the paramount consideration in each single case and thus try to give prizes, grades, rewards, and the like to those who deserve them instead of those who qualify for them (when these are different) would be to abrogate the controlling rules, overload officials with dangerous discretion to be used as they see fit, and thus, in the long run, given human fallibility, generate more injustice than is avoided. It may not be just (in some cosmic sense) for a prize to go to the second fastest runner rather than to his unlucky superior who pulled up lame. But, if judges were given discretion to award the prize to competitors whom they regard as most deserving even when they do not qualify under the rules, it would cause bitter resentment and bickering (utilitarian consideration) and lead to inevitable injustices.[22] Desert is always an important con-

[22] This is a truth which the Greeks learned the hard way, as they experimented with ever-more-elaborate systems of rule-governed activity, while the values of an earlier desert-oriented Homeric society stubbornly persisted:

> Systems of values, however, persist while societies develop; and the Homeric system conflicts violently with any form of society which attempts to allot reward or punishment to an action simply on the basis of the characteristics of that action, irrespective of any other claims to consideration the agent may possess. The persistence of the one system is certain to confuse any attempt to introduce the other.
>
> Signs of such confusion existing already in Homer may be seen in the chariot race of *Iliad* xxiii. We regard a race as a trial of prowess on a particular day. Whether or no the best man wins, the winner deserves the first prize, the second the second prize, and so on; but when Eumelus comes in last, Diomedes, who won, is given the first prize, but Achilles proposes to give the second prize to Eumelus, since "The man who is *aristos* has finished last." (*Iliad,* xxiii. 536. Clearly it would be unreasonable for the winner not to receive the first prize.)
>
> Everyone approves of Achilles' decision except Antilochus, who finished second. His protest is successful, but he does not say "This is

sideration in deciding how we are to treat persons, especially when we are not constrained by rules or where rules give us some discretion; but it is not the only consideration and is rarely a sufficient one.

DESERT AS MORAL ENTITLEMENT

The final kind of mistake precluded by this analysis tends to be committed by philosophers who hold a parajuridical conception of morality. These philosophers take legal institutions as their models, consciously or not, in explicating puzzling moral concepts and then obscure the distinction between the moral and the legal (or institutional) by interpreting the former as an eccentric species of the latter.[23] In the case at hand, the distinction between entitlement and desert is obscured by making desert a peculiar *kind* of entitlement, rather than a notion in essential contrast with entitlement. Desert confers rights, says this theory, but not the ordinary kind of right of the sort winners of competitions and claimants of rewards have, for example, but rather "moral rights," as assigned by special "moral rules," which in

---

unreasonable. I never heard of such a thing," but "Eumelus should have prayed to the gods, and anyway you can easily give him another prize." That is to say, he does not regard it as unreasonable that, even in a race, a man's *arete* should be held to be more important, for the purpose of distributing prizes, than his actual performance. On the other hand, though Menelaus *is* "mightier in *arete* and in strength," he insists that this must not be the reason why he should be placed second rather than Antilochus; the reason is that Antilochus has broken the rules by crowding and crossing. And yet he also says to Antilochus, "You have brought shame upon my *arete*"; and nothing is more important than this.

This is a hopeless tangle of values. Unless the allotment of prizes bears some relation to the result of the race, there is no point in running at all, since the prizes could be distributed before the race starts. Accordingly, some attention must be paid to the result; and yet clearly in this society some attention must be paid to the *arete* of the respective competitors as well. Such a situation can only lead to doubt, confusion, and argument. In a chariot race, this may be unimportant; but we have here in a microcosm the tangle of values which prevailed in the Athenian law-courts and assembly, with such disastrous results. The problem is a serious one. . . ." A.W.H. Adkins, *Merit and Responsibility* (1960), pp. 55–56.

[23] For a more detailed discussion of this philosophical practice, see my "Supererogation and Rules," *Ethics* (July 1961).

turn are implicitly treated as regulations of a special "moral institution." There are, of course, a variety of legitimate uses of the expression "moral right,"[24] but this is almost certainly not one of them. The defeated presidential candidate who deserved to win, for example, is not by that token entitled to the office, nor does he have any right to it. These are conferred by votes, not by deserts. And I fail to see how matters are clarified by qualifying the alleged entitlement as moral. The defeated candidate has no right to the office, moral or otherwise, unless of course "moral right" is simply another, eccentric, way of referring to his deserts. "Deserve," "fitting," and "appropriate," on the one hand, and "right," "entitlement," and "rule," on the other, are terms from altogether different parts of our ethical vocabularies; they are related in such a way that there is no paradox in saying of a person that he deserves (it would be fitting for him to have) certain modes of treatment which, nevertheless, he cannot claim as his due.

This analysis has attempted to show in just what sense the moral notion of desert is prior to a system of public bestowals (one of the aims of the latter is to give people what they deserve) and in what sense it is not (bestowals can often be most justly conferred if the system is governed rather strictly by qualifying rules). We have also seen the variety of conflicts which are possible between desert and desert and between desert and entitlement. These conflicts within the category of justice are as subtle and difficult as any others in ethics, and it is doubtful that general principles can be formulated to dictate a priori the necessary manner of their resolution in every case. But if desert and entitlement are not distinct in nature, the question of their relation cannot be difficult or complicated; for in that case there could be only "real," or "higher," entitlement (desert) and "lower," or "inferior," entitlement (qualification), and in cases of conflict the higher must always vanquish the lower. This is what comes of efforts to compare the incomparable by positing a special cosmic institution in which the one has a subordinate and the other a higher place, of attempts to unify contrasting ethical and institutional concepts by locating them at opposite ends of a common

[24] See H.L.A. Hart, "Are There Any Natural Rights?" *Philosophical Review*, LXIV (1955); reprinted in F. Olafson, *Society, Law, and Morality* (1961).

scale. It is important to emphasize then, in concluding, that desert is a *moral* concept in the sense that it is logically prior to and independent of public institutions and their rules, not in the sense that it is an instrument of an ethereal "moral" counterpart of our public institutions.

6

CONSTITUTIONAL LIBERTY AND THE CONCEPT OF JUSTICE

JOHN RAWLS

An essential part of the political form of constitutional democracy is provision for certain fundamental liberties. These liberties may be contained in a bill of rights or in other clauses of a written constitution interpreted by a supreme court with the right of judicial review; or they may be secured by certain constitutional conventions and statutes which the supreme legislature would in no circumstances violate or override. There are, of course, various kinds of arguments which may be used to support the institutional forms embodying these constitutional liberties. In this essay, however, I should like to examine those arguments which derive from the concept of justice alone.

Justice is but one of many virtues of political and social institutions, for an institution may be antiquated, inefficient, degrading, or any number of other things without being unjust. The notion of justice is not to be confused with an all-inclusive vision of a good society; it is only one part of any such conception. When applied to an institution (or a system of institutions), justice requires the elimination of arbitrary distinctions and the establishment within its structure of a proper balance or equilibrium between competing claims. The principles of justice specify when the balance or share is proper and which distinctions are arbitrary; they do this by formulating restrictions as to how an institution may define offices and positions and assign thereto powers and liabilities, rights and duties. Here, the concept of justice will be considered solely as it applies to (political) institutions, that is, publicly recognized systems of rules which are generally acted upon and which, by defining offices and positions, rights and duties, privileges and penalties, give social activity its form and structure. I shall not, then, discuss justice as it applies to particular persons or to their actions.

One may distinguish the various kinds of constitutional liberty as liberty of the person, liberty of conscience and freedom of thought, political liberty, freedom of movement, and equality of opportunity. It is characteristic of these liberties in a constitutional democracy that they are equal liberties; in respect to these liberties, no person is favored over another. Since the constitution is the foundation of the social and political structure, the highest-order system of positive rules regulative in relation to other institutions, the constitutional liberties define and establish an initial position of equal liberty for all citizens within the basic social system in which everyone must begin to have a place.

Our question, then, is the following: what arguments does justice provide for these constitutional liberties; what distinguishes these arguments from those which invoke other moral concepts and, in particular, from those which invoke the concept of social utility? I shall try to show that the concept of justice provides conclusive arguments for these liberties (although I shall consider only liberty of the person and of conscience), whereas the notion of social utility does not and, moreover, that the concept of justice represents the minimum and the most secure moral concept for achieving this result. In a free society, in which a wide divergence of religious and political belief is to be expected, the concept of justice is, therefore, the most rational ground for a common public understanding of the basis of these fundamental liberties.

To deal with our question, I shall formulate in this and in the next section a concept of justice which may be called "justice as fairness." [1] I shall then consider the manner in which this concept provides arguments for liberty of the person and freedom of conscience. The discussion of these two forms will display a general method of argument which applies equally well to the other constitutional liberties and which illustrates the special aspects of the concept of justice.

The concept of justice which I shall use may be stated, for the moment, in the form of two principles: first, each person participating in an institution or affected by it has an equal right to the most extensive liberty compatible with a like liberty for all; and, second, inequalities as defined by the institutional structure or fostered by it are arbitrary unless it is reasonable to expect that they will work out to everyone's advantage and provided that the positions and offices to which they attach or from which they may be gained are open to all. These principles express the concept of justice as relating three ideas: liberty, equality, and reward for services contributing to the common advantage.

The term "person" is to be understood in a general way as a subject of claims. In some cases, it means human individuals,

[1] For a more detailed discussion of this concept of justice, see "Justice as Fairness," *Philosophical Review*, LXVII (1958), 164–194. This concept of justice is closely related to the theory of the social contract; in particular, there are close similarities, as I have only recently come to realize, to Rousseau's concept of the general will in *Le Contrat social*. If space permitted, I should like to discuss briefly the relation of the argument of this essay to that of James Buchanan and Gordon Tullock in their book *The Calculus of Consent* (1962), which appeared after the meetings at which this paper was read. Both arguments are similar in that in each case an attempt is made to formulate a general principle to apply to the choice and design of a constitution, and the decision on a constitution is to be made first in the absence of certain kinds of information and is to regulate subsequent decisions and actions. The approaches differ in that Buchanan and Tullock use as the principle of choice Pareto's criterion as adjusted to apply to institutions, and they are mainly concerned with that part of the constitution having to do with legislative procedure, for example, with the advisability of majority rule; they take the fundamental constitutional liberties more or less as given. In this essay, I try to connect the principle of constitutional choice with the principles of justice (one part of the second principle having a formal resemblance to Pareto's criticism) and to illustrate their application to the basic constitutional liberties.

but in others it refers to nations, corporations, churches, teams, and so on. Although there is a certain logical priority to the case of human individuals, the principles of justice apply to the relations among all these types of persons, and the notion of a person must be interpreted accordingly.

The first principle holds inviolably only given an assumption of *ceteris paribus,* that is, although there must always be a justification for departing from an initial position of equal liberty, and the burden of proof is on those who would depart from it, nevertheless, there can be and often is a justification for doing so. The principle does indeed imply, for example, that there is a presumption against the distinctions and classifications made by legal systems and other social institutions to the extent that they infringe on the original and equal liberty of the persons participating in them. The second principle defines how this presumption may be put aside by specifying the kinds of inequalities which are permissible.

By "inequalities," it is best to understand not any differences in the institutional structure between offices and positions and the rules defining their rights, duties, powers, and privileges, but differences in the benefits and burdens attached to them either directly or indirectly, such as prestige, wealth, and liability for taxation and compulsory services. Players in a game do not protest against there being different positions, nor do the citizens of a country object to there being different offices of government. They are not differences of this kind that are normally thought of as inequalities, but differences in the resulting distribution established by an institution or made possible by it of the things men strive to attain or avoid. Thus, they may complain about the pattern of honors and rewards set up by an institution (e.g., the privileges and salaries of government officials), or they may object to the distribution of power and wealth which results from the various ways in which men avail themselves of the opportunities allowed by it (e.g., the concentration of wealth which may develop in a free-enterprise economy allowing large entrepreneurial and speculative gains).

It should be noted that the second principle holds that an inequality is allowed only if there is reason to believe that the inequality will work to the advantage of every person engaged in or affected by the institution which defines or permits it. Since this principle applies to institutions, the representative man in every office or position defined by an institution, when he views it as a going concern, must find it reasonable to prefer his condition and prospects with the inequality to what they would be under the institution without it. The principle excludes, therefore, the justification of inequalities on the grounds that the disadvantages of those in one position are outweighed by the greater advantages of those in another position. It is at this point that the principles of justice differ from the principle of social utility, which incorporates no such restriction.

Finally, it is necessary that the various offices to which special benefits or burdens attach should be open to everyone. It may be, for example, to the common advantage, as just defined, to attach special benefits to certain offices. Perhaps by doing so the requisite talent can be attracted to them and encouraged to give its best efforts. But any offices having special benefits must be won in a fair competition in which contestants are judged on their merits. If some offices were not open, those excluded would normally be justified in feeling unjustly treated even if they benefited from the greater efforts of those who were allowed to compete for them. If one can assume that offices are open, it is necessary only to consider the design of institutions themselves and how they work together as a system. It is a mistake to focus attention on the varying relative positions and well-being of particular persons, who may be known to us by their proper names, and to require that every change of position and well-being, as a once-for-all transaction viewed in isolation, be in itself just. It is the system of institutions which is to be judged, and judged from a general point of view. Unless one is prepared to criticize the system of institutions from the standpoint of a representative man holding some particular office, one has no complaint against it.

Put another way, the principles of justice do not select specific distributions of desired things as just, given the wants of particular persons. This task is abandoned as mistaken in principle, and it is, in any case, not capable of a determinate answer. Rather, the principles of justice define the constraints which institutions and joint activities must satisfy if persons engaging in them are to have no complaint against them. If these constraints are satisfied, the resulting distribution, whatever it is, may be accepted as just (or at least as not unjust).

These two principles may be interpreted as those which rational persons would acknowledge when the constraints of having a morality are imposed on them in circumstances which give rise to questions of justice, that is, in circumstances in which persons make conflicting demands on the design of their common institutions and in which they regard themselves as representing or possessing legitimate interests, the claims of which they are prepared to press on one another. Questions of justice and fairness arise when free persons, who have no authority over one another, are participating in their common institutions and settling or acknowledging among themselves the rules which define it and which determine or limit the resulting shares in its benefits and burdens. An institution is just or fair, then, when it satisfies the principle which those who participate in it could propose to one another for mutual acceptance in an original position of equal liberty. To see how the two stated principles are quite likely the best candidates for these principles, consider the following analytic construction.

Imagine a society of persons in which a certain system of practices is already established. These persons, let us suppose, are mutually self-interested, that is, their allegiance to their established practices is normally founded on the prospect of self-advantage. One need not suppose that, in all senses of the term "person," the persons in this society are mutually self-interested. The relations between nations, churches, and families is often mutually self-interested even though there is intense loyalty and devotion on the parts of individual members. A more realistic conception of such a society might construe its persons as mutually self-interested families or some other association.

Imagine also that these persons are rational: they know their own interests more or less accurately; they are capable of tracing out the likely consequences of adopting one practice rather than another; they are capable of adhering to a course of action once they have decided on it; they can resist present temptations and the enticements of immediate gain; and the bare knowledge or perception of the difference between their condition and that of others is not, within certain limits and in itself, a source of great dissatisfaction. Only the last point adds anything to the usual definition of "rationality." Finally, assume that these persons have roughly similar needs and interests or needs and interests in various ways complementary, so that there exist schemes of cooperation which are mutually advantageous.

Since these persons are conceived as engaging in common practices which are already established, there is no question of our supposing them to be deciding how to set up their institutions from the start. Yet we can imagine them considering whether any of them has a legitimate complaint against their established institutions. Suppose that, in doing this, they try first to arrive at the principles by which complaints and thus institutions themselves are to be judged. They do not begin by registering complaints; instead, they try to settle on the standards by which a complaint is to be counted as legitimate.

Their procedure for this is the following: each person is allowed to propose the principles on which he wishes his own complaints to be tried, this privilege being subject to three conditions. It is understood (1) that, if the principles one proposes are accepted, the complaints of others will be similarly tried; (2) that no one's complaints will be heard until everyone is roughly of one mind as to how complaints are to be judged; and (3) that the principles proposed and acknowledged on any one occasion are binding, failing special circumstances, on all future occasions. Thus, each person will be wary of proposing a principle which would give him a peculiar advantage, in his present circumstances, supposing it to be accepted. Each knows that he will be bound by it in future circumstances, the peculiarities of which cannot be foreseen and which might well be such that the principle is then to his disadvantage. The main idea of the procedure is that everyone be required to make in advance a firm commitment which others also may reasonably be expected to make and that no one be given the opportunity to tailor the canons of a legitimate complaint to fit his own special condition and then to discard them when they no longer suit his purpose. Hence, each will propose principles of a general kind which preclude any attempt to take advantage of particular conditions as they may be known at one time or another. These principles will express the standards in accordance with which each person is the least unwilling to have his interests limited in the design of institutions, on the supposition that the interests of others will be limited in the same way. The restrictions which would so arise may be thought of as those a person would keep in mind if he were resigning a social system in which his enemy were to assign him his place.[2]

The elements of this analytic construction can be divided into two parts with the following interpretations. The character and situations of the parties can be taken to represent the special features of circumstances in which questions of justice arise, for these questions arise when conflicting demands are made on the design of an institution and where it is assumed that each person will insist, so far as possible, on what he considers his rights—all of which sets the problem of finding a proper balance, or equilibrium, between these claims. On the other hand, the procedure whereby principles are proposed and acknowledged can be taken to represent the constraints of having a morality. A person who has a morality expresses in his thought and conduct an acceptance of general and universal principles which restricts the pursuit of his own interests. He regards these principles as conclusively binding on himself as well as on others in virtue of his and their nature as human persons. Thus, one's being subjected to the imagined procedure results in constraints analogous to those of having a morality.

There is the following argument for holding that the two principles would be acknowledged given the conditions of the analytic construction. Since there is no way for anyone to win special advantages for himself, each would consider it reasonable to acknowledge the first principle (that of equal liberty) as an initial principle. There is, however, no reason why they should regard this position as final, for, if there are inequalities which satisfy the second principle, the immediate gain which equality would allow can be considered as intelligently invested, in view of its future return. If, as is quite likely, these inequalities work

[2] It will become clear later that this way of putting the matter is appropriate not because persons are assumed to avoid taking chances or to share a pessimistic view of the future, but rather because, in the case of the basic structure of the society in which each must begin, the possibility of a real and equal sharing of risk does not obtain; people have obligations, religious and familial, which restrict the acceptance of risk.

as incentives to better efforts, the members of this society may look on them as concessions to human nature; they, like us, may think that people should ideally want to serve one another. But, since they are mutually self-interested, their acceptance of these inequalities is merely the acceptance of the relations in which they actually stand and a recognition of the motives which lead them to engage in their common practices. They have no title to complain of one another. Provided that the conditions of the principle are met, there is no reason why they should not allow such inequalities. Indeed, it would be short-sighted of them not to do so and could result, in most cases, only from their being dejected by the bare knowledge, or perception, that others are better situated. Each person will, however, insist on an advantage for himself and thus on a common advantage, for none is willing to sacrifice anything for the others.

This argument is not, of course, sufficient to prove that persons conceived and situated as the conjectural account supposes and required to adopt the procedure described would settle on the two principles of justice. For such a proof a more elaborate argument would have to be given. There is, in particular, one natural objection which comes to mind. I wish to consider this objection as a way of introducing the arguments for liberty of the person and liberty of conscience which are founded on justice. Together with the argument of the analytic construction, the discussion of the natural objection is intended as a sketch of a proof of the proposition that, when the logical subject is the fundamental structure of the social system in which everyone must begin, the two principles of justice are those which would be acknowledged when the constraints of having a morality are imposed on rational persons in circumstances which give rise to questions of justice. Since the fundamental structure of the social system is the most important subject of questions of justice, being that part of the social order regulative of the rest, the two principles are not inappropriately referred to as the principles of justice, although there are other principles constitutive of the concept when it is applied to other subjects.

The natural objection to the argument for the two principles is roughly as follows. Suppose that a caste system is defined as one in which society is divided into a number of distinct groups arranged in a definite order of political authority and power, each group having its special occupations, and in which caste membership is hereditary and intermarriage forbidden. In particular, suppose such a system to include a caste of slaves. Given this definition, it does not seem impossible that rational individuals should acknowledge principles which allow of a caste system. Imagine that a group of such individuals finds a caste society already in being and that they are to decide whether to enter it. If the prospect of being in the upper caste greatly attracted them, might not they agree to contract into this society on the condition that their place in it be assigned by a chance device which gives them a certain likelihood of their being placed in the upper caste? It seems possible that they would prefer to take this option rather than to contract into a society satisfying the two principles of justice. (Such a society, I shall call an "open society," in view of the conditions stated in the second principle.) To be sure, such a preference between these two types of society may be unlikely, but it does not seem inconsistent with the notion of rationality. If not, there can be, one might think, no proof that the two principles are, in the sense explained, the principles of justice.

This natural objection rests, however, on a presupposition which does not obtain, namely, that there is the possibility of a real and equal sharing of risks in the case of one's initial place in the basic structure of the social system in which everyone begins. For this reason it fails. Before discussing the place of this presupposition in more detail, it is worthwhile to consider why the preference for a caste system is unlikely. Discussion of this matter will help clarify the nature of the two principles.

The preference for a caste system over an open society may be seen to be unlikely in the following way. Assume, as the first possibility, that the persons in question are human individuals without obligations to any other individuals and that they do not know their own talents and abilities. That is, they have no knowledge of how they will fare in the competition for positions in an open society. There are two main reasons against their agreeing to contract into a caste system. For one thing, whatever chance device is used, the chances must accord with the actual numbers of persons occupying the positions of the system. If but one person in a hundred is in the highest caste, there is but one chance in a hundred of entering it. On any realistic assumption, the likelihood of entering the upper caste is small, and the chance of being in one of the lower castes is high. The other consideration is that an open society may be assumed to be more efficient. Not only is this plausible on theoretical grounds, since a caste system will not place talent where it is most needed or encourage it to make its best contribution, but historical experience seems to support it. Thus, even if a caste society is not less affluent in all corresponding positions, a person's expectation of achieving well-being in a caste society must be less (taking this expectation as given by the expression $\Sigma p_i w_i$, where p_i is the percentage of persons in the ith position and w_i is an index of the average level of well-being of those in the ith position). If these individuals choose between the alternatives on the basis of this expectation, they would not prefer the caste system.[3]

A second possibility is that these individuals do know their talents and abilities. Before, the differences between persons did not enter, and the argument could be carried out from the standpoint of a single representative man. With the knowledge of talents, the case changes, since a gifted person will not evaluate the alternatives in the same way as an ungifted person. An open society must be evaluated according to the series of positions a person may expect to hold in it over time and not simply by the position in which he is likely to start. In the case of a talented person, since he can usually count on improving his place, his expectation is greater than the expectation estimated by initial positions, whereas for the untalented the opposite is true. Indeed, for one without talents, taking a chance in a caste system may be the only possible way of reaching the higher ranks. To simplify things, fix attention on two representative men, one for the upper and one for the lower ranges of ability. Between them there is a possible conflict of interest. If one assumes, in accordance with the conditions of the analytic construction, that unanimity is necessary before these individuals can contract into

[3] It is not necessary to assume that rational individuals would decide between alternatives on this basis alone. They may well consider such other features of the distribution as variance and range. But making allowance for these possibilities would not, I think, affect the substance of the argument.

one society or the other, how is this conflict of interest to be resolved?

If the two principles of justice are acknowledged, the understanding is, in effect, that those favored in the natural lottery (that is, the lottery of native talents and abilities) and who know that they have been favored undertake to gain from their good fortune only on terms that improve the condition of those who have lost out. They are not to win advantages simply because they are more gifted, but only to cover the costs of the necessary efforts of training and cultivating their endowments and for putting them to use in a way which benefits the losers. The more able propose, then, to the less able that the latter give up what is in any case a slight chance for an upper place in a caste system, and in return the more able agree that any inequalities they are to enjoy are for efforts which make a contribution to the less gifteds' well-being, so that the less gifted prefer the system with these inequalities. Accepting a society in which the two principles are satisfied is, then, the best way for the less gifted to overcome their misfortune in the natural lottery. The offer of the more gifted man to acknowledge the second principle would probably be accepted, since doing so would strike the ungifted as a fair way to take advantage of the natural fact of differing native endowments. There would, then, most likely be an agreement to contract into the open society.

It is, however, a mistake to reply to the natural objection by showing that, even if it is true, an agreement to enter a caste society is unlikely. As previously noted, one of the assumptions of the natural objection is that there is a real and equal sharing of risks prior to the assignment of one's place in the caste society. But this assumption is not satisfied in the case of the social system in which everyone begins. Arguments which presuppose a real and equal risk are, therefore, without weight against the reasoning of the analytic construction.

That the natural objection does presuppose a real and equal acceptance of risks may be shown quite easily. Suppose that, in a society where slavery exists, a slaveholder were to try to justify his position to his slaves by claiming that, if given an option between a slave society and an open society, he would take his chance on becoming a slaveholder and willingly run the risk of becoming a slave. He may sincerely hold, although he is probably mistaken in doing so, that one's expectation of well-being (as previously defined) is higher for the slave society. On both these grounds, he says that slavery is not unjust and that he is not being unjust in holding slaves and in supporting the institution.

The reply to this is, first, that there has been no actual taking up of options to which everyone agreed and in which real and equal risks were shared. The slaves have had no chance to be anything but slaves, and therefore it is irrelevant what options the slaveholder would accept if certain real chances were offered. Since there has been no equal sharing of risks, the slaveholder's position is an inequality which could not be acknowledged from an original position of equal liberty. Again, it is irrelevant, even if it is true, that the expectation of well-being for a slave society is higher. If slaveholders are so well off that this is so, this is no justification to slaves who have never had any opportunity to reach that position. It is necessary in order for the slaveholder to make his case that, from an initial position of equal liberty, he (and his slaves) should have accepted, at the age of reason, the option of a slave society and should have submitted to the same real chances. One could imagine a society in which those who become slaves are chosen at birth or at some later time by some random device; but in this variant of slavery the slaveholder's case would not be any better. Finally, how is one to know whether the slaveholder is sincere in his claim? Indeed, how is he to know, given the manifest temptations to self-deception? Where sincerity of conviction is essential for the sense of community it cannot be gathered from opinions voiced from positions of secured advantage, but only by everyone's being in a real initial position of equal liberty from which, by reference to principles generally acknowledged, each can justify to every other the position in which he stands. This is the mark of a just society. In a free society, this initial position is represented in real institutions by that of equal citizenship.

It is possible to imagine special forms of slavery which allow of a real and equal risk. Suppose that city-states which previously have not taken prisoners in war but have always put them to death agree by treaty to hold prisoners as slaves instead. Although the concept of justice does not allow justification of the institution of slavery on the grounds that greater gains to some outweigh the losses to others (that is, justice is opposed to the principle of utility), it does allow that an institution may have to be tolerated as necessary or as the best possible advance on previous institutions. In the present special case, assume that these three conditions hold: (1) that the servitude in question is not hereditary, (2) that the citizens of the city-states signing the treaty approved of it, and (3) that the city-states have a roughly similar military force or capacity. Then the form of slavery imagined might even be said not to be unjust. In this case, the slaveholder could say to his slaves that he prefers the present to the previous arrangement and that he does not consider it unjust. He could claim that he has run and continues to run a real and equal risk of becoming a slave himself. As a citizen of his city, he upholds the treaty and has no complaint against it.

This example shows that situations are possible in which there is a real and equal risk of becoming a slave and that in these special cases slavery need not be unjust. (Of course, the historical forms of slavery have not satisfied these conditions, for example, that it not be hereditary. It may therefore be misleading to call the imagined form slavery at all; it might be better to refer to it as a form of contractual servitude.) This is because it satisfies the conditions of the concept of justice, for it is in accordance with what has been mutually acknowledged from an original position of equal liberty. The persons concerned are, by hypothesis, equals as equal citizens of equal city-states, and they have each approved their city joining the treaty. One may, of course, question whether the requisite conditions are ever likely to be satisfied, or whether, if they were satisfied, this form of slavery (or contractual servitude) would not soon be abandoned for a more humane institution, such as the exchange of prisoners. Surely it would be better to have one's loved ones returned than to hold aliens as slaves. But for the moment this is irrelevant. The essential thing is that the equal citizenship of equal city-states permits citizens of these states to do whatever they consent to do as long as they do not infringe on the like liberty of others. If, having this special institution accepted as the best possible advance on previous institutions, they do not abandon it for a more liberal practice, one may think them callous and unfeeling, but one may not think them unjust to one another.

This example is perhaps overly hypothetical, but it illustrates the following point. The correct reply to the natural objection is not to argue that rational individuals, whether or not they know their talents and abilities, would most probably not contract into a caste society. The correct reply is that this objection assumes a real bearing of risk and the possibility of accepting it in connection with our initial position in the social system and that there is no such risk or real possibility. To satisfy the concept of justice, there must then exist in society a position of equal citizenship within which the liberty of the person is secured and which will express in institutions the satisfaction of the first principle. Given this equal liberty, there will exist a position from which the application of the second principle may be discussed and a sense of community maintained.

One can then formulate a further principle as follows. If rational individuals have willingly and knowingly joined a cooperative scheme from an original position of equal liberty (represented by the position of equal citizenship), if they have borne equal risks in doing so, and if they persist in their willing cooperation and have no wish to retract or no complaint to make, then that scheme is fair or at least not unfair (see footnote 3, *supra*). This principle itself would be acknowledged; it is simply an extension of the first principle of justice and permits the establishment of any voluntary scheme which does not interfere with the liberty of those outside it. In view of this principle, which may be referred to as that of free association, an account of the concept of justice need not pass judgment on those forms of cooperation in which rational individuals are willing to engage from a position of equal liberty. In this way, by establishing and preserving a position of original equality and by allowing a liberty to set up cooperative schemes and other associations which may be freely joined, the free decisions of individuals may be left to determine the form of institutions (so far as the concept of justice applies). But, in the case of the basic features of the social system in which each begins (the constitution and the main economic and social forms), the two principles of justice must be satisfied. In the absence of the actual decisions of rational persons under conditions of equal liberty, one must be guided by those principles of which it can be shown that rational persons, when subject to the constraints of morality, would acknowledge them. The principles of hypothetical arrangements which persons might agree to under conditions of real risks are irrelevant.

The discussion of the natural objection may be summarized in the following way. Together with the argument of the analytic construction, this discussion is intended to sketch a proof of the proposition that, when the logical subject is the fundamental structure of the social system in which everyone must begin, the two principles of justice are those which rational persons would acknowledge when subject to the constraints of the concept of morality in circumstances giving rise to questions of justice. But a natural objection to this conjecture is that rational individuals might agree to take a chance on entering a caste system in preference to an open society. They might agree to do this if they each found their expectation of well-being in the caste system sufficiently attractive. Although it is unlikely that they would find it sufficiently attractive, it is not impossible. This objection proposes, in effect, that rational individuals might accept the principle of social utility rather than the two principles as the standard of justice, for, as the measure of expectations was defined, expectations will vary with social utility and will be highest when social utility is maximized.[4]

The refutation of the natural objection is that it presupposes a real risk and the possibility of accepting it in the case of the

[4] Recall that the expectation was defined as $\Sigma p_i w_i$, where p_i is the percentage of persons in the ith caste and w_i is the corresponding measure of well-being. Social utility is defined as $\Sigma n_i w_i$, where n_i is the number of persons in the ith caste and w_i the same as before. If $\Sigma n_i = n$ is the total number of persons, the expectation is simply the social utility divided by n. The argument in the text assumes that those outside the society take as welfare indexes those of the groups in the society. Relevant here is Jerome Rothenberg, *The Measurement of Social Welfare* (1961), pp. 267–269. Rothenberg argues that an earlier proposal of Harsanyi's, similar to that of the natural objection, is equivalent to the principle of utility. For this proposal, cf. J.C. Harsanyi, "Cardinal Utility in Welfare Economics and in the Theory of Risk-Taking," *Journal of Political Economy,* LXI (1953), 434–435, and "Cardinal Welfare, Individualistic Ethics, and Interpersonal Comparisons of Utility," *ibid.,* XLIII (1955), 309–321.

basic structure of the society in which each must begin, but this presupposition does not hold. Therefore, the natural objection fails as an argument against the two principles as the proper standard of justice in the case of the fundamental form of the social system. Once given a social system satisfying the two principles of justice in its basic structure and so securing an equal liberty of the person, rational individuals may, if they wish, decide which voluntary schemes to engage in by estimating their expectation of well-being. The principle of utility so understood may be used by individuals within the framework of a just society, but it is not the correct principle of justice to apply to the constitution of the social system itself.

Although the natural objection fails as an argument against the two principles of justice, the discussion of its presupposition of the possibility of a real and equal risk has brought out the necessity for a real position of equal liberty in actual institutions. In this way, the concept of justice may be seen to require in the constitution of society liberty of the person and to exclude caste systems and slavery. There is another assumption of the natural objection to which I shall now turn. The consideration of this assumption will show the manner in which the concept of justice also requires an equal liberty of conscience in the constitution of society.

The second assumption of the natural objection is that the persons who are to acknowledge principles before one another have no obligations, that they are free as individuals to do as they please. If they wish to take a chance on attaining a high place in a caste system, they may do so. But, if the persons in question have obligations as fathers, heads of nations, or of religious sects have obligations, the situation changes. Even if a man would, for his part, agree to take a chance on entering a caste system, he cannot and would not be willing to if he is a father and if the position of being lower-caste will be inherited by his children. For a man to face his children, he must insist on the two principles of justice.

The same is true of the heads of religious sects (whether these authorities are represented by a single person, a council, or whatnot). They cannot take chances with the future of their religion. For heads of churches to conduct themselves in any other way would imply, given the concept of religion, that they do not take their religion seriously. If one supposes them to gamble winner take all, as two autocrats might gamble for the rule of certain territories or city-states, they could not be taken as religious persons. They might, perhaps, regard themselves as possessors of certain means of influence to which they had proprietary rights and which they could dispose of as their interests required. Admittedly, the concept of religion might be specified in various ways, but any plausible determination of it would imply that a person under a religious obligation must regard this obligation as binding absolutely in the sense that he cannot qualify his fulfillment of it for the sake of personal advantage. In particular, the obligation to preserve the truth of one's religion and the obligation to live up to its injunctions cannot be compromised for the sake of secular interests.

It might be argued that religious bodies could not acknowledge any principles at all which would limit their pressing their claims on one another. The obligation to religious truth and divine law being absolute, no understanding among persons of different religions is permissible from a religious point of view. Certainly, religious sects have often acted as if they accepted this doctrine. There is no need, however, to argue against it. One may simply observe that, if any principle can be acknowledged, it must be that of equal religious liberty, since the concept of religion is such that each understands that he could not expect another to accept less than an equal liberty. A person may think that another ought to belong to the same faith that he does and that by not doing so the other person is in mortal error. But anyone understanding the concept of religious obligation cannot expect another of a different faith to accept without coercion less than an equal liberty. Much less can it be expected that another will permit him to be the arbiter of the proper interpretation of religious obligations. One may add that, if God wills justice among men (as expressed by the concept of justice as fairness) and if God prefers the worship of men in a free society, then acknowledging an equal liberty is surely permissible, even given the absolute character of religious obligations. In this way, the argument for liberty of conscience from justice may be supported on theological grounds.

These conclusions are further supported by recalling that the relevant acknowledgment is not that which would be made by representatives of religious sects, but that which would be accepted between members of differing sects as citizens. If one supposes that the fundamental position is that of citizenship, then one should ask what rational individuals in the original position could acknowledge as principles to regulate the liberties of the citizen. In this case, it is equally clear that they can acknowledge only an equal liberty of conscience and that this initial position must be final. If each person is thought to regard himself as in general subject to religious obligations (although he may expect that these obligations will change over his life if his religious views change), then he can only acknowledge the principle of equal religious freedom; otherwise he would be violating his interpretation of his religious obligations. A person can accept a less-than-equal religious liberty only if there is a threat of coercion which it seems unwise to resist from the standpoint of these obligations. That is, without resistance, the prospect is that one's religion will be tolerated, but resistance will bring greater repression.

Once each understands that a less-than-equal liberty can be acquiesced in only under these conditions, it will be recognized that equal liberty of conscience is the only principle which can be acknowledged from an original position of equal liberty and thus is the principle which must regulate the liberties of the fundamental office of citizen. It is the only principle which is consistent with a sense of community, for, where there is not equal liberty of conscience, the religious convictions of some citizens are given a priority which those citizens not so privileged cannot acknowledge consistent with their own beliefs. They can only acquiesce in their inferior status under a threat to resist which would put their religion in jeopardy. A sense of community, insofar as it depends upon the concept of justice, is possible only where the rights and privileges of all can be acknowledged by each without anyone's being required to violate what he understands to be his obligations. The principles of justice and in particular equal liberty of conscience (as a special case of the first principle) are the only possible principles in matters of religious toleration which, given the concept of religion, are consistent with a sense of community.

It is now possible to comment on why it is characteristic of the constitutional liberties that they must be equal; why, in respect to these liberties as defined by the structure of the social system in which each begins, no one can be favored. Their role is to mark off and to define a part of the social structure distinct from that part which allows differences in rights and powers and a varied distribution of good things in accordance with the second principle. Roughly, the distinction between these two parts of the social structure is that the first part—the constitutional liberties—expresses in institutions the original position of equal liberty; it represents the position from which the application of the second principle may proceed among persons secure in their fundamental equality. The second part of the social structure contains those distinctions and hierarchies of political, economic, and social forms necessary for the efficient and mutually beneficial arrangement of joint activities; but such distinctions can be acknowledged only in matters of secular and personal interests or, roughly speaking, in matters of welfare.

Given these equal liberties and certain other conditions secured by institutions—in particular, equality of opportunity and a social minimum—any one of a wide range of distributions of good things taking place as a consequence of legitimate inequalities of the second part of the social structure is acceptable to justice. In this way, the social structure provides the latitude necessary in the performance of a well-ordered society.[5] The unifying feature, then, of the constitutional liberties is that they are equal liberties. They are essential features of the position of

---

[5] The essential idea here is that the problem of distributive justice, in the case of the basic structure of the social system, should be viewed as a problem of distributing or assigning rights in the design of the general systems of rules defining and regulating economic activities. It is not a problem of distributing given amounts of income or batches of goods to given individuals with certain patterns of tastes and wants. If one assumes that law and government effectively act to keep markets competitive, resources fully employed, property and wealth widely distributed over time, and maintains a reasonable social minimum, then, if there is equality of opportunity, the resulting distribution will be just or at least not unjust. It will have resulted from the workings of a just system, one against which no one can complain, since it would satisfy principles acknowledged in the original position. For example, since it cannot be supposed that everyone will have sufficient private wealth to tide him over disasters that may befall him, a social minimum is simply a form of rational insurance and prudence. Given a just system, one need not complain or worry about particular outcomes.

equal citizenship and as such define the first and primary part of the social structure in a way which is necessary for a sense of community.

Suppose, then, that the concept of justice permits these arguments for an equal liberty of conscience as found in a constitutional democracy. The existence of this liberty means that, according to the constitution, there is freedom of religious belief, worship, and conduct save as limited by the state's interest in public order and security, that the state will favor no particular religion, and that no penalties or disabilities, as expressed in political or legal rights, are attached to any religious affiliation or lack thereof. Particular religious associations may be organized as the members wish and may have their internal discipline, subject to the restriction that members be given the choice of affiliation in the sense that the public order provide the right of sanctuary, that is, that apostasy is not recognized, much less penalized, as a legal offense. In this way, the state secures the original position of equal liberty expressed in institutions by the office of equal citizenship.

Liberty of conscience is limited, everyone agrees, by the state's interest in public order and security. This limitation also is readily derivable from the concept of justice; it does not presuppose the notion that public interests are superior to private (or to ecclesiastical) interests. The acceptance of this limitation does not imply that the state is prepared to ignore private or religious matters as things indifferent or to claim the right to suppress or curb them when they conflict with its own affairs. Rather, given the concept of justice as here understood, the state is viewed as the association of citizens to regulate their pursuit of their profoundest interests and their fulfillment of their most solemn obligations and to give form to their relations in a manner acceptable to each from an original position of equal liberty.

From this position, each recognizes that an interference with the security of public order is an infringement on the liberty of all. This follows once the maintenance of the public order is understood as a necessary condition for every person's achieving his ends (whatever they are, within certain limits) and for his fulfilling his interpretation of his obligations which all would have a right to do if anyone did. To limit liberty of conscience at the boundary, however inexact, of the state's interest as expressed in the police power is a limit derived from the principle of equal liberty itself; it marks the limit acceptable to those in an original and equal position as being the terms on which persons so placed as the analytic construction supposes would agree and acknowledge before one another. In this conception, then, the state's right to maintain public order is derivative; it is an enabling right, a right which it must have if it is to carry out its duty of impartially supporting the conditions necessary for everyone's pursuing his interests and fulfilling his obligations as he understands them.

Again, liberty of conscience is to be limited only when there is a reasonable expectation that not doing so will interfere with the security of public order; this expectation must be established by evidence and ways of reasoning acceptable to common sense, that is, by observable and provable consequences and by modes of thought which are generally recognized as correct. This reliance on the methods of common sense (and on the methods of rational scientific inquiry generally, where they are not controversial) and this limitation on what can be established and known by all does not imply any particular metaphysical doctrine as to the nature of the world. It does not imply, for example, that what exists is only what can be observed or evidenced by common-sense methods of investigation or that everything is, in some sense, a logical construction of what can be observed or evidenced by rational scientific inquiry. Such a metaphysical view is, one may suppose, sufficient to derive the reasonableness of this restriction to what can be established by common sense; it is not, however, necessary.

Rather, the acceptance of the standard of reasonable expectation as that of common sense is required by the concept of justice, for it is an appeal to what everyone can accept, if any principle can be accepted, in an original position of equal liberty. It is an appeal only to what in fact all have in common in their knowledge and understanding of the world, so that the acceptance of this standard does not infringe on the equal liberty of anyone. A departure from the principles of common sense would involve giving a privileged place to the views of some over others which could not be acknowledged in the original position. Finally, in holding that the consequences for the security of public order should not be merely possible or even probable, but reasonably certain and imminent, there is no implication of any particular philosophical analysis of the concept of knowledge, for this requirement may be understood as an expression of the high place which everyone must accord liberty of conscience and the urgency of religious obligations.

It follows, then, from the concept of justice as applied to the fundamental structure of the social system in which each must begin, that there should be equal liberty of conscience limited only where common sense establishes a reasonably certain interference with the essentials of public order. By this elementary principle alone, many grounds of intolerance given in past ages may be rejected as fallacious. Thus, Aquinas accepted the death penalty for heretics on the ground that it is a far graver matter to corrupt the faith, which is the life of the soul, than to falsify money, which sustains life.[6] So, if it is just to put to death forgers and other criminals, heretics may a fortiori be so dealt with. But the premises on which Aquinas relies cannot be established by the methods of common sense. It is a matter of dogma that faith, as the Roman Church defines it, is the life of the soul and that the suppression of heresy—that is, departures from orthodoxy in defiance of ecclesiastical authority—is necessary for the safety of souls.

Again, the grounds given for limited toleration often run afoul of this elementary principle. Thus, Rousseau thought that people would find it impossible to live in peace with those they regard as damned, for to love them would be to hate God, who punishes them. One who regards another as damned must either reclaim or torment him. Rousseau believed that those who regard others as damned cannot, then, be trusted to preserve civil peace, and he would not tolerate, therefore, those religions which say that outside their church there is no salvation. But the consequences of dogmatic belief which Rousseau conjectures are not borne out by experience; however plausible the a priori psychological argument may be, toleration must not, to accord with the concept of justice, be abandoned on anything but consequences securely established.[7] There is, however, this difference

[6] Cf. *Summa Theologica* II–ii. Qu. 11. Art. 3.

[7] Cf. *The Social Contract* iv. 8.

between Rousseau and such others as Bayle and Locke, who advocated a limited toleration, on one side, and Aquinas and the Protestant reformers, on the other, namely, that they limited toleration on the basis of what they supposed were clear and evident consequences for the security of public order. More experience would presumably have convinced them that they were mistaken. With Aquinas and the Protestant reformers, the grounds for intolerance are themselves matters of faith, and this difference is more fundamental than the limits actually drawn to toleration. One view recognizes the priority of principles which can be acknowledged in an original position of equal liberty, whereas the latter does not.

That religious liberty is limited by the necessity of securing public order but that its interference with the public order must be established by the principles of common sense is a principle itself derivable from the concept of justice. In acknowledging this principle, one does not commit oneself either to a particular metaphysical view of the world or to a particular philosophical account of knowledge. One is, rather, committed to it by the requirements of justice.

Finally, one may ask whether the concept of justice implies that a religious sect which rejects the principle of equal liberty should itself be tolerated, that is, given that constitutional liberty which it would deny, had it the means, to others. There may certainly be many reasons for toleration; for example, it may be impossible, if the sect is strong in numbers and influence, not to tolerate it without a divisive civil conflict. But I am concerned with reasons of justice alone.

Several questions must be distinguished—first, whether the intolerant sect would have any title to complain if it were not tolerated; second, whether the tolerant sects have a right not to tolerate the intolerant sect; and, finally, whether, having the right, it should be exercised? In considering the first question, it seems that the intolerant sect has no title to complain. This follows if it is assumed that a person has no title to complain of conduct of others toward him which is in accordance with principles which he would, in similar circumstances, follow in his conduct toward them. A person's right to complain is limited to violations of principles which he himself acknowledges. It may be said that members of the intolerant sect profess the principles that God should be obeyed and truth accepted by all. Their complaint, then, is that they but not others act on this principle.

The reply is that, from the standpoint of the original position, no particular sectarian interpretation of religious truth could be acknowledged as binding on citizens. In that position, each person must insist on an equal right to understand what religion requires of him. Thus, the right to complain is further limited to violations of those principles which one accepts and which would be acknowledged in a position of equal liberty. An intolerant sect would not, it seems, have title to complain; its representative member claims, as a citizen, an authority to determine what is true and binding in matters religious which would not be acknowledged and which he would not grant to another in the original position.

Because the intolerant sects do not have a right to complain, it does not, I think, follow that tolerant sects have a right to suppress them. For one thing, others may have a right to complain. To simplify the question, assume that the tolerant sects would have the right not to tolerate the intolerant sects in at least one circumstance, namely, when they sincerely and with reason believe it necessary for their own security. This right follows readily enough from the concept of justice, for, as the circumstances giving rise to questions of justice are defined, no one is required to watch idly while the basis of his existence is destroyed. Therefore, what is in question is the wider restraint, that is, whether there is a right on the part of tolerant sects to curb the intolerant when they are of no danger to the equal liberties of others. This question should be answered from the point of view of the tolerant sects and on the assumption that they each accept the principles constitutive of the concept of justice. It is then clear, I think, that they would not regard themselves as having any such right.

An intolerant sect may be said to authorize others to suppress it in the sense that it cannot complain should it be suppressed. But why should the just act on the authorizations of the unjust? Do the just enjoy, as it were, suppressing the unjust? On the contrary, acceptance of the concept of justice as the basis of a free society requires one to act so far as possible to establish justice throughout society. This means that the fundamental position of equal citizenship, with all its constitutional liberties, should be upheld as far as possible without putting liberty itself in danger. It is from the position of equal citizenship that persons join the various sects, and it is from this position that persons should view one another. However intransigent ecclesiastics and theologians may be, their strength depends in part on the convictions and numbers of the laiety. Citizens in a free society should not be held by one another incapable of a sense of justice failing a clear necessity for doing so. Justice and equal liberty of conscience should be upheld to persuade the intolerant (that is, those citizens who belong to the intolerant sect) to justice, this persuasion working on the psychological principle that, other things equal, those whose liberties are secured by a just system will acquire an allegiance to it. The intolerant ecclesiastic is, then, secure through the rights of the citizens whose institutions of faith he administers and whose rights and capacities for justice cannot without the most urgent of reasons be denied.

The conclusion, then, is that an intolerant sect does not itself have title to complain of intolerance and that, although tolerant sects have a right not to tolerate an intolerant sect when they sincerely and with reason believe that their own security and that of the institution of liberty is in danger, they have this right only in this case. What must be the principle of their action is the concept of justice, which requires the establishment for all of the position of equal citizenship with an equal liberty of conscience. The just must be guided by the concept of justice and not by the authorizations of the unjust. They are bound above all else to see that just institutions flourish, and they must not punish the unjust simply because the unjust cannot reproach them.

So much, then, for a brief and all-too-abstract discussion of the arguments derivable from the concept of justice for the two constitutional liberties—liberty of the person and liberty of conscience. What does this discussion suggest is the special sense of the concept of justice, as distinct from other moral concepts? In particular, how does the concept of justice differ from the concept of social utility? I should like to think that the discussion confirms the initial idea that, as applied to social institutions, the sense of the concept of justice is essentially that of the elimination of arbitrary distinctions and the establishment within the structure of an institution of a proper balance, share, or equilibrium between the competing claims of persons prepared to press their rights on one another and that the general characterization of the principles constitutive of the concept is that they are the principles which rational persons, when subject to the constraints of morality, would propose and acknowledge before one another in an original position of equal liberty. This characterization states the just way of defining and limiting people's rights with respect to one another in their claims on institutions, and an institution is just only if it satisfies principles which could be so accepted. If the argument of the analytic construction is correct, it follows that the basic structure of the social system in which everyone begins must satisfy the two principles of justice and therefore that these principles may without impropriety be called the principles of justice.

The peculiar feature of the concept of justice is that it treats each person as an equal sovereign, as it were, and requires a unanimous acknowledgment from a certain original position of equal liberty. This is a strong condition, ostensibly too strong. I have tried to show, by examining the arguments for liberty, that it works out well enough. In contrast to the conception of social utility, the concept of justice excludes the possibility of arguing that the violations of the claims of some is justified (rendered just) by compensating advantages to others. If there is any disadvantage which cannot be acknowledged, an institution is unjust.

The concept of justice is distinct from that of social utility in that justice takes the plurality of persons as fundamental, whereas the notion of social utility does not. The latter seeks to maximize some one thing, it being indifferent in which way it is shared among persons except insofar as it affects this one thing itself. The conception of utility extends the principle of rational choice for one person to the case where there is a plurality of persons, for one person may properly count his advantages now as compensating for his own losses earlier or subsequently, but justice excludes the analogous kind of reasoning between persons. The plurality of persons must construct among themselves the principles in accordance with which they are to decide between institutions, and the general characterization of the circumstances of this construction and the respective positions of persons within it is given by the analytic framework by which the two principles of justice were derived. Moreover, a necessary condition for the moral worth of the people of any society is that they be moved by the principles of such a construction, however hypothetical.

A strong case can be made for the view that the arguments for constitutional liberties founded on the concept of justice are the most fundamental ones and that these arguments ought to be recognized as the surest basis of a free society. It is both unwise and unnecessary to found liberty of conscience and freedom of thought on, say, indifference to religion or philosophical skepticism. These are at best fragile bases for these liberties. They are open to theological and philosophical objection and cannot attain a wide measure of assent in a free society, where diversity of opinion is to be expected. But an examination of the essential parts of the concept of justice as fairness would show, I think, that it is not impossible that a broad understanding might be reached on this concept and on its constitutive principles and thus on the general constraints and forms which the concept requires in the framework of the social structure.

Aristotle thought that it was a peculiarity of man that he had a sense of the just and the unjust and that participation in a common understanding of justice makes a *polis*.[8] Analogously, one might show that participation in the understanding of justice as fairness makes a constitutional democracy.

---

[8] Cf. *Politics* i. 2. 1253a15.

7

JUSTICE AND LIBERTY

CHARLES FRIED

Mr. Rawls's thesis, in his paper, "Constitutional Liberty and the Concept of Justice," puts us in mind of what it is to be concerned with justice. It is not to describe, classify, or analyze existing laws and practices. Still less can we say that it is justice which is the concern of those thinkers whose theories on this topic, though portentous enough in tone, propose no dispositive criteria of judgment and indeed lack even that determinacy which concentration on the actual and identifiable lends. Rawls's thesis is important, first of all, because it has bite; he would not allow one to espouse his thesis and still eschew the judgment that a particular institution is demonstrably just or unjust.

But Rawls's thesis is important for another reason: it identifies as requirements of justice itself some of the tenets of constitutional democracy, and this vindication of assumptions we all share presents fruitful ground for comment in its application to particular legal controversies. For instance, one may well ponder whether the courts or at least scholars have not in recent times given short shrift to the claim that the limitations of justice have relevance to readjustments and regulations of interests apart from those connected with liberty of conscience. The model of justice we are now considering thus may have important bearing on the doctrine of the "preferred position" of First Amendment liberties. Although a direct consideration of such practical issues would be fruitful, I nevertheless find it necessary for my own understanding of the basis and full purport of Rawls's thesis to consider it primarily at the level of abstraction at which it is presented.

Rawls's conception of justice has two principal features: (1) it is formal, in the sense that it does not propose a complete system of ideally just institutions, practices, or acts, singly or in the alternative, against which existing and proposed institutions and the like are to be judged; and yet (2) it is substantial, in the sense that it purports to dictate a form of justification by which particular institutions and the like in a given context must be deemed just or unjust, and then absolutely.[1] As I have indicated, the second feature of the argument is necessary in order to make any conception of justice worth considering at all.

In this paper, I shall consider to what extent it is possible for an analysis of justice to yield substantial judgments and yet be formal in that it prescinds from the types of philosophical controversy (of which Plato's *Republic* is the paradigm) that have been concerned with substantial speculations as to human nature, human purposes, and human goods.[2] Thus, we may paraphrase Seneca's question: "If I turn the inquiry to why nature brought forth man and why she set him above the other animals,

---

[1] See Roderick Firth, "Ethical Absolutism and the Ideal Observer," *Philosophy and Phenomenological Research,* 12 (1952), 317–319, for a discussion of the term "absolutist."

[2] Radbruch was of the opinion that justice is a formal concept and that it yields no substantial results. "For while justice directs us to treat equals equally, unequals unequally, it does not tell us anything about the viewpoint from which they are to be deemed equals or unequals in the first place; moreover it determines solely the relation, and not the kind, of the treatment." Radbruch, *Legal Philosophy* trans. Wilk (Twentieth Century Legal Philosophy Series, 1932), p. 107.

would you then judge me to have left our topic, the question of justice, far behind?" [3]

I

The inquiry I propose must seem excessively abstract. In order to make it more concrete, I shall begin by suggesting two test situations. In determining what judgment Rawls's concept of justice would require us to pass on the proposals in those situations, it is my hope that some more general questions about Rawls's thesis may be raised and some more general answers suggested.

It is determined in good faith and on the most convincing evidence that, with the advent of automation and the short work week, the intellectual resources of those whose time is thus liberated are simply inadequate to cope with the ensuing leisure. A program of adult education is considered a full solution to this problem. Would it be unjust to make such a program compulsory although considerations of social utility might well justify the compulsory manipulation of beliefs or preferences? Note that the sole or at least the intended beneficiaries of such a compulsory program are the same people whose title to complain of its injustice is in issue.

A still less sympathetic proposal is this one. Again in good faith, it is determined either that religious beliefs in general or some particular religious belief are the cause of great unhappiness to those who hold them. Would a regime be unjust in suppressing those beliefs if the suppression is undertaken—unlike the punishment of heretics to which Rawls refers—solely for the benefit of the suppressed?

The concrete form, then, of the abstract question I have raised is: By what standard would Rawls require the condemnation as

[3] The passage from Seneca, *Letters* 121. 3, reads: "Cum quaeritur, quare hominem natura produxerit, quare praetulerit animalibus ceteris, longe me iudicas mores reliquisse? Falsum est. Quomodo enim scies, qui habendi sint, nisi quid homini sit optimum inveneris, nisi naturam eius inspexeris." (When the inquiry turns to why nature brought forth man and why she set him above the other animals, do you judge me to have left the discussion of morals far behind? That is wrong. For how are you to know what practices would obtain if you do not discover what is best for man, if you do not consider his nature?)

unjust of the two practices I have hypothesized? He explicitly rejects the standard of classical utilitarianism, that is, "the most efficient design of institutions to promote the general welfare," since it contains no requirement that inequalities in the distribution of benefits and burdens work out for everyone's benefit and thus would permit, for instance, justification of slavery on the ground that the unrelieved misery of some is outweighed by the benefits to the slave-owners. This rejection is perhaps the distinctive feature of Rawls's analysis. However, the rejection of such a crassly utilitarian argument seems to be required as much by the vacuity of the principal notions of classical utilitarianism—"pleasure," "pain," and "general welfare"—as by Rawls's model. The suffering of the slave and the advantages of the slaveholder are essentially incommensurable in the absence of some common, extrinsic standard which assigns to each an identifiable value. But classical utilitarianism aggressively rejects any such extrinsic standard.[4]

The problem of incommensurability is solved by Rawls by the notion of consent, for, if the question is changed from the essentially meaningless one of whether the sufferings of X number of slaves outweighs the ease of Y number of masters into an inquiry whether rational people would arrange their common affairs in such a way that some would run the risk of becoming slaves, an answer to the problem of justice seems close at hand. It also appears that the notion of consent has dispensed with any appeal to extrinsic standards of the good life for man or of the good state. Since rational men are unlikely to consent to the risk of slavery, slavery is excluded as an unjust practice with no apparent consideration of the compatibility of slavery with an ideal state or an ideal life for man.

In Part II, I shall examine the basis of the notion that consent is a sufficient and perhaps a necessary condition of the justice of

[4] "It is . . . not [on] the principle of utility, that the most abominable pleasure which the vilest malefactor ever reaped from his crime would be reprobated, if it stood alone." Bentham, *The Principles of Morals and Legislation,* Chap. II, § iv; quoted in John Rawls, "Justice as Fairness," *Philosophical Review,* 67 (1958), 164; reprinted in F. Olafson, ed., *Justice and Social Policy* (1961).

To allow reference to Rawls's earlier paper in either source, citations will be made by section.

a practice or, put otherwise, that a justification which ultimately refers to consent is a valid form of justification. In Part III, I shall argue that the model from which we drew our conclusions as to the primacy of consent can be only a model and that in any actual society most of the crucial decisions which affect, and affect adversely, its members must rest on a justification only remotely related to consent. The inevitable concomitant of this remoteness is the inconclusiveness of any argument as to the justice of some of the most crucial arrangements in any society. In Part IV, I shall consider the claim, which is the thesis of Rawls's paper, that, as to some actions and some practices, the principle of consent retains full force even in an actual society, namely, where what is involved is liberty of conscience. Rawls faces us with the familiar claim, therefore, that, though a society which is in general fairly organized may justly operate on a variety of principles (including the principle of utility) in many matters, still, in some matters, a society must observe stringent limitations.

It is at this point that the test of what could reasonably be agreed to reappears as a very real, rather than a remote, factor in Rawls's analysis. But it is just at this point that the most serious question about the status of consent in the concept of justice must be raised. My two hypothetical situations are intended to pose that question, since on their face, at least, they do not involve the *same* necessity for balancing incommensurables which makes the utilitarian calculus so inadequate. I shall argue in Part IV that, in order for the notion of consent to do service in my hypothetical situations, the whole status of the argument from consent must be altered. It is no longer possible to argue simply from the plausibility of a model based on consent to the conclusions which such a model compels or suggests. Rather, the appropriateness of the model itself is radically challenged, and it becomes necessary to assert that consent—or, what comes to the same thing, liberty—is not merely a neutral feature of a formal model, a simple heuristic principle, but a substantial moral principle in its own right, asserting a (necessary) view of the good life and a good society and imposing this view from an objective standpoint outside any system. I shall argue that, to this extent, at least, it is not possible to develop a theory of justice without first asserting something about at least one intrinsic right on which any formal system must build. Only by positing liberty as an intrinsic right which is logically prior to any procedure intended to yield just results may we conclude that consent is not only a sufficient but a necessary condition of justice.

II

In the *Ethics,* Aristotle says: "As the unjust man is one who takes the larger share, he will be unjust in respect of good things; not all good things, but those on which good and bad fortune depend." [5] And again, in speaking of money, he says: "it is necessary that all commodities shall be measured by some one standard. . . . And this standard is in reality demand, which is what holds everything together, since if men cease to have wants or if their wants alter, exchange will go on no longer, or will be on different lines." [6] Aristotle's analysis of justice, then, concentrates on a particular area of human behavior, and it is the same area to which Rawls's conception of justice as fairness applies most aptly.

> Justice is the virtue of practices where there is assumed to be competing interests and conflicting claims and where it is supposed that persons will press their rights on each other. . . .[7] [1] These persons have roughly similar needs and interests, or needs and interests in various ways complementary, so that fruitful cooperation among them is possible; and . . . [2] they are sufficiently equal in power and ability to guarantee that in normal circumstances none is able to dominate the others.[8]

I would suggest two further requirements: [3] that, though the needs of each person are identical or complementary, it will not

---

[5] *Nicomachean Ethics* V. i. 9 (Loeb ed.).

[6] *Ibid.* V. 11. The Greek word translated as "demand" is *xpeia,* which has a meaning closely akin to "need" or "lack." Thus, the kind of demand Aristotle is discussing is not necessarily any demand a person may choose to make, but particularly such a demand as corresponds to an acknowledged human need. Similarly, in the passage quoted above Aristotle explicitly refers not to an imagined good or even to a good which necessarily involves the kind of moral judgment he is discussing in the *Ethics.* Rather, he seems to be referring to such undoubted goods as money, food, health, etc., as to which wrong, or at least injustice, only becomes relevant when any person takes more than his share. In short, no moral argument is needed to establish the status of these things as goods.

[7] "Justice as Fairness," § 4.

[8] *Ibid.,* § 3.

be possible to meet every need to the fullest extent; that is to say, there is a condition of scarcity; and [4] the participants in the model procedure cannot have full knowledge of the future circumstances in which the specific applications of the adopted or proposed practices will have to be made.

The requirement of incomplete knowledge is stated, though not as a requirement, at several points by Rawls.

> [E]ach person will be wary of proposing a principle which would give him a peculiar advantage, in his present circumstances, supposing it to be accepted. Each knows that he will be bound by it in future circumstances, the peculiarities of which cannot be foreseen. . . .[9]

The requirement of a situation of scarcity is implicit in what has been said; where no person's claims need be subordinated to those of any other person, surely the need to adopt a procedure for subordinating them disappears.

As Rawls no doubt acknowledges, what has been sketched here (the pursuit of common or complementary goals in a situation of scarcity and of mutual dependence without full knowledge of all contingencies) represents an incomplete but accurate picture of certain human facts. It is true that we do have certain (important) purposes which cannot be accomplished at all or as well without cooperative effort. Furthermore, this cooperative effort, at least as to some purposes, must be a voluntary effort, and coerced cooperation can only refer to a marginal, parasitical situation. This is what is meant by the hypothesis that the participants in a practice "are sufficiently equal in power and ability to guarantee that in normal circumstances none is able to dominate the others." [10]

An important and perhaps the paradigmatic case of a practice growing out of these conditions is the practice of promising.[11] In Kant's phrase, this "possession of the active free-will of another," [12] that is, the practice whereby a person voluntarily agrees

---

[9] John Rawls, "Constitutional Liberty and the Concept of Justice," this volume.

[10] "Justice as Fairness," § 3.

[11] I am indebted to the discussion of promising in an unpublished paper of Miss G.E.M. Anscomb, "On Acting in Good Faith," for the light it casts on the relation of this practice to justice.

[12] Kant, *Philosophy of Law*, trans. Hastie (1833), p. 100.

to relinquish to some degree his prior freedom of action, is obviously a crucial technique for persons accomplishing an enormous number of things which they could not otherwise accomplish. And, of course, that the keeping of a promise may in particular circumstances prove disadvantageous (this is putting it too mildly, for surely the *keeping* of a promise will in almost every case prove disadvantageous) is inadmissible as an excuse for not keeping it, unless perhaps it is urged that this is not the kind of disadvantage bargained for. Perhaps such other practices as making gifts may be adduced; indeed, Kant builds his whole theory of law and state on such reasoning.

But the plausibility of this example as showing the type of practice which must be considered just depends on this—that the sacrifices which are made by each individual are by hypothesis less than the gain to that individual. Furthermore, we need not determine whether any individual has in fact received full value, and more, for his sacrifice, since as the practice is defined, it is the individual himself who approves the exchange.

Since the subordination of claims which is accomplished under such a practice is precisely that subordination to which the participant agreed in making and receiving the promise, he can have no moral title to complain of that subordination. We may conclude, then, that consent to the *particular* subordination of one's claim is a sufficient condition (though not, so far as we can yet see, a necessary condition) of the justice of that subordination. We may also conclude that a practice, such as promising, which in every instance requires no other subordination than that to which the claimant consents meets this sufficient condition of justice. Such a practice will be referred to as a "first-order consensual practice."

III

Let us pass, however, from such practices as promising and making gifts, where the practice permits the participants to choose what they will sacrifice and holds them to their choice, to such practices as punishment or military service, where it is the practice itself which defines the sacrifices to be made. And, of course, they are these practices (which shall be referred to as second-order practices because of the relation in which they stand to first-order practices) which make up the actual institutions, laws, and customs of a society.

It appears that Rawls would solve the question of justice as to second-order practices on the analogy of first-order practices, that is, he would ask whether this is the kind of sacrifice which a rational man would make. This is why he admits a kinship to the contractualist tradition—the test of the justice of a practice involving sacrifices is the plausibility of a rational man contracting for such sacrifices in return for the benefits he can expect.

But it is important to see how radically different the argument has become; in the first type of case, there could be no legitimate claim of injustice, since each participant got only what he chose, and the practice imposed no other sacrifices than those the participant chose to make, whatever they might be. That everyone must accede to such a practice must follow from the mere assumptions that most persons consider themselves able to choose and to choose what they want. But no such simple assumptions will do where the practice itself specifies the sacrifices and only limited choice is permitted to the participant once the practice has been adopted. Of course, it is no great stretch to imagine a fictitious contract by all citizens to each other that promises shall be obeyed, since there can be so little question of all citizens acknowledging such a practice, and since little more is involved than the formalization of first-order practices, which are undoubtedly just.

But the testing of most other types of social practice by such a fiction is far more questionable, since what must be imagined is not all members of a society agreeing to abide by their promises, but all members of a society making certain specific promises to one another, albeit often promises about procedures for resolving disputes, subordinating claims, and so on. Indeed, among the promises which we must imagine to be made by all to each are promises under the terms of which society acquires the title to interfere in the making of promises, punishing some and denying all or partial effect to others. This is a long step from first-order practices, but it is nevertheless one which Rawls must be prepared to make if his analysis is to have more than the most limited application.

All that was needed to make the argument apply to promises or gifts were certain scarcely arguable assumptions about the human condition, namely, interdependence, the need for voluntary cooperation, and the condition of scarcity. From these assumptions, the necessity of the practice followed almost inexorably. But from these assumptions very little follows necessarily when the question is which particular promises would be made. Thus, before we can decide which other practices, besides such first-order practices as promising, would be fully accepted, we must know more about the participants in such practices.

To begin, we must know the kind of things these participants want, for otherwise we cannot even tell whether the proposed practice confers any benefits on anyone other than the proposing party. Further, we must know what would count as a sacrifice before we know whether a problem of justice arises at all. But, most difficult of all, we must have a fairly accurate notion of the relative importance of the benefits and burdens imposed or proposed, as viewed by the various participants. Indeed, there is an important aggravation of the importance of the last point. The condition of incomplete knowledge introduces the notion of risk, so that even if we might suppose that a certain sacrifice—say, slavery or death—would almost certainly be considered disproportionate to some proposed benefit and therefore that that benefit would not justify the sacrifice, still we would have to consider many situations where the benefit is accorded in return only for a risk of the sacrifice. Or, what is more complicated still, the benefit itself may have to be discounted by the probabilities of its realization.

What, for instance, does a contractualist analysis of justice hold as to a practice permitting a decision to hold atomic-weapons tests? On one hand, the benefits are the benefits derived from national security against a feared enemy; on the other, there is the sacrifice of a known number of unknown persons to various diseases and defects. What is certain is that, if atomic testing were demonstrably indispensable to forestall imminent defeat, the choice would be easier, and so would it be if the persons whose health and lives were to be sacrificed were known beforehand. Similarly, compulsory military service in wartime must appear tolerable at least partially because those to be killed are not selected beforehand, so that what must be balanced off is only a *risk* of being killed.

Rawls fully recognizes the complexity of such situations and applies his analysis to them at least to clarify the confusion created by one sort of argument. In his discussion of slavery, he excludes the argument that the pleasures of mastery can ever be urged in justification of the miseries of slavery. The question must be viewed in terms of the benefits to each participant as weighed against his sacrifice, so that, if it is the chance of being a master that justifies the risk of being a slave, then the procedure is just only if all the participants in the situation take the chance and run the risk. Compulsory military service in wartime is an approximation of such a situation, when all who could contribute to the national defense run the risk of serving in the military.

Though we know that the practice is plainly unjust if there is no attempt at a fair apportionment of the risks, an important question is still left unanswered: how do we know that all the participants would consider the risk worthwhile and therefore that they would consider the risk fairly apportioned? How can we know that the person who does in fact die of leukemia caused by increased radiation would have considered the risk so slight at the time of the making of the decision as to be worth the benefits? Per contra, can we be sure that everyone would consider the one-in-ten chance of being a slaveowner as clearly not worth the risk of being a slave? Rawls properly withholds judgment on the practice, were it to impose the risk but impose it on all alike, for then it *might* be just.

It is apparent that, if the principle of justice requires that all departures from a position of equal liberty be justified by a showing that the inequality in imposition works out to everyone's advantage, then some standard must be found for judging what that advantage is. Nor are we aided by the point that it is the judgment of a *rational* man which is operative in the model, for we know nothing more about the rational man on this score, except that he knows his own advantage.[13] Of course, this does not tell *us* what that advantage is, unless a rational man is defined as

[13] See Note 23, *infra*, and accompanying text.

having certain specified views on what precisely constitutes his own advantage. But, if that is the case, then the analysis of justice will depend directly on the establishment of a scale of advantages with the weight to be assigned to each, which scale would be the standard of the rational man. But Rawls does not suggest that the rational man so conceived should serve as the norm. All we can say is that some hypotheses as to the advantage of others are plainly untenable and certain forms of *argument* inadmissible. Still, in most practical situations, the balance of chance of gain and risk of loss will be close enough so that a man could reasonably suggest that many a particular practice of doubtful credentials works out to everyone's advantage.

In these typical situations of justice, what is apparently needed is some measure of what everyone would in fact consent to. Perhaps the ideal of consent might be preserved by the promissory adoption of a procedure to which everyone does in fact consent, and this procedure would in turn either yield a rough-and-ready determination of everyone's advantage or the procedure would result in the development of secondary procedures which would eventually yield a rough-and-ready determination of everyone's advantage. Thus the participants, when they have reached an impasse or when meaningful consultation on individual proposals are evidently impracticable, may all agree to abide by a vote or even a throw of the dice. Or they may set up a constitutional convention, which in turn establishes a legislature, which in turn determines particular issues. But, if this route is chosen, it becomes apparent that the connection between the notion of consent at one end of the process and justice at the other will have become highly tenuous.

To reach the state at which unanimous consent (and not simply some majority consensus) can meaningfully be postulated, we must surely attain the level of the hypothetical, the social contract which never took place. And, at the lowest level of the particular decision, it is obvious that the society will be intolerably unjust if the individual legislators do not make a serious attempt to vote their view of what is just in the particular case. But how is one to guide them in this virtuous instinct? Surely, the same model of attenuated and delegated consent by virtue of which they are placed in their quandary will often prove inadequate as a guide in particular cases.[14] Indeed, the two most likely interpretations by individual legislators of their mandate will be in terms either of their own interests and the interests of those they represent or in terms of some version of "the greatest good of the greatest numbers."

Are we to conclude, then, that the notion of appraising the justice of a practice by the standard of the consent of a rational man is pointless because where it works—in the situation of maximization of advantage in first-order consensual practices—it is unnecessary, and where it is necessary it does not work? At least it would seem that the propriety of passing from the justice of practices which allow each participant to choose those interests he will sacrifice and those he will further to the justice of practices which make that choice for him will depend on some view of the relative importance of those interests either absolutely or to each participant. In passing now to the third type of situation with which Rawls's thesis must be confronted, we shall examine to what extent the estimation of the relative importance of interests is an objective, philosophical estimation of intrinsic value and to what extent it is a consensual one, i.e., depending on each participant's own estimation.

IV

It is in respect of liberty of conscience, Rawls's paper argues, that a consensual model leads necessarily to substantial,

[14] "The individualistic view uses as illustration the analogy of the contract. . . . The contract doctrine does not apply to the actual state. It means, not that real states have been created deliberately by way of contract, but only that a right state must be able to be conceived as originating in a contract between its members. The contract 'is by no means necessarily to be presumed as a fact'; 'rather is it a mere idea of reason, which however, has its undoubted practical reality, viz., to bind every legislator so to make his laws that they *could* have originated in the united will of a whole people, and to regard each subject . . . *as if* he had agreed to join in such a will. For this is the touchstone of the legality of any public statute.' (Kant). So the contract theory declares the state justified not because, but rather if, it may be conceived as originating in a contract, because only then, indeed, it may be regarded as in the interest of every one of its members. Therefore, wherever the contract theory uses the term 'will,' one must insert the term 'interest' for which the former figuratively stands, if one is to understand the contract theory correctly." Radbruch, *op. cit.*, pp. 94–95 (footnotes omitted). Cp. Rawls, "Justice as Fairness," § 4.

rather than formal, conclusions. And so it will be in respect of liberty of conscience that the legislator, even the legislator whose position is assigned him by just institutions, must feel most acutely those limitations which Rawls's consensual model of justice imposes, for the nature of those limitations will no longer be a matter of conjecture.

> Admittedly, the concept of religion might be specified in various ways, but any plausible determination of it would imply that a person under a religious obligation must regard this obligation as binding absolutely in the sense that he cannot qualify his fulfillment of it for the sake of personal advantage. In particular, the obligation to preserve the truth of one's religion and the obligation to live up to its injunctions cannot be compromised for the sake of secular interests.[15]

Thus, however difficult it may be to estimate what risk a rational man, or any man, might take when faced with some alternatives, if he is a religious man there are certain risks he would never take, certain things to which he would never consent. His religious obligations have such a status for him that no prospect of gain can justify a commitment to compromise those obligations. And, by this route, we seem to come to the conclusion that at least the second of the two hypothetical practices suggested at the outset of this discussion must be stigmatized as unjust. By hypothesis, no rational man would consent to the compulsory reformation of his present most deeply held convictions.

In this situation, at least, a smooth transition from first-order consensual practices to second-order consensual practices seems possible, since we know by hypothesis the precise value to be placed on the particular interest involved; it is absolute, we are told.

If we consider what this evaluation as an absolute entails, it must appear that there really is a more general point to be made here than the one Rawls makes. Surely, Rawls does not wish to say that no person who has religious beliefs would ever or has ever sacrificed them to "secular interests," for common experience belies such an assertion. Nor is it open to him to say that no religious person *should* so sacrifice his religious principles. In a sense, that is none of Rawls's business.

The point that is to be made is a quite different one, and it is

[15] "Constitutional Liberty and the Concept of Justice," *op. cit.*

brought out by considering my first hypothetical, that of the compulsory re-education. Is it really open to us to judge less unjust the purpose in the first hypothetical than the purpose in the second, where they are religious beliefs which are being tampered with, simply because most people would object less to a program of compulsory education cutting into their unenlightened idleness than to an interference with their religious beliefs? What if some religious persons cherish their idleness more; is that any of Rawls's business? The point I am making is that Rawls is only entitled to say that both impositions are equally clearly unjust; they really involve, in the only relevant respect, the same interest—the interest to determine for oneself what is in one's own best interest, be it idleness or superstition.

This interest, then, should be contrasted to the kind of interests sacrificed in first-order practices and the kind sacrificed in second-order practices. In the former, we did not have to concern ourselves with the status of the interest; the participant is able to perform this function for us. In the latter, the status of the interest is generally unspecified, and the model of justice is largely formal as a result. And, in the type of situation we are now considering, where liberty of conscience—in the sense of the liberty to define one's own interests—is concerned, the interest itself defines its own status, so that we may deduce how those who have this interest would bargain in respect of it. Accordingly, a contractualist model appears to work as to this interest, at least in the sense that it yields a substantial answer.

Yet, this answer is obtained only by virtue of having ignored one important feature of the hypothetical situations I have proposed—that the sacrifice demanded is exacted for the benefit solely of the victim. And, indeed, I think it may be demonstrated that cases of interference with liberty of conscience, if not always, then typically, are intended for the benefit of a victim who is denied a fully free choice.[16] This feature distinguishes the problem of

[16] Consider even the case Rawls puts: the persecution of heretics lest they "corrupt the faith." *Ibid.* Although such a practice does not aim primarily at the good of the heretics, it is clearly aimed at the good of those who might be "corrupted." But corruption of the faith is not like physical corruption, it is in fact a change of mind or a change of heart. Therefore, to guard someone's faith from corruption by such means is simply to interfere with that person's choice as to what he will believe and thus his liberty to define his own interests.

justice raised by my hypotheticals from the types of situations considered so far.[17] For, even in second-order situations, if there were doubts as to the value to be ascribed to interests advanced and sacrificed, this was only because we could not be sure what value would be ascribed to them by the individual participants. Thus, justice has previously been conceived in terms of competitive situations of scarcity, where the vice lay in wanting too much of a good thing, indeed, more than one's share. And a consensual model of justice as fairness seemed plausible as a way of determining what that fair share is.

But interference with liberty of conscience poses a different sort of question; the contest does not appear to be between two claimants to an insufficient quantity of an acknowledged good, but between two claimants pressing their views of what the good for one of them is. In effect, they both want the good of the same person. What does Rawls's consensual model provide here?

At first, it might seem that the problem is an easy one, indeed, that it follows a fortiori from the conclusion that it is unjust to interfere with the peaceful, conscientious convictions of others for one's own good. But, in fact, no such conclusion is possible without an important additional hypothesis, since it is not clear how the case I put concerns a situation of justice at all. There is no condition of scarcity, no issue as to fair distribution, but only a dispute about a matter of principle, perhaps a matter of fact—what is the good for you or me or both of us. And what does consent, if it is to be the real consent of real men, have to do with such a dispute?

An answer might take this form: there is even here a situation of opposing claims, the parties to the dispute seeking to accomplish incompatible things. One seeks to go on believing as he does—necessarily so, as we have seen—and the other seeks to impose his views on the other by forcing him to change his views. And, if this is so, why can we not employ the same model of the consent of the rational man to solve this dispute?

The same model is inapplicable because heretofore liberty has merely been a hypothesis for adjusting conflicting claims of per-

---

[17] Previously, we spoke of demands or claims which expressed acknowledged and undoubted needs. See notes 5 and 6, *supra,* and accompanying text.

sons seeking to advance acknowledged interests; but in this situation the essence of the dispute is about the status of the interest itself as an interest. However much liberty may be the proper hypothesis for an adjustment of claims involving recognized interests, it does not follow that liberty is also a proper hypothesis for establishing the legitimacy of the claim of an interest to be considered as such. It does not follow, that is, unless liberty is itself accorded the status of a substantial interest on the same logical level as the material interests we have been considering so far. But it is obviously illicit to establish the claim of liberty to recognition as an interest by reference to liberty as a mere logical presupposition of our model. It makes sense to say that your interests may be limited and your claims allowed only on a principle that you yourself acknowledge as working out to your general advantage, but it is circular to say that the issue of what is in fact to your advantage can justly be decided only by reference to principles you do in fact acknowledge, since then there could either be no dispute or you would be certain to win it.

The circle may be broken if we are prepared to assume that liberty is an important need or interest in itself and not just a hypothesis for adjusting conflicts among other acknowledged needs. Thus, the argument has three distinct logical levels. There is the level of first-order consensual practices as to which the issue of the status of various interests does not arise. There is the level of second-order consensual practices, the justice of which depends at least on a guess at what value each participant would accord his various interests. And, finally, there is the level at which some assumption must be made as to the existence and status of certain of these interests, perhaps only liberty,[18] by which in turn assertions about one's own or another's interests may be judged. At least this one interest or right, then, must be posited by us for the individual, since only if he enters the situation of justice armed with this single interest, which he could not have won for himself by his own assertions, will his position in asserting any other interest for himself be impregnable to the kind of objection I have raised here. This is what would be needed to show that consent is both a necessary and sufficient condition of justice, rather than only a sufficient condition.

[18] See Part V, *infra*.

Rawls's models and arguments, though plausible and acceptable in their conclusion, thus seem to me to fail to bring into sufficient prominence what is really at stake here, namely an analysis of justice as based on a conception of the moral status of the individual man and, more particularly, on the role of liberty in defining that status. To be sure Rawls does say, "The peculiar feature of the concept of justice is that it treats each person as an equal sovereign," [19] and thus that justice "is simply . . . one of the forms of conduct in which the recognition of others as persons is manifested." [20] But it is not so clear from what is said that perhaps the crucial, the defining feature, need, or capacity of a human person is liberty. The individual "sovereign" notion may only take one as far as affirming that the interest of this person may never be sacrificed to those of others; at most, he may gamble them away when the risks are fairly apportioned. But this says nothing about who is to decide what these interests are, nothing about a conflict between the individual's view of his interest and another's view of his interest, urged, as it were, in the individual's best interest. And that is what is needed to make the argument go.[21]

V

The consequence of granting human liberty an ontological rather than a logical status in the concept of justice is that something considerably more concrete can be said than that:

---

[19] "Constitutional Liberty and the Concept of Justice," *op. cit.*

[20] "Justice as Fairness," § 5.

[21] It may be well to consider in this connection the relation between justice and that other virtue of men and their institutions—conformity to the truth, to things as they really are. It seems odd at first that the just, which is in Aristotle's term the "proportionate," should allow an equality between such plainly unequal quantities as a man who propounds the truth and a man who propounds a falsehood or between an interest which is based on an error and an interest based on a true appreciation of the facts. Surely the proportion between truth and falsehood, truth and error is 1:0. Yet, the just proportion between the two proponents may still be one of equality, not because we need dissimulate a nonexistent doubt or espouse some philosophical skepticism, but because the proportion to be established is not between the two propositions, but between their proponents. And, if it is indeed true that liberty, even liberty to err, is the defining feature of a person's moral status, then equality surely is the only just proportion.

> The term "person" is to be understood in a general way as a subject of claims. In some cases, it means human individuals, but in others it refers to nations, corporations, churches, teams, and so on. Although there is a certain logical priority to the case of human individuals, the principles of justice apply to the relations among all these types of persons, and the notion of a person must be interpreted accordingly.[22]

It must appear quite exactly what the "certain logical priority" is. Thus, if, in my two hypothetical situations, the impositions were not on individuals but on states or groups which were in turn imposing on individuals, justice, though it might not require the forceful remedy, need not foreclose it. What would have to be considered would be the extent to which even the coercive aspects of a state are the articulations of cooperative schemes for the maximization of liberty and other interests and the extent to which the effectiveness of the state as such a cooperative practice would be undermined by outside intervention. But, unless we are to be guilty of the absurdities of Kant's theory on this score, we must be prepared to say that at some point it is no injustice to the individuals who suffer from an unjust (on Rawls's analysis) regime to destroy that regime by force. And, if it is no injustice to the individuals, it is irrelevant that it may appear to be an injustice as between the states viewed as metaphorical individuals.

In order to make his model work, Rawls found it necessary to posit that the participants in his procedure were rational in the sense that:

> They know their own interests more or less accurately; they are capable of tracing out the likely consequences of adopting one practice rather than another; they are capable of adhering to a course of action once they have decided upon it; they can resist present temptations and the enticements of immediate gain; and the bare knowledge or perception of the difference between their condition and that of others is not . . . a source of great dissatisfactions.[23]

Since Rawls is concentrating at that point on justice in situations where the maximization of shared or complementary purposes is

---

[22] "Constitutional Liberty and the Concept of Justice," *op. cit.*

[23] "Justice as Fairness," § 3; "Justice and Liberty," § 5.

possible for each participant in a practice, these assumptions are necessary to make the model work.

But, if these conditions of rationality, and particularly the condition of knowing one's own interest, were taken at full value as necessary conditions of a situation of justice, it would be otiose to add, as I think we must, a notion of liberty as being one of several interests which individuals do in fact have. Furthermore, these conditions would render the concept of justice inapplicable in many important situations, for in many situations precisely what is claimed is that the "victim" does not know his own interests and hence is not rational. If we were to exclude situations where such claims could be made, the applicability of the concept would be drastically reduced. That is why justice must include the liberty to define—even incorrectly—one's own interests.[24]

The ontological status of this liberty as an interest is further revealed by the fact that we think we know when the interest is present. It is present at least presumptively in an adult, but not in a child, at least not fully, and not in lunatics. But an adult is free to be wrong, free to do himself dreadful harm, and justice demands that he be free even in this. Is there not implicit in this a notion that recognition of this liberty is part and parcel of a recognition of another as a fully human person and that this recognition is not dependent on that other's knowing his own interests, even generally?

The point which has been made here is not new. Kant bases his whole moral philosophy on this view of man's moral nature.

---

[24] An analogous point obtains as to Rawls's requirement that the factual basis of claims and the arguments put forward to support them, as well as their conformity to the model of justice, be tested by the criterion of common sense. Common sense in this context, however, can mean nothing more than a criterion of judgment acceptable to all concerned, and thus it is but an application of the consensual model to a particular step in the argument being made from that model. And, though it is proper in and necessary to Rawls's scheme, it can scarcely solve the problem created by an assertion that the consensual scheme is inadequate to deal with claims that a certain imposition is justified by what is in the best interests of the person imposed on. For such a claim, in denying the right of the victim to define his own best interests, presumably simultaneously denies the validity of the thought processes leading to a contrary view in the victim. One might say that the victim is asserted to lack common sense; certainly there is no sense common to him who imposes and him who is imposed on.

H.L.A. Hart has advanced the thesis that, if there is any such thing as a natural right, it is the equal right to be free.[25] What I have attempted to do in this paper, therefore, is not to propound a novel doctrine. The point has been, rather, a logical one: that the model of justice Rawls has presented and the results it yields depend on a prior hypothesis about what is important to men. I certainly do not suggest that Rawls would reject the proposition that his view of justice depends on granting a pre-eminent status to man's right to determine his own advantage and interests.

[25] "Are there any Natural Rights?" *Philosophical Review,* 64 (1955), 185.

8

JUSTICE AND FAIRNESS

JOHN W. CHAPMAN

In a series of articles, remarkable both for their lucidity and cogency, John Rawls advances the proposition that fundamental to the concept of justice is fairness.[1] The significance of Rawls's work is that it makes reciprocity and not equality central to the interpretation of justice. My purpose is to examine this interpretation in a critical way, and I shall argue that Rawls's analysis is deficient in that it fails to give sufficient weight to considerations of need and rights. These deficiencies I shall trace

[1] See Rawls, "Justice as Fairness," *The Philosophical Review,* LXVII (1958), 164–194, reprinted with revisions in Frederick A. Olafson, ed., *Justice and Social Policy* (1961), pp. 80–107. A shorter version of Rawls's interpretation of justice is presented in "Justice as Fairness," *The Journal of Philosophy,* LIV (1957), 653–662. In "Constitutional Liberty and the Concept of Justice," this volume, he develops the arguments for liberty that may be derived from his analysis of justice. See also his "Two Concepts of Rules," *The Philosophical Review,* LXIV (1955), 3–32, in which he sets forth his conception of rules and practices, for his concern is with the justice of practices or institutions.

to the manner in which he attempts to explain the concept of justice, to his "analytic construction," and to the assumptions upon which that is based.

According to Rawls, the fair is to be seen as what free and rational men could reasonably be expected to agree on in their dealings with one another. Fairness is essentially right dealing or, more precisely, reciprocity in institutionalized relationships, and it is the possibility of mutual acceptance that is the test or criterion of fairness as this standard is applied to institutions or practices. Further, according to Rawls, mutual acknowledgment and acceptance of the standard of fairness is a manifestation on the part of those concerned of their mutual recognition of one another as persons. Such recognition, however, does not preclude the practice of slavery under certain specified circumstances, provided only that the agreement establishing this institution is reached by people who start from an initial condition of equal freedom or autonomy. Indeed, it would appear that any practice which could conceivably meet the test of the possibility of mutual acceptance is to be judged fair. And a fair practice is, or becomes, a just practice when it is authoritatively established. Justice, then, on Rawls's interpretation, is essentially the legal or political counterpart of the ethical concept of fairness. Justice has to do with the political and the authoritative, whereas the criterion of its ethical foundation, fairness, is the free and voluntary way in which agreement upon what is deemed fair is reached. An institution or a practice is just, therefore, if it meets the test of fairness and is also authoritatively established.

Hence, central and fundamental to both fairness and justice is the notion of reciprocity between autonomous persons who initially confront one another from positions of moral sovereignty.[2] It is this conception of justice which Rawls finds at the heart of social contract theory and which he compares favorably with the utilitarian theory of justice to which equality in an important sense is central. That sense of equality has to do not with reciprocity between morally autonomous persons but rather with equality of treatment of persons who differ in respect of wants and needs. It is the contractualist conception of equality as

[2] Rawls refers to his interpretation of justice as ". . . the conception of justice as reciprocity." "Justice as Fairness," *op. cit.*, p. 661.

reciprocity that is at the root of Rawls's interpretation of justice.

I propose to appraise this view of justice from three distinctive standpoints, namely, the historical, the linguistic, and the metaethical, and from these standpoints to offer reasons which suggest a conception of justice less narrow than that which Rawls provides. Each of these directions of investigation could be pursued for its own sake and might be expected to produce results not necessarily convergent. But in the case of justice, I shall hope to show that they do converge in a manner that illuminates some features of that concept which Rawls's analysis, on the basis of his "analytic construction" and in terms of reciprocity, of necessity neglects. The justification for my procedure is that in dealing with a concept as large and as amorphous as that of justice it is perhaps advisable, as far as possible, to test the results of one line of investigation against the results of others. Although this procedure may risk a certain loss of analytical precision, I believe that compensations are to be found in its comprehensive character, which in turn may be expected to reveal the extent to which historical, linguistic, and metaethical considerations reinforce or diverge from one another in the explanation of the meaning of justice.

From a historical standpoint, there may be more to be said for the utilitarian conception of justice than Rawls allows. I do not contest his claim that his analysis is fatal to the attempt to derive the principle of justice from the principle of utility. For justice is a primitive or basic moral conception, and, as he quite rightly points out, the utilitarian theory reduces justice to a sort of efficiency, without regard for the moral relations that exist among the persons concerned.[3] Rawls's interpretation of justice as fairness does have the very great merit of displaying this weakness of the utilitarian theory from an analytical and moral standpoint, for he reveals with striking clarity the fact that justice has to do with moral, and not merely economic or efficiency, relations among persons. In this respect, unquestionably his contractualist approach to the meaning of justice is markedly superior to the utilitarian theory of justice as a means to the achievement of the greatest sum total of satisfaction or happiness. Utilitarianism overlooks the fact that society consists of a plurality of persons

[3] See *ibid.*, pp. 184–193.

and the fact that the claims of each cannot be assessed apart from the claims of all. Both of these facts are fully taken into account by contract theory and by Rawls's conception of justice as reciprocity.

There is a difference, however, between what may be called the analytical and the historical relations of contractualism and utilitarianism, a difference which I think deserves notice, and the significance of which will become fully apparent only in the light of what I shall have to say about justice from the linguistic and metaethical standpoints. Although it may be the case that the contractualist conception of justice as reciprocity, insofar as it directs attention to the plurality of persons and to the moral relations that exist among them, is superior analytically to the utilitarian theory, historically precisely the opposite may be true, for utilitarianism represents in an important respect an expansion of the meaning of justice as compared with contractualism.

Consider the fact that neither a contractualist such as Locke nor Rawls is prepared to give weight to considerations of need in their analyses of justice.[4] But utilitarianism does insist that needs be taken into account simply because it proposes to appraise institutions, in the light of the principle of diminishing marginal utility, by their contribution to human satisfaction. Historically, this insistence would appear to have been an advance on Locke's complacency in the face of massive inequalities. Evidently for Locke the plurality and moral equality of persons did not imply that they should be accorded equal treatment with respect to equally central needs. Their theory may well have made utilitarians insensitive to the moral characteristics of human relations; indeed, given their assumption of psychological egoism, there are,

---

[4] On John Locke's view of justice, see his *Second Treatise of Civil Government,* and especially the chapter on property. Rawls says:

> The conception of justice which I want to develop may be stated in the form of two principles as follows: first, each person participating in a practice, or affected by it, has an equal right to the most extensive liberty compatible with a like liberty for all; and second, inequalities are arbitrary unless it is reasonable to expect that they will work out for everyone's advantage, and provided the positions and offices to which they attach, or from which they may be gained, are open to all. These principles express justice as a complex of three ideas: liberty, equality, and reward for services contributing to the common good. (*Ibid.,* pp. 165–166.)

strictly speaking, no such characteristics. But they are sensitive, in a way that Locke was not, to the claim of each person to a basic equality of treatment.

Examine Locke's general view of the conditions under which and the principles according to which property may be rightfully acquired and held. If property is acquired in accordance with his interpretation of the principles of natural law and natural rights, then it is fairly or justly acquired, and no further question as to the fairness or the justice of the resulting distribution of property may legitimately be raised, even though this distribution be vastly unequal. Property may be taken only with the consent of its holders. Locke would appear to have been interested almost exclusively in the process of acquisition, and, if this process meets his principles of justice, then the resulting distribution is just and cannot be altered except on the basis of consent. No doubt Locke was concerned for the possibility of culture in the face of scarcity, and it is also true that he does not speak much of justice as such. Nevertheless, property which is acquired in accordance with his conception of natural law and which does not infringe on the natural rights of others as he understands them is, on Locke's reasoning, immune to the charge of injustice on the ground that some are much more able to satisfy their needs, including their relatively peripheral needs, than are others. Indeed, from the standpoint of Locke's justification of the institution of property, great inequalities in its distribution are not only expedient but also must be recognized as just. No question could rightfully be raised about either the fairness or the justice of the distribution provided that it had come about under rules that could be defended as fair or just, that is to say, as long as the parties involved all have had, or have, an equal chance at amassing wealth or the ancestors from whom they have inherited property have had, in some sense, an equal chance at it.

Would it not be appropriate and natural to say that, according to Locke's theory of property, if the game of property has been fairly played, then no separate and independent appraisal about its outcome may be made on the grounds of right and justice? The demands or the requirements of justice are fulfilled in what I think we should today naturally refer to as the fairness of the competitive process itself. Assessment of the fairness of this process requires no attention to needs; they are irrelevant. In this light, the mission of utilitarianism historically appears to have been to focus attention on the consequences of institutions and to assert that these consequences be subjected to independent appraisal in terms of need and satisfaction. In effect, this is to enlarge the conception of justice beyond what it apparently meant to Locke and to insist that the question of justice be raised not only about the ways in which property could rightfully be acquired but also about the resulting distribution of wealth.[5] Considerations of need become relevant to questions of justice as contract theory historically gives way to utilitarianism. The human sense of justice has deepened or broadened to include something more than reciprocity among competitors, namely attention to the needs of the human personality itself.

When placed in historical perspective, the greatest-happiness principle reveals an aspect of justice which seems today unduly minimized by an interpretation that makes fairness and reciprocity, rather than equality, fundamental to the concept of justice. Utilitarianism implies that a judgment be made not only upon institutional processes but also upon institutional outcomes in the light of human satisfaction. Maximizing satisfaction is what counts for the utilitarian, and this cannot be estimated without taking account of needs. Now, if utilitarianism is correct in taking account of needs, then either Locke held a view of justice that todays strikes us as rather narrow and limited,[6] or he was mainly concerned with what we should ordinarily refer to as fairness.

---

[5] This, I think, it is true to say about utilitarianism as a political and moral theory, despite the rather narrow conception of justice held by some utilitarians such as Hume, who is closer to Locke on the question of the scope of justice than he is to later utilitarians such as John Stuart Mill and Henry Sidgwick. On this point, see Gregory Vlastos, "Justice," *Revue internationale de philosophie,* XLI (1957), 329–330.

[6] William K. Frankena says:

> One of the chief considerations which not only justifies but also establishes as *just* differences in the treatment of human beings is the fact that the good life (not in the sense of the morally good life but in the sense, roughly, of the happy life) and its conditions are not the same for all, due to their differences in needs and potentialities. I am inclined to think that it is this fact, rather than that of differences in ability, merit, and the like, which primarily justifies differences in the handling of individuals.

"The Concept of Social Justice," in Richard B. Brandt, ed., *Social Justice* (1962), p. 15.

When I say that Locke appears to have been concerned with what we should call fairness, I mean simply that he thought that, if the competition for wealth was conducted fairly, there was nothing more to be said on the matter. The outcome of the competition could not be challenged on the ground of justice. It is the way in which the competition is carried on, not its results, that counts for Locke. This concern with the process of competition is most aptly described, in my opinion, as a concern for fairness, and it avoids or evades recognition of the claims of need. It is these claims which are recognized by utilitarianism.

Historically, I think utilitarianism is best viewed as ambiguous with respect to contractualism. On the one hand, there is a loss of grasp on the principles of the plurality and moral autonomy of persons; on the other, there is an advance on contractualist thought, whether this advance be interpreted as an enlargement of the meaning and scope of justice or as a shift in meaning from justice as fairness to justice as equality. On either interpretation, justice is seen as something more than reciprocity and fair play, and this something more involves recognition of the claims of need. I suggest, therefore, that Rawls's contractualist interpretation of justice shares both the strength and the weakness of the idea of justice as reciprocity. Justice as reciprocity makes sense only if society is seen as a plurality of persons and not, as the utilitarian would have it, as a sort of single great person. But reciprocity would appear to be only one aspect of justice in the light of the utilitarian insistence upon equality as equal treatment of persons.

I shall now consider Rawls's interpretation of justice as fairness from a linguistic standpoint. My aim is to discover what dimensions there are to the distinction between the two concepts. And I shall argue that linguistic considerations—reflections upon what we should naturally say when—do lend support to my contention that in judgments of justice claims of need cannot be ignored.

According to Rawls, there is but a single dimension to the distinction between justice and fairness. The former is a political or legal concept, whereas the latter is an ethical concept. He says: "The question of fairness arises when free persons, who have no authority over one another, are engaging in a joint activity and amongst themselves settling or acknowledging the rules which define it and which determine the respective shares in its benefits and burdens." [7] Fairness ". . . relates to right dealing between persons who are cooperating with or competing against one another, as when one speaks of fair games, fair competition, and fair bargains." [8] For Rawls fairness is connected with the voluntary in a double sense. First, mutual acknowledgment of a principle or a rule is the test of its fairness; acceptability is the guarantee of reciprocity. Second, fairness is said to be ordinarily applied to practices in which there is an option on the part of the participants whether or not to engage in the practice. Justice, on the other hand, he contends is the concept we use to talk about fairness in relationships where no option may be said to exist. This, I take it, is the implication of the following statement:

> If, in ordinary speech, fairness applies more particularly to practices in which there is a choice whether to engage or not, and justice to practices in which there is no choice and one must play, the element of necessity does not alter the basic conception of the possibility of mutual acceptance. . . .[9]

Rawls thus distinguishes between types of practices, those which are voluntary and those which are authoritative, and ties the distinction between fairness and justice to this distinction between practices.

The question I raise here is whether our ordinary way of talking supports Rawls's claim that it reflects the distinction which he makes between justice and fairness. Does an analysis of usage reveal that the difference between these two concepts is only or primarily the difference between the ethical and the voluntary, on the one hand, and the political and the authoritative, on the other? Certainly I think that we may grant immediately that this is one of the dimensions to the distinction between the two concepts, but there may be others which are equally if not more important to an understanding of justice.

As an example of usage, consider the following statement by H.L.A. Hart: "We speak not only of distributions or compensations as just or fair but also of a judge as just or unjust; a trial

[7] Rawls, "Justice as Fairness," *op. cit.*, p. 178.
[8] *Loc. cit.*
[9] *Ibid.*, p. 658.

as fair or unfair; and a person as justly or unjustly convicted."[10] In this statement four different applications of the concepts are envisaged, and in each case Hart's usage would appear to be natural and correct. His assertion that we use just and fair interchangeably with reference to distributions and compensations is borne out by the following quotations from a British Labour Party document:[11]

> We are not, of course, just concerned to share out more fairly what is already produced. We wish to see the most rapid possible increase in our total production, simultaneously with its fairer distribution. . . .
>
> Left to itself the capitalist system distributes income in a manner that is manifestly unjust.

But now notice that while it seems natural to refer to a judge as just or unjust, trials are fair or unfair, and convictions are just or unjust. Is it not reasonable to detect in these examples a tendency to use fair when a process is involved, including the authoritative and legal process of a trial? Is not fairness the notion we naturally and appropriately use to appraise an activity, the doing of a something, like playing a game? The contrast which I wish to make is that between the fairness of a trial and the justice of its outcome—the justness of the verdict. Here there would appear to be an additional dimension to the distinction between fairness and justice. In the concept of justice, there is a note of finality which is lacking in the concept of fairness, and this is why I think that we readily apply fair in the context of a process and we tend to reserve justice for use with reference to outcomes alone.

Comparison of the concepts of justice and fairness in the light of the concept of practices obscures the note of finality about justice. For we naturally refer to the practice or the institution of trials as just, but in the case of the individual trial we break it up into a process and an outcome and, just as naturally, say about a specific trial that although it was fair the verdict was unjust. The finality of justice contrasts with the note of activity

[10] Hart, *The Concept of Law* (1961), pp. 154–155.

[11] The Labour Party, *Towards Equality: Labour's Policy for Social Justice* (n.d.), pp. 4, 11. Throughout this paper, the concepts of justice and fairness are used interchangeably with reference to the distribution of income and wealth.

that seems intrinsic to fairness. This dimension of the distinction between the two concepts is not adequately specified in terms of the difference between the ethical and the legal, the voluntary and the nonvoluntary practice. Rawls's concept of a practice includes both process and outcome and so tends to hide this dimension.

Another way in which the meaning of fairness would appear to diverge from that of justice has to do with what we mean by fair play. Fairness and fair play appear to be intimately bound up with the notion of reciprocity, and the principle of reciprocity may be violated even though it would make sense to say that the violation was made in the interests of justice. According to Isaiah Berlin:

> The notions of equality and fairness are closely bound up: if as a result of breaking a rule a man derives benefits which he can obtain only so long as other men do not break but keep the rule, then no matter what other needs are being served by such a breach, the result is an offence against a principle best described as that of fairness, which is a form of desire for equality for its own sake.[12]

Here notice that it is the principle of reciprocity which has been violated and that the natural way to describe this violation, as Berlin points out, is to say that it offends against the principle of fairness or what Rawls calls the "duty of fair play." [13] The idea of reciprocity and the idea of fairness would both seem to be especially appropriate in usages having to do with an activity defined by or governed by rules, whereas the question of justice may arise with reference to considerations, such as needs, essentially extraneous to the activity itself. Berlin's statement implies that the requirements of reciprocity may be met or violated without settling the question of justice. Indeed, would not our sense of justice be offended if reciprocity were insisted upon in the face of gross disregard of the claims of need? More generally, reciprocity in the shape of the requirement of fair play would appear to be the distinctive note in the concept of fairness and as such contrasts with the note of equality in the sense of equality of treatment, which is distinctive of justice. Indeed, if Berlin's sense of the

---

[12] Berlin, "Equality as an Ideal," in Olafson, *op. cit.*, p. 144.

[13] Rawls, "Justice as Fairness," *op. cit.*, pp. 180–182.

matter is correct, reciprocity and fairness are not so much fundamental to justice as they are manifestations of a desire for equality which itself may be fundamental to both fairness and justice.

Another dimension to the distinction between justice and fairness has to do with the difference between the simple and the complex. Where there is a balancing or a weighing of considerations and values that are in some degree competitive with or alternative to one another, the language of justice seems to be more appropriate. By comparison, judgments of fairness appear relatively simple and hence easier to make. These judgments have to do with conformity to rules—reciprocity or fair play among participants—and with the fairness of the rules of a game or a practice themselves. In none of these cases does there enter the kind of weighing of claims and values that is involved in a judgment in which the essentially disparate considerations of need and contribution confront one another. In contrast to judgments of fairness, judgments of justice are likely to possess the special characteristics of comprehensiveness and complexity. And they are more difficult to make just because they call for a weighing of considerations that are relevant and yet not readily reducible to reciprocal conformity to rules. By way of illustration of this point, let us consider another statement by Isaiah Berlin:

> We seem to choose as we choose because one solution seems to us to embody a blend of satisfaction of claims and desires (or to contain or omit other factors) which we prefer as a total pattern to the blend provided by the other solution. Indeed the intervention of considerations of equity in the rigorous workings of some deductive legal system are due to our desire for justice that we are not always able to analyse too closely, into which the principle of "every man to count for one" does indeed enter, but without any clear understanding whether he is to count for one in the sphere of legislative rights, or of responsibility for action, or the receipt of benefits, or other respects, between any of which conflict all too easily occurs.[14]

Here justice appears as a more vague, a more complex, and a more comprehensive notion than that of fairness. We desire justice, but we do not really know what it is that justice requires. An equality of treatment is at stake, but this may be achieved in different ways, among which a choice must be made. We cannot

[14] Berlin, *op. cit.*, p. 148.

make this choice except by testing alternative "blends" against our considered preferences, Berlin suggests. His use of "blend" and his reference to a "total pattern" both express what I mean by the element of complexity which seems characteristic of judgments of justice. A judgment is being made upon net results, and the concept of reciprocity does not seem adequate to describe this type of judgment. I think that ultimately we have to test alternative patterns of institutional practices against our sense of justice, and into such judgments considerations of reciprocity do indeed enter, but in itself the standard of reciprocity is not sufficient to provide a basis for the judgment. Hence the language of justice rather than that of fairness feels more appropriate and expresses our sense of the weighing and the choosing that are involved in judgments on a "total pattern."

What is the significance of these reflections on natural usage for Rawls's interpretation of justice? It would seem that there are dimensions to the distinction between fairness and justice other than the one which he specifies. The difference between voluntary reciprocity and authoritative reciprocity does not appear to exhaust the distinction in meaning of the two concepts. To be sure, we do not use the concept of justice to refer to or to appraise behavior in the purely voluntary activity of a game. But, on the other hand, we do use the concept of fairness to appraise the conduct of a trial which is a legal process. Justice and fairness seem equally applicable to questions of distributing wealth or income, in which both voluntary and nonvoluntary practices are involved. Justice, however, seems most at home in judgments that involve equality of treatment, that have a note of finality, that are complex and comprehensive, and that require a weighing of disparate considerations and claims. The language of justice feels least appropriate in the context of an ongoing activity where the concepts of reciprocity and fair play are applicable. On the other hand, fairness seems most at home precisely where a process or an activity is being judged and least appropriate where a weighing of claims that are both disparate and competitive is involved. At the very least, linguistic investigation does suggest that the distinction between fairness and justice is less clear-cut and less closely tied to types of practice than Rawls's interpretation would allow. The distinction appears multidimensional in that it contains not only an ethico-legal dimension but also dimensions which may be described in terms of the contrasts between reciprocity and equality, continuity and finality, simplicity and complexity.

It is of special interest that these additional dimensions define the distinction between the two terms that emerged in the comparative historical analysis of utilitarianism and contractualism. The contractualist conception of justice had to do with reciprocity and fairness in competitive processes. Utilitarianism requires of justice judgments that institutional results be evaluated in the light of need with a view to obtaining equality of treatment. These historical and theoretical differences are in some degree reflected in the ways we use the concepts of fairness and justice, and this is so whether we interpret the difference between contractualism and utilitarianism as an enlargement of the meaning and scope of justice or as a shift in the meaning of justice in which the principle of equal treatment displaces the principles of reciprocity and fair play. In either case, both historical and linguistic considerations suggest that Rawls's interpretation of justice in terms of reciprocity and fairness does not reveal the full meaning of the concept.

It may well be that behind our apparently natural ways of using the concepts of fairness and justice lies the fact that language makes provision for talk not only about voluntary and nonvoluntary practices but also for talk about the flow of activity, a flow which we break into processes and outcomes for the purpose of appraisal. In this connection notice that J.L. Austin in his analysis of excuses—a much more tightly patterned area of discourse than the one with which we are dealing—discovered that excuses are precisely and appropriately related to certain stages in the course of an activity or project.[15] More generally, Austin calls attention to the fact that we may and do split up courses of action in various ways, one of which he describes with the words "stretch" and "consequences." He points out that ". . . a single term descriptive of what he did may be made to cover either a smaller or a

[15] Austin says, for example: "Inattention, carelessness, errors of judgment, tactlessness, clumsiness, all these and others are ills (with attendant excuses) which affect one specific stage in the machinery of action. . . ." "A Plea for Excuses," in J.O. Urmson and G.J. Warnock, eds., *Philosophical Papers* (1961), p. 141.

larger stretch of events, those excluded by the narrower description being then called 'consequences' or 'results' or 'effects' or the like of his act." [16] What I am suggesting is that Austin's findings on the way we talk about the action of an individual have their counterparts in the way we talk in our appraisals of practices and institutions. If we do break up the actions of individuals into "stretches" and "consequences," it would seem reasonable to expect that we should do the same sort of thing with institutions and so look at institutional activity as a flow punctuated by outcomes for each of which there is an appropriate language of appraisal.

We refer naturally to fair play, fair procedures, fair dealing, fair competition. Justice, however, with its notes of finality, complexity, and comprehensiveness, refers not so much to the way of doing something, to what goes on in the stretch of activity under appraisal, as it does to the results of the activity or set of activities. Complexity emerges at this level of evaluation simply because some claim or value, such as that of need, enters the appraisal and must be weighed with other claims and values if equality of treatment is to be achieved. In the case of need, its claims may be introduced only at the concluding stage of judgment, for the claims of need do not arise within the activity itself, as do claims based on relative contribution, which are, so to speak, intrinsic to the process or activity. As long as the claims that are to be balanced are intrinsic to the activity, Rawls's concept of a practice and the standards of reciprocity provide an adequate account of the judgments involved. But the claims of need and contribution, because of their disparate nature, require a weighing type of judgment that comes appropriately at the stage where the activity is completed and so eludes description in terms of reciprocity or fair play.[17]

It is of interest to note that in the realm of games, where the

---

[16] *Ibid.*, p. 149.

[17] In his essay "Justice and Personal Desert" in this volume, Joel Feinberg refers to ". . . the variety of conflicts which are possible between desert and desert and between desert and entitlement." He goes immediately on to suggest: "These conflicts within the category of justice are as subtle and difficult as any others in ethics, and it is doubtful that general principles can be formulated to dictate a priori the necessary manner of their resolution in every case."

concepts of fair and fairness are most applicable, the contrasts between reciprocity and equality, continuity and finality, simplicity and complexity, are simply irrelevant. If the rules that define a game are fair and the game itself is fairly played, it makes no sense to raise a question, either in terms of fairness or justice, about its outcome. What counts, and all that counts, is the performance of the contestants in the light of the rules that define and govern the game. No independent appraisal is to be made of the outcome of the game as we should wish to do in the case of a trial. Now compare a game with that system of cooperative and competitive processes that we call an economy. Entry into the system is voluntary, or at least quasivoluntary. Assume further that fair dealing is characteristic of the behavior of all the participants in the system and that all the requirements of reciprocity have been met. We should still wish to raise a question, either in terms of fairness or of justice, about the treatment of individuals. And here it is that claims based on need must be weighed against claims based on relative contribution. Now, claims based on relative contribution may be settled in the light of reciprocity, but, short of the requirement of the equality of treatment that is owing to us as moral persons, there would appear to be no standard by which to weigh claims based on contribution against claims based on need. And the claims which we do make as moral beings seem somehow both different from and larger than the claims we make as either players in a game or participants in a practice. Is not this difference that between equality of treatment and reciprocity?

Earlier we noted that appraisals of the distribution of income may be made in terms of either fairness or justice, and it is now in order to try to determine the significance of this interchangeability of concept. Does this interchangeability lend support to Rawls's argument that fairness and reciprocity are fundamental to justice? Now claims of need are taken into account in distributing or redistributing income, and, if this implies that what is being aimed at is equality of treatment however roughly that may be conceived, then I suggest that what is being done is not properly described in terms of the concept of reciprocity. If we do use the concept of fairness to evaluate distributions of income, then we are using it in a sense different from that in which we use it when we are talking about games and practices. The concept of fairness is being used not as an equivalent for reciprocity but as a substitute for justice, for weighing of claims of a disparate nature is involved, and the judgment partakes of the elements of finality and complexity which we found to be characteristic justice judgments. If justice were being used as an equivalent to or substitute for fairness, one would expect that only the standard of reciprocity was involved. But this cannot be the case, for the claim of need is the claim of the moral personality and not one advanced by participants in a common practice. Interchangeable usage does not, therefore, support Rawls's interpretation of justice as a brand of fairness. Rather, interchangeability is based on a shift in the meaning of fairness toward the way in which we ordinarily use the concept of justice.

My analysis of interchangeability assumes, of course, that a weighing of the claims of need against those of contribution is present in judgments on the distribution of income. And I think this is inescapable for the reason that human personalities differ not only in terms of ability but also in terms of need and that practices which accommodate the claims of talent and contribution—and so can be designed in the light of the standard of reciprocity—do not also necessarily and automatically meet the claims of need. Needs such as those for education and medical attention exert a demand upon us which is independent of the criterion of performance within the context of a practice. They are grounded in human personality and take the shape of a demand for equality of treatment and not mere reciprocity.

The comparison between a game and an economy points, therefore, to an asymmetry in usage which is important for Rawls's interpretation of justice. The concept of fairness we do use as a substitute for that of justice, but, where we do so, we mean fairness as equality of treatment, not fairness as reciprocity. This use of fairness may well be an extended use in which a concept we normally use in the context of an activity is used in appraisal of the outcome of the activity or set of activities, both cooperative and competitive, where considerations not intrinsic to the activity are introduced. If the idea central to the concept of fairness is reciprocity and if we use fairness as an equivalent to justice when equality of treatment is at stake, it does not, of course, follow that reciprocity is fundamental to the concept of justice. This could be the case only if reciprocity and equality of treatment meant the same thing. Rather, what we are concerned with is fairness in two senses, reciprocity and equality, the former of which appears to be its primary meaning and the latter its extended meaning. That reciprocity may appear to be fundamental to the concepts of both fairness and justice is the result of ignoring the dimensions of the distinction between the two concepts—dimensions which are obscured by an analysis in terms of the concept of practice and which are revealed by an analysis of usage. It is by ignoring these dimensions that the difference between reciprocity and equality of treatment is blurred. And the multidimensional character of the distinction between fairness and justice emerges only when this distinction is viewed in a light other than that provided by Rawls's analytic construction based upon the concept of the practice. Within the confines of this concept, reciprocity does indeed appear to be fundamental to justice for the reason that the distinctive features of the concept of justice—equality, finality, and complexity—remain hidden. Only when these features of the concept of justice are brought to light does it become apparent that judgments of justice require a weighing of considerations, and it is this above all that differentiates them from judgments of fairness.

So far I have argued that on both historical and linguistic grounds there are good reasons to regard Rawls's explanation of justice as authoritative reciprocity as deficient. I wish now to attend directly to his tool of explanation, the analytic construction, and to ask whether this conceptual framework may be expected to reflect accurately our ethical thinking.

From a metaethical standpoint, there are two features of Rawls's analytic construction that deserve notice. The first is that it is based on the concept of the practice, the rule-defined activity or institution. And the second is that it makes no provision for the confrontation and weighing of the claims of need and contribution. In consequence, the multidimensional character of the distinction between justice and fairness does not emerge, and Rawls is able to explain justice as reciprocity. This explanation does not, however, reflect the fact that, in making judgments of justice, we do engage in weighing competing considerations.

Rawls's use of the concept of the practice does have the merit of enabling him to divide institutional activity into the voluntary and the authoritative. This division is accomplished, however, at the expense of the distinction between institutional processes and outcomes, for apparently the notion of a practice, as it is used by Rawls, includes the distinction between an activity and its outcome. He assumes that the people he is talking about ". . . are capable of tracing out the likely consequences of adopting one practice rather than another. . . ."[18] For them the distinction between an activity and its outcome does not arise empirically. Moreover, he assumes that ". . . these persons have roughly similar needs and interests, or needs and interests in various ways complementary, so that fruitful cooperation amongst them is possible. . . ."[19] The effect of these assumptions is both to dissolve the distinction between an institutional process and its outcome and to prevent the confrontation of need and contribution. If the results of practices are known in advance, no independent judgment upon them is required, and, if needs are similar or complementary, they become a constant and not a variable factor in judgments. On both these scores, Rawls's analytic construction seems ill-designed for the purpose of reflecting the realities of moral deliberation and institutional evaluation. Ethical thinking becomes purely a matter of reaching agreement upon standards to be applied to practices; the possibility of mutual acceptance becomes the test of justice. Since all that is at stake is an assessment of rewards for contributions, there is no need for a weighing of the competing claims of need and contribution in order to achieve equality of treatment. Justice can be nothing other than reciprocity; the analytic construction is designed to display this interpretation of justice and can accommodate no other.

It seems to me that Rawls's analytic construction tends to distort the process of ethical reflection in two distinct and yet related ways. In the first place, it blurs the distinction between institutional processes and the evaluation of their results. Rawls does notice this distinction, but he absorbs it in his assumption that a single judgment may be made upon both a practice and its

[18] Rawls, "Justice as Fairness," *op. cit.*, p. 655.
[19] *Ibid.*, p. 171.

results. Differences in need are reduced to insignificance by his assumption that they are similar or complementary. Second, the analytic construction makes agreement upon principles central to the process of ethical deliberation and decision. Indeed, the test of fairness—and so by implication also the test of justice—is the possibility of mutual agreement. In practice, principles themselves, I should think, are not only tested against the possibility of mutual acceptance, but are also evaluated in the light of their implications, that is to say, the results of their application. Now, taken separately, neither of these features of Rawls's analytic construction could be said to involve serious distortion of how we actually think about ethical questions. We do employ standards and principles in making judgments, and the test of mutual agreement as a test of fairness of a principle would in itself seem reasonable and sound. However, when these metaethical theses are taken in conjunction with his claim that justice is the authoritative reflection of fairness, then the implication emerges that the criterion and the ground of justice is mutual agreement. Not only does this conception of justice as reciprocity preclude the sort of weighing of considerations of need and contribution to which usage points, but it also implies that any practice upon which agreement could be freely reached is a just practice. This implication raises the question of the relation between justice and rights.

In certain specified circumstances, Rawls contends, free men could agree to accept the practice of slavery, and, if they so agreed, then that practice would not be unjust. His example is that of citizens of city-states who have been accustomed to killing captives of war and who agree to substitute for this practice the practice of enslaving prisoners. This substitution is seen as an advance, and Rawls goes on to say: "This example shows that situations are possible in which there is a real and equal risk of becoming a slave and that in these cases slavery need not be unjust." [20] According to Rawls:

> This is because it satisfies the conditions of the concept of justice, for it is in accordance with what has been mutually acknowledged from an original position of equal liberty. . . . The essential thing is that the equal citizenship of equal city-states permits citizens of

[20] Rawls, "Justice and Liberty," *op. cit.*

> these states to do whatever they consent to do as long as they do not infringe on the like liberty of others.[21]

Thus the practice of slavery in these circumstances is not unjust because the practice has been agreed upon from an initial condition of equal freedom. Slavery has met the test of mutual acceptance. Therefore, it is fair, and, if it is fair and also authoritative, it must be just, or at least not unjust. I wish to suggest that it would be more natural, more in accordance with our sense of the meaning of the concepts, to describe the agreement on the practice of slavery as making it fair. I doubt that we should be prepared to call it just.

By calling slavery under the conditions that Rawls sets forth fair, I mean to say that anyone who became a slave after having freely agreed to the rules according to which one could become a slave could not complain of unfair treatment. He is a party to the agreement, others have run the same risk, reciprocity has been satisfied, and the requirements of fair play have been met. Everyone has taken his chances; hence, on the ground of fairness no one can complain of his status as a slave. Indeed, all who are slaves prefer this condition to the alternative. But cannot anyone raise the question of the justice of the practice on the ground that it involves a violation of a fundamental right, say the right to moral freedom, a right which, it is asserted, cannot be infringed by any practice no matter how voluntary the agreement upon it may be? The slave could say that, although he had agreed to the practice and had done so freely, at best it was still an expedient thing to do and the question of the justice of his condition is not settled by his having agreed to the practice. The fact remains that his right to moral freedom, a right which he claims as a moral personality, is being infringed, and this infringement is unjust.

The implication of Rawls's argument that under these circumstances slavery need not be unjust is that there is no distinction to be made between our sense of fairness and our sense of justice, for it is a logical implication of his interpretation of justice that, if a practice is mutually acceptable, it must be fair, and, if it is

---

[21] *Ibid.* Also note his statement: "The peculiar feature of the concept of justice is that it treats each person as an equal sovereign, as it were, and requires a unanimous acknowledgment from a certain original position of equal liberty." *Ibid.*

fair, it must also be just. The question of justice cannot arise as a separate question, for justice is entirely derivative from fairness. This means that there are no rights which could impose a limit upon the scope of agreement, no rights so fundamental that they cannot be bargained away. So long as there is reciprocity, the requirements of justice are satisfied; all that is owing to us as moral personalities is reciprocity of treatment. Rawls's concept of justice has swallowed the concept of rights. This, I suggest, is to do violence to our sense of justice, for that sense depends, in part at least, upon our conception of ourselves as moral beings possessed of rights.

According to Rawls, our recognition of one another as persons manifests itself in the willingness to deal fairly with one another and in acceptance of the principles of justice. Now, if both fairness and justice depend upon mutual acceptance, does it follow that whatever is agreed upon from an initial condition of freedom involves mutual recognition as persons? The answer to this question, according to Rawls, is yes. Mutual agreement upon the practice of slavery is consistent with such recognition. But does this not imply that, in Rawls's view, mutual recognition as persons is not so much displayed as exhausted in the test of mutual acceptability? Mutual consent is not only, therefore, the test of fairness and of justice but also the criterion of mutual recognition as persons. Apparently, no rights are implied in that recognition other than the right to make agreements freely. Again, I suggest that the idea of reciprocity is being used in a manner that is not consistent with our moral experience, in this case our experience of ourselves as moral persons and our sense of what is owing to us as such. What it means to be a person, in the moral sense of that term, does not depend upon the notion of reciprocity of treatment, but rather upon how we conceive of ourselves, upon how we think and feel about ourselves. By making reciprocity the criterion of mutual recognition of moral personality, Rawls ignores this feature of our moral experience.

Again, in the slavery example, we see that, in his interpretation of justice, Rawls makes no distinction between the process by which an institution is established and the effects of the institution. If the establishment meets the test of mutual consent, then the resulting practice must be either fair or just. But if the mutual recognition of persons implies that persons have rights and that it would be wrong to violate their sense of what is owing to them as moral persons, then it seems to me proper to say that it would be unjust to place them in a condition of slavery, whatever else may be said about that condition—that it was equally risked, that it was expedient, or that it was fair. Rawls's conception of moral personality as essentially moral autonomy implies that there is only one constraint upon persons in their dealings with one another and that constraint is the requirement of reciprocity. Indeed, the requirement of reciprocity is now to be seen as only the reflection of his conception of moral personality as moral autonomy, equal moral sovereignty. Equal moral sovereigns dealing with one another under the conditions and the assumptions specified by Rawls's analytic construction can settle their arrangements only on the basis of reciprocity. His interpretation of justice as reciprocity is but the shadow of their absolute autonomy. But this interpretation of justice does not appear to be consistent either with the way we use the concept or with our sense of justice. We think ourselves unjustly treated not only when reciprocity is violated but also when we are not accorded the treatment that we think is owing to us as moral persons, whether this be expressed in terms of our needs or of our rights.

To summarize, there are reinforcing considerations of a historical, linguistic, and metaethical nature that render Rawls's interpretation of justice as fairness and reciprocity dubious. He is surely right that the contractualist approach to justice does take account of the plurality of persons in a way that the utilitarian theory does not. But contractualism does not provide for a weighing of claims based upon need against claims based upon contribution to the common good. Here the utilitarian conception of justice as equality of treatment would appear to be an advance upon the contractualist conception of justice as reciprocity; a historical expansion of our sense of justice has taken place. From a linguistic standpoint, this expansion of our sense of justice would appear to take the shape of distinctions between justice and fairness other than that which Rawls specifies in terms of types of practice. Special to our use of justice are the connotations of equality, finality, and complexity, all of which point to a weighing aspect of justice judgments that is not present in judgments of fairness. Rawls's analytic construction, by means of which he attempts to explain the concept of justice, diverts attention from this special feature of weighing, the feature which above all distinguishes justice judgments from fairness judgments. Thus mutual consent is held to be the common test of both justice and fairness, and the test of mutual consent is itself grounded in a conception of moral personality as moral autonomy and sovereignty. This conception of moral personality implies no rights other than that of reciprocity in treatment and would appear to be inconsistent with our sense of justice or what is owing to us as moral beings. Rawls's conception of moral personality is made a derivative of the idea of reciprocity. Thus Rawls's interpretation of justice as reciprocity is not so much the outcome of an analysis of our moral experience—whether this be viewed historically, linguistically, or directly—as it is the reflection of the assumptions which he incorporates in his analytic construction.

As an alternative to Rawls's interpretation of justice as fairness, I should like to suggest that fairness has to do with reciprocity and justice with equality of treatment; that both our concern for fairness and our concern for justice are rooted in the moral nature of personality; that both give expression to our feelings of what is owing to us as moral persons. But neither fairness nor justice is fundamental to the other. Fundamental to both is the nature of moral personality. In the light of our moral experience, it is not a matter of justice as fairness but of justice and fairness.

9

LAW, JUSTICE, AND THE PUBLIC'S ASPIRATIONS

CLARENCE MORRIS

The thesis of this paper is twofold: (1) there can be no justice without law, and (2) justice is not ordinarily intentionally created except by lawmakers acting as agents of the public (and not acting as its masters).

(1) Though there can be law without justice, justicc is realized only through good law; justice is the quality that makes just law just. This may be made clearer by two analogies. Literary merit makes good literature good. There are poor poems, novels, dramas, and so on, but there could be no literary merit if literature were not written. Pulchritude is a quality of some people. Many people are plain, but, in an unpeopled world, no pulchritude would exist. Literary merit can be thought of with no specific writing in mind; standards of pulchritude can be formulated with no specific person in view; justice can be discussed without focusing on a particular statute, decision, or legal obliga-

tion. But, in a world that knew no law, justice would not exist. When the word "justice" is used in other senses (e.g., "a just father," "a just employer"), its use is metaphoric. Of course, there are preconditions of justice; there could be no literature—good or bad—without language, no just law of real property without land.

(2) Justice is not likely to be actualized except when a lawmaker has intended to advance the public's aspirations as the public's agent, though the law of tyrants can be in some respects accidentally just. Of course, the public aspires to goals other than justice (e.g., beauty and truth), but these are not the goals of lawmakers. Conscientious lawmakers do not always understand and succeed in advancing the public's aspirations. But the public's aspirations do, in fact, exist.

I am not expert in detailing or defining the public's aspirations, but nearly all thoughtful people have some sketchy notion of their ambit. Desires too unworthy to be called public aspirations (even though widely held) are selfish, unreasonable, or even the result of widespread mental illness. The public's true aspirations are deep-seated, reasonable, nonexploitative. They are not entirely unchanging, but many are relatively permanent, and, when change occurs, it is slow. New public aspirations develop as the social scene changes and human capabilities and techniques develop. The realization of aspirations must sometimes await technical developments—know-how. The scope of the public's aspirations is difficult to delimit for four reasons. (1) No one is experienced and wise enough to blueprint them *in extenso.* (2) Some of the public's aspirations are inchoate and thus can be well formulated only by the most prescient of experts. (3) Technical methods of plumbing the public's aspirations are still crude and misleading. (4) The aspiring public changes and expands, and some of its aspirations are constantly in flux.

One more introductory point: only when law is defined broadly can the realization of justice be said to depend on law. A definition restricting law to the government's general commands will not do. Though justice can and does result from legislators' statutes and ordinances, nevertheless justice is sometimes created by judges deciding cases. The definition of law for my present purposes should be wide enough to include law originating in judicial (and quasijudicial) decisions. My definition of law must also cover more than governmental intervention in affairs, for justice can result from social recognition of legal obligations, which sometimes occurs without governmental prompting. I do not really quarrel with those who define law more narrowly. I could (less conveniently) use a narrower definition, but then my discussion of the nature of justice would be still more cumbersome than it now is.

To promote clarity, I shall discuss separately the relationship between justice and (1) law as rules enacted by legislators, (2) law as decisions made by judges, and (3) law as obligations arising in society.

Since legislators can be lazy, mistaken, stupid, capricious, selfish, intolerant, and tyrannical, their enactments can be unjust. Even well-qualified and well-meaning legislators (to whom none of the above adjectives apply) may forget that they are the public's agents and not its masters and may (by substituting their own values for the public's aspirations) legislate unjustly. Even capable legislators who are eager to forward only the public's aspirations may nevertheless be hampered by awkward procedures and lean resources and so fail to enact just laws.

Several great philosophers, however, find a font of justice in legislation. All of them, of course, admit that enacted law can be poor law. Aristotle's "conventional justice" arises when a lawgiver promulgates rules on matters previously indifferent.[1] Such enactment, however, prescribes law rightly only insofar as the law has been rightly enacted, and "not so well if it has been made at random." [2] Hobbes, who says that the Leviathan lawmaker cannot be unjust, nevertheless admits that Leviathan can be iniquitous [3] or inept.[4] Hume, to whom justice is human artifice, implies that rules of enacted law can work poorly and need reformulation.[5] I

[1] Aristotle, *Nicomachean Ethics,* Rackham trans., 1949, 295; Clarence Morris, ed., *The Great Legal Philosophers* (1959) (hereinafter cited as *Great Philosophers*), p. 21.

[2] Aristotle, *op. cit.*, p. 259; *Great Philosophers,* p. 17.

[3] Thomas Hobbes, *Leviathan* (1904), p. 122; *Great Philosophers,* p. 121.

[4] Hobbes, *op. cit.*, p. 252; *Great Philosophers,* p. 132.

[5] David Hume, *A Treatise of Human Nature,* Vol. 11, Book 111, #549 Everyman's Library, 1911, 226; *Great Philosophers,* p. 207, says, "As the obligation of promises is an invention for the interest of society it is warped into as many different forms as that interest requires." If this is so, the technical job of formulating it may be done badly.

am not unmindful that other great philosophers do not look on legislation as a font of justice. Cicero used Roman public law to illustrate justice in the third book of *The Laws,* but he nevertheless believed that the justice of the Roman system existed before its enactment, that both justice and law worthy of the name exist in the gods' right reason before men enact good law.[6] Earthy Montesquieu (in one of his untypical moods) also said that the potentiality of justice pre-exists its historical actuality.[7]

Both these views seem to me to overlook the newly created justice that promulgated legislation can and sometimes does accomplish, justice unrealized and not fully understood *as justice* until the processes of enactment are, in fact, completed. An example may clarify: British judges have recently held (as have judges in several American states) that common-law crimes may be punished, i.e., that, without a legislated, preannounced rule, a court may nevertheless find an accused guilty of a crime and order him punished.[8] This would have delighted ancient Confucians. When Tzu-chan promulgated criminal laws in 536 B.C., Shu-hsing, a scholar in a neighboring kingdom, wrote him that he was flouting the example of the ancient kings, who abjured announced general laws of punishment to avoid contention. Shu continued, saying that, when exact laws are known, the people lose their awe of their superiors, argue about the ambit of statutory terms, and become unmanageable.[9]

In eighteen of the United States, the courts' power to punish common-law crimes has been expressly abrogated and replaced by legislated penal codes.[10] In the other states, the situation is like that in Britain, i.e., the courts' power to develop common-law crimes theoretically still exists, but the courts show a marked re-

[6] Cicero, *Laws,* trans. Keyes (1928), p. 317; *Great Philosophers,* p. 44.

[7] "Before laws were made there were relations of possible justice. To say there is nothing just or unjust but what is commanded or forbidden by positive laws, is the same as saying that before describing a circle, all radii were not equal." Montesquieu, *Spirit of the Laws,* trans. Nugent (1873), p. 2; *Great Philosophers,* p. 161.

[8] *Shaw* v. *Director of Public Prosecutions,* 2 All E.R. 448 (1961); discussed in *Modern L.R.,* 24 (1961), 626. The punishment was nine months' imprisonment for publishing a lurid directory of prostitutes. Common-law grounds for the holding were alternative with statutory offenses.

[9] Ch'u, *Law and Society in Traditional China* (1961), p. 170.

[10] "Common Law of Crimes in the United States," *Col. L.R.,* 47 (1947), 1332.

luctance to innovate or apply ancient and obscure precedents; [11] in these states, the only common-law crimes are a few petty offenses.[12] For example, in 1924 in my state of Pennsylvania, a Court of Common Pleas (note the court's appropriately archaic name) fined, without statutory authority, a woman for being a common scold.[13] It can be said on the court's behalf that the only point argued by her defense counsel was that the state's evidence was unconvincing.

Wherein, however, are criminal statutes creative of justice? How can they be said to embody any new justice, since they were, for the most part, enacted long after the conduct interdicted was first thought unlawful and justly punished? No American legislature invented the classic crimes. Every state legislature has, by defining crimes, developed limitations on the authority of officials who detain, try, and punish accused persons. No doubt our criminal laws and procedures are unjust in many particulars. But the point I am stressing here is that new criminal justice was created when modern criminal law embodied in the formulated texts of statutes limits on authority that was fluid before those statutes were enacted.

I am, of course, not unmindful of criminal statutes drawn so loosely that they do not channel the judgments of courts "applying" them. Obscenity and conspiracy statutes often fall into this class. No doubt, from time to time, other criminal statutes are interpreted in ways that surprise both legislators and citizens.[14] However, one significant twentieth-century development is the change in judges' attitudes toward legislation. Whenever any nineteenth-century American judge doubted the legislators' wisdom, he usually managed a statutory interpretation thwarting the legislature's purpose.[15] Nowadays, most of our judges do their best to effectuate the legislature's intentions.

[11] *Ibid.*, p. 1334. See also Warren and Brandeis, "The Right to Privacy," *Harv. L.R.*, 4 (1890), 193, 219, in which a new civil remedy for invasion of privacy is proposed, but the authors say that a criminal action would not lie without legislation.

[12] *Loc. cit.*

[13] *Commonwealth* v. *Smith, alias Quinter,* 17 Berks 40 (1924).

[14] Witness, e.g., *Caminetti* v. *U.S.*, 242 U.S. 470 (1917), in which the Mann Act, passed to combat commercial vice, was turned against amateurs.

[15] See Roscoe Pound, "Common Law and Legislation," *Harv. L.R.*, 21 (1908), 383, 385.

The substance of classic criminal law interdictions is so centrally an expression of public aspirations that legislators move with warranted assurance when they interdict, for example, murder, theft, and arson. But the limiting force of legislative definition of crimes is equally a response to another public aspiration—the public aspiration for preformulated, deliberate, clear, promulgated criminal law. The significance of that aspiration lies in the public's distrust of the ability of single judges to objectively define crimes extemporaneously when the guilt of an accused individual (who may be unattractive or unappealing) is at stake. Even when only petty offenses are involved, we recoil from procedures permitting a finding of guilt unless a clear criterion has been legislatively enacted before the crime was committed.

This public aspiration for impersonal definition of crime might conceivably be realized in some other way. In a static society, perhaps a common law of crimes could become so fully developed and so frozen that (after a period of development) most of the criteria of guilt would be fixed in advance of trial. But no such system has, in fact, existed, and in all civilized countries legislative definition of nearly all crimes has forwarded the public's aspirations for promulgated criminal law. I venture to say that, as a practical matter, justice of this sort can probably be accomplished in no other way. If this is so, then the legislative definition of crimes illustrates both (1) a justice that could not exist without law and (2) a justice that came into being when the public's agents, as agents, endeavored to advance the public's aspirations. In the Confucian system, Tzu-chan, who believed that officials should be masters, also believed that promulgated criminal laws would embarrass official power. In his system, therefore, the justice of promulgated laws could happen, if at all, only accidentally, as it did when the later legalists thought promulgation better deterred misconduct and that they could be more effective masters by using the device of promulgation.

I have given only a comparatively trivial illustration of creation of justice depending on legislators, rather than on judges or on nongovernmental forces. There are, of course, innumerable areas in which the development of justice is uniquely legislative. Other institutions have, for example, struggled with economic insecurity, but, without legislation, modern social security would have advanced haltingly, if at all. Similarly, the development of just regulation of business and traffic, just military conscription, and just taxes falls solely on the legislator.

Of course, not all enactments are creative. Every legislative session is spent, in major part, on allocation of appropriations and other pressing but routine business—not improving the administration of justice. Bills introduced compete for attention; no session of any modern American legislature lasts long enough to consider all the meritorious bills introduced. Sometimes, trivialities attract and debilitate legislators. Even when they are not diverted, their output of justice is only a trickle—and courts, administrators, and nongovernmental power-wielders must constantly create justice if our lives are to be tolerable. Even if legislators tried to solve all problems of justice in advance, they could not completely anticipate the inevitably novel future.

I turn now to justice originating in judicial decision. Judges' work is even more often routine than is the work of legislators. When cases involve only disputes of fact, judges are about as creative as doctors engaged in mine-run medical treatment; a sensitive and imaginative doctor's day-to-day therapy is above average, but an average doctor treats ordinary illnesses reasonably well. The judge dealing with ordinary cases has only an occasional chance to be mildly creative.

When a legislature is faced with a puzzling proposal, it postpones action until it knows what to do; a court, however, cannot properly refuse to dispose of a perplexing case. If the operative facts of a case are undeveloped in some respect, assigned burdens of proof arbitrarily determine which litigant must suffer from lack of proof. The same burdens also function (at least in theory) when conflicting proofs are evenly balanced. Once facts are settled, if the court cannot convince itself that the law should lie with one litigant rather than the other, it usually refuses to interfere with the *status quo* and dismisses the suit, leaving the disputants where it found them. Of course, in none of these cases is the court's decision creative, and a fortiori in none does any new creative justice arise. On the contrary, even future creativity is embarrassed in one of these instances, i.e., the cases in which, once the facts are known, the court makes no decision on the merits because it does not know which litigant the law should favor. The force of tradition in our common-law system tends to keep courts from reconsidering the merits of unsolved problems in justice. When, at a later date, the way to justice might be clearer, undue respect for precedent or tradition may blind the court's eyes.[16] Utter lack of precedent, too, has an intimidating effect; courts citing precedents for virtually all their decisions become uneasy when no precedent favors realization of a public aspiration.[17]

The judiciary, of course, does not have the office of implementing all the public's aspirations. But what is now good, routine common law had its creative beginnings. Before the middle of the nineteenth century, neither the British Parliament nor the American legislatures concerned themselves much with administration of justice in private affairs, and, when they did, they responded to dissatisfactions of small moment. Not until the turn of our century did the compiled statute books of American states grow fat and divide into multivolume sets. Only in response to special and politically respected voices were our legislatures stimulated to develop systematic and extensive codes on negotiable instruments, corporations, insurance, etc. Over the long haul of history, the common law has been the principal font of justice in England and America.

Common-law judges no doubt borrowed from other legal systems and adopted both customs of trade and other everyday social patterns. But their willingness to strike out on their own often produced novel recognitions of public aspirations, aspirations that were unlikely to be actualized in any other way. This creativity is well illustrated by the judicial invention of the rule against perpetuity, i.e., the seventeenth-century rule interdict-

---

[16] See, e.g., *Union Pacific* v. *Cappier,* 66 Kan. 649, 72 Pac. 281 (1903)—a wrongful death action in which the plaintiff alleged that, after the defendant railroad ran over the decedent, railroad employes failed to come to his aid promptly and, as a result, he bled to death. Held: the railroad had no duty to come to his aid.

The judicial deaf ear to justice sometimes also has failed to hear just defenses to claims. This was so in the common-law courts in the period immediately before their adoption of equitable defenses. See Walsh, *Treatise on Equity* (1930), p. 99.

[17] See, e.g., *Roberson* v. *Rochester Folding Box Co.,* 171 N.Y. 538 (1902), in which the court refused to recognize that an advertiser who without permission put a pretty girl's picture in his ads violated her rights.

ing those restraints on alienation of property operating beyond lives in being plus twenty-one years. The judges who developed this clear-cut bar to frozen ownership had to predicate their invention on two premises, i.e., (1) perpetuities are evil and (2) judges are enfranchised to combat that evil. They made no trivial change [18] like that, for example, made by twentieth-century judges who were first willing to enjoin spite fences.[19] The seventeenth-century judges circumscribed the planning power of landed proprietors who wanted durable posthumous control of their family properties. These judges were themselves elder members of the propertied class; their natural sympathies lay, to some extent, with those whose bent they curbed. But they also thought that they knew that the British public's postfeudal aspirations were against a strait-jacketed property system and favored a dynamic, developing society.

The remarkable aspects of this judicial creativity were that the judges did not hesitate to deal with so central and complicated a problem and that they could agree to draw the arbitrary line where they did, even though it could have been drawn as wisely at some other point. Perhaps the times both emboldened the judiciary and diverted other governmental forces from concern. Earlier and later common-law creativity seems to be less calculated, more interstitial, more intuitive, more a product of the institutional ingenuity of judges and lawyers. The development of the fictions in ejectment and trover exemplify.

Ejectment was at its birth a trivial thirteenth-century addition to the common-law actions for regaining possession of land after wrongful ouster. Important landowners when wrongfully ousted used the appropriate "real" action. No real action lay, however, to protect tenants, and the new ejectment writ was invented to plug this loophole. The new remedy was, perhaps accidentally, classified as trespass and not as a real action and was both fast and simple. The real actions were complicated and slow-going. Not long after ejectment was invented, nontenant land occupants found a way to substitute faster ejectment for their more torpid real actions. An ousted landowner would execute a lease to a friend. Since that friend had not been ousted (a prerequisite of

[18] See Gray, *Rule against Perpetuities* (4th ed., 1942), especially §§ 169–170.
[19] See, e.g., *Hubbard* v. *Halliday*, 58 Ok. 244, 158 Pac. 1158 (1916).

ejectment), a second friend would purport to oust him. First Friend then, as an ousted tenant, sued Second Friend in ejectment. Second Friend notified the real occupant that the suit was pending and told him that Second Friend did not intend to defend the suit and that therefore, unless the occupant defended, he was likely to have a brush with the sheriff putting First Friend into possession. This brought the occupant into court. Whether such hocus-pocus was invented by lawyers[20] or was in some measure inspired by judges is difficult to tell. In any event, the judiciary countenanced the make-believe and ruled that any occupant who wished to defend an ejectment action brought by a nominal lessee could do so only if he admitted the lease, entry, and ouster. After this, the farce became fiction, and eventually even the fiction was abolished.[21]

Enlargement of ejectment was merely a procedural reform; a faster remedy was substituted for a slower one. But relief speeded by two or three years was a real boon over the injustice of real action delay and no doubt advanced the public aspiration for more effective justice against unlawful ouster from real property. Today, we would hail a similar gain in automobile accident litigation, in which defendants are often unwilling to make substantial settlements until cases are near trial, sometimes years after they were first docketed.

Enlargement of trover effected a substantive advance. The action originally lay only against a finder who refused to deliver lost property to the true owner. Eventually, however, there were trover cases in which plaintiffs alleged that they casually lost such property as, for example, forty tons of coal, which the defendant found and refused to deliver.[22] Loss and finding had, as a result of lawyers' and judges' connivance, become fictitious, and the enlarged action lay against any wrongful converter of personal property.[23]

Advocates not only help the desirable spread of old remedies to new cases, but, by standing outraged, they also check judicial

---

[20] "*Lawyers* saw an opportunity to secure the trial of title to realty without the expense and delay of the old real action . . . ," says Edmund Morgan, *The Study of Law* (1926), p. 82 (italics mine).

[21] *Ibid.*, pp. 81 *et seq.*

[22] *Mast* v. *Goodson*, 3 Wilson 348, 351 (Common Pleas, 1772).

[23] See Morgan, *op. cit.*, pp. 80 *et seq.*

temptations to innovate unjustly. This aspect of the value of lawyers is best illustrated by what can happen in a judicial system in which advocacy was forbidden—the system of imperial China. In an early wills case, a dying father of an infant son and of a mature married daughter bequeathed to his daughter all his property except his sword, which the son was to have on his fifteenth birthday. When the son turned fifteen, the daughter refused to deliver the sword, and the son brought suit for it. Ho Wu, the judge, said that he found the daughter violent and domineering and her husband greedy and low-minded. The dead father, said Ho Wu, feared that this couple would harm the son if the estate were left to him; therefore, the daughter was given temporary custody of the estate until the son was old enough to use a sword, when he would also be mature enough to take independent action and appeal to the authorities if need be. Ho Wu held that not only the sword but all the property must be delivered to the son.[24]

A bequest leaving an estate to a daughter by a father who also had a son was odd in imperial China. Ho Wu, however, did not hold that such a bequest could not be made. He refused to respect this ostensible bequest because the testator, he thought, had symbolically indicated a different intention. Suppose Ho Wu, the superior man, did catch aright the true meaning of the testator. Should Ho Wu, the judge, have the office of attaching legal force to this cryptogram? Would he have done so had the daughter been championed by a phlegmatic advocate insisting that some value inheres in less imaginative methods of interpretation? (Ho Wu's opinion, I must add, was much admired and was reported in a casebook compiled about a thousand years ago for the guidance of Chinese magistrates.)

It is not easy to demonstrate that judicial innovation sometimes is and always should be an attempt to actualize a public aspiration.[25] Judges are not representative in the same sense that legislators are; even where they are elected, they announce no platforms, make no campaign promises, offer no allegiance to party programs. This is so because, largely, the judicial role is

---

[24] Van Gulik, *T'ang-Yin-Pi-Shih* (1956), p. 176.

[25] A court interpreting a statute or a written constitution has a somewhat different function; analysis of this function is not covered in this short paper.

thought of as administrative, rather than creative. In most cases, it is believed, the law's direction has already been fixed, and the good judge's job is to even-handedly apply or to adapt existing law to the case. Only occasionally do judges properly innovate to any great extent, and even then they should be objectively non-partisan, i.e., they should move only in directions that they believe command approval of the corporate public. The examples I have given seem to fall into this category. Public aspirations were advanced a little when the torpid procedures of the real actions were superseded by the faster justice of ejectment and when trover's vindication of rights in personal property was extended to all misappropriations. These two innovations, however, merely extended the justice of pre-existing law to sensible limits; the innovations were only triumphs of function over history. The rule against perpetuity, too, advanced public aspirations. The boldness of the invention of the rule against perpetuity, however, seems to me another story; seldom do common-law judges strike out so much on their own. And, in our time, exemplification of such clear-cut judicial policy-making, unconnected with statutory or constitutional text, is difficult to find.

Learned Hand noted a contemporary tendency against judicial innovation; he said that common-law judges of earlier times innovated more easily because the self-conscious elements in society were homogeneous and likely to agree on where justice lay.[26] He goes on to say: "All this has changed . . . [new] demands are vocal that before were dumb. . . . If justice be a possible accommodation between the vital and self-conscious interests of society it has taken on a meaning not known before." [27] So the more varied private value systems of modern times greatly reduce the palatability (and hence the likelihood) of newly made judicial justices.

Twentieth-century judges have not, however, abjured creativity. They have made both corrections and advances. Two modern examples make the point; one is a rectification of case-law foolishness, the other a development of a new right.

(1) In the nineteenth century, a carriage-maker contracted with the British postmaster general to maintain mail coaches.

[26] Learned Hand, "The Speech of Justice," *Harv. L.R.*, 29 (1916), 617, 619.
[27] *Loc. cit.*

Thereafter, a mail coach cast a wheel because of the carriage-maker's negligent failure of maintenance. The driver was injured and sued the carriage-maker. In 1842, the Court of Exchequer held that, since the maintenance obligation grew out of a contract to which the driver was not a party, no duty was owed the driver.[28]

The resulting "privity-of-contract" rule protected all sorts of careless suppliers of goods and services from liability to third persons. The doctrine was so obviously unjust that minor exceptions developed quickly. But the doctrine endured in America for more than seventy years. In 1916, however, Cardozo repudiated it and held the Buick Motor Company liable for an injury resulting from the negligent manufacture of a car sold by a dealer to a customer with whom the Buick Company had made no contract.[29] Cardozo's lead emboldened judges in virtually all the following American cases, and the privity doctrine soon became history instead of law. Cardozo, it seems to me, bespoke justice where those not trained in the law hardly knew that the law was unjust.

(2) My other example is the twentieth-century development of the right to privacy, not known (at least by that name) until championed in an imaginative and persuasive article published in the *Harvard Law Review* in 1896.[30] The article inspired many state courts to develop new protections against advertisers' unpermitted use of names and pictures, wire-tappers, public dunning of debtors, and so forth. The state courts' developments of these rights (rarely aided by legislation) are both impressive, needed new protections and admirable avoidance of overenthusiasm.

Courts also constantly formulate or reformulate law interstitially with an eye on justice. The process is so pervasive that single examples would mislead by their specificity. Of course, wooden technicality, unwarranted conservatism, and blindness are also pervasive and are enemies of justice—enemies hidden in the chinks of our case law. Judicial failure to do justice may, indeed, be more significant than judicial creative advancement of

---

[28] *Winterbottom* v. *Wright,* 10 M. & W. 109 (1842).

[29] *MacPherson* v. *Buick Motor Co.,* 217 N.Y. 382, 111 N.E. 1050 (1916).

[30] Warren and Brandeis, "The Right to Privacy," *Harv. L.R.,* 4 (1896), 193.

justice. My own conviction does not lie with Cardozo's easy optimism about courts when he says: "Not all the progeny of principles begotten of [judicial] judgment survive . . . to maturity. Those that cannot prove their worth and strength by the test of experience are sacrificed." [31] I find myself closer to Traynor when he says:

> There is now wide agreement that a judge can and should participate creatively in the development of the common law. Yet each time he does so, he must reckon with the ancient suspicion that creativeness is a disturbing excess of skill, at odds with circumspection; darkly menacing the stability of the law. . . . The real concern is not the remote possibility of too many creative opinions but their continuing scarcity. . . .[32]

So, though judges create justice, our need for justice will not be met entirely by courts. Judges have neither the mobility nor the resources to create all the justice we need; they have neither the obligation nor the competence to bespeak justice as individuals consulting only their own consciences. If judges are idiosyncratic, they disrupt the system of justice and flirt with impeachment. If they are egoistic and clever, they may persuade their benchmates that they see new justice not visible to a sleeping public, but seldom will their successors follow their novel holdings when those holdings conflict with the public's aspirations. Only when judges stay within both their competence and their trust can they advance justice, rather than threaten stability. If, however, they are too slow in their proper sphere of creativity, their failures will be doubly unjust; the doctrine of *stare decisis* will tend to make the evil they do live after them.

The sum of all governmental justice (judicial, legislative, and executive) does not, without more, produce a just society; so now I turn to the justice of legal obligations recognized without direct governmental intervention. In Savigny's historical philosophy of law (as set out in his one systematic book on jurisprudence),[33] law is pictured as developing like language—naturally and in response to folk character. Each society produces its own unique,

---

[31] Benjamin Cardozo, *The Nature of the Judicial Process* (1921), p. 22.

[32] Monrad Paulsen, ed., *Legal Institutions Today and Tomorrow* (1959), pp. 48, 50.

[33] Savigny, *Of the Vocation of Our Age for Legislation and Jurisprudence* (1814), esp. chapters I and II; *Great Philosophers*, pp. 290–293.

binding customs, which are embedded in popular faith. Since such law is not consciously invented, it is therefore "created" only in a metaphorical sense.[34] This law can seldom be properly or profitably restated as official, promulgated, formal rules, because the process of reducing it to abstract words deadens it and obscures its meaning. Governmental lawmakers function well only after they have prepared themselves by historical study, so that, when a rare need for clarifying the law arises, their enactment will accurately reflect the folk spirit. Without such a background, lawmakers promulgate rules divorced from folk wisdom, rules that are unable to inspire folk loyalty.

Though the word "justice" seldom occurs in Savigny's discourse,[35] he implies that good (and, therefore, just) law can never be a product of official creativity. Though officials are enfranchised to find and apply the law on occasions (and, once in a long while, to restate it officially in a rule), a folk exudes its justice, a justice that exists as a historical fact which good officials learn and then gratifyingly apply to problems as they arise.

Savigny was no Rousseau; though his appeal to folkways did purport admiration for the public's unconscious wisdom, he was actuated more by fear of elite lawmakers turning away from the tangible historic scene to make abstract formulas bearing little on contemporary conditions, needs, or desires. He argued against attempts to capture universal and permanent justice because he feared that the resulting structure of doctrine would be only a false front, behind which foolish officials would bumble and self-willed ones would try to rule according to caprice.

In our time, it seems to me, we need not fear that Anglo-American legislators will embark on abstract codification; they are unlikely to try to restate either the natural law or the *jus gentium*. In our complicated world, we would wait long and usually in vain if we relegated all our important needs for justice to folkways for solution. We often prefer more active and professional lawmaking. We live in hope that hard-working, trained,

[34] But see Carl J. Friedrich, "Law and History," *Vand. L.R.*, 14 (1961), 1027, 1035.

[35] And, when it does it is usually in the phrase, "administration of justice," by which he usually means only the application of law to cases without regard to how just that law may be.

expert officials will be skillful enough to hasten realization of some of the public's aspirations. Nevertheless, Savigny's thesis has lessons for us. Since genuine culture [36] results only in communities affording widespread participation in vital social decision-making, the creativity of legislators and judges is most welcomed when it recognizes and draws on the corporate public's values and tries to realize the public's, and not their own, aspirations. Savigny also points up for us the important fact that some obligations are, in fact, developed in society itself, without intervention of government.

In some respects, however, Savigny's metaphor of folk creativeness is misleading; it pictures the social forces that create legal obligations as both monolithic and unconscious. Though he says that mores vary from province to province, he nevertheless gives to each locality a unified character which uncalculatingly spawns a single set of folkways.

Savigny's twentieth-century follower, Ehrlich, built on a more sophisticated sociology; he saw society as pluralistic, and the men in Ehrlich's groups often intentionally develop those legal obligations that will serve their purposes. Like Savigny, however, he believes that the bulk of men's legal obligations arise without governmental intervention and are respected without thought of official sanctions.

> . . . Man lives in innumerable legal relations and . . . , with few exceptions, he quite voluntarily performs the duties incumbent upon him because of these relations. One performs one's duties as father or son, as husband or wife, does not interfere with one's neighbor's enjoyment of property, pays one's debts, delivers that which one has sold, and renders to one's employer the performance to . . . which one has obliged himself. . . . As a rule, the thought of compulsion by courts does not even enter the minds of men. . . . Would an employer sue a servant girl for not tidying the house? [37]

A spectacular example to add to Ehrlich's is the law originating in the substance of collective bargaining agreements and their

---

[36] I borrow this phrase and the idea from Bertram Morris's brilliant *Philosophical Aspects of Culture* (1961).

[37] Eugen Ehrlich, *Fundamental Principles of the Sociology of Law,* trans. Moll (1936), pp. 21–23; *Great Philosophers,* p. 440.

private interpretation and enforcement. A single pact between management and labor in, for example, the automobile industry channels the lives of more people than do most statutes.

Justice (defined in this paper as resulting from attempts of the public's agents to actualize its aspirations) is rarely thought of in privately negotiated legal transactions. Each trader is, of course, interested[38] in protecting his own fortunes, and, when a continued course of dealing is expected, each trader has an incentive to treat his vis-à-vis fairly. Concern for those with whom one deals can, of course, transcend selfishness, but often the government intervenes to discourage unfair dealings with, for example, such statutes as pure food laws, antitrust laws, standard insurance policy laws, etc., or with such administrative supervision as that of the Securities and Exchange Commission, the Federal Trade Commission, and so on.

Rarely are private business or professional activities calculated to advance the interests of those not immediately involved. In routine dealings, occasions on which the traders can show concern for strangers seldom occurs.[39] Some private dealings, however, profoundly affect nonparties, and the decisions made by the parties may, therefore, tend to thwart or advance the realization of public aspirations. This was recently spectacularly the case with the collective bargaining in the steel industry. Should those who struck that bargain have had any concern about inflation, and should they have tried to forestall it by agreeing on terms that could be met without a price rise? Should the public have been represented at the bargaining table during the negotiations? The answers to these questions are beyond my competence, but the fact that such questions can be asked demonstrates that we

[38] At least in the sense that his interest is involved. Cf. John Austin, *Lecture on Jurisprudence* (3rd ed.; 1869), p. 162; *Great Philosophers,* p. 350: "[Generally] every individual person is the best possible judge of his own interests: of what will affect himself with the greatest pleasures and pains. Compared with his intimate consciousness of his own peculiar interests, his knowledge of the interest of others is vague conjecture. Consequently, the principle of general utility imperiously demands that he commonly shall attend to his own rather than to the interests of others; that he shall not habitually neglect that which he knows accurately in order that he may habitually pursue that which he knows imperfectly."

[39] See John Stuart Mill, *Utilitarianism* (Everyman's Library; 1951), p. 28; *Great Philosophers,* p. 368.

live with nongovernmental processes fraught with the capacity both to perpetrate injustice on us and to create justice for us. This conclusion is more easily appreciated when two simpler examples from organized medicine are considered.

In a recent Delaware Supreme Court case, an unprecedented question was raised, i.e., has a hospital the duty to render emergency aid to a stranger applying for it at the hospital's emergency ward? The court answered this question in the affirmative.[40] The decision, of course, was governmental intervention; but the significant point is that neither the lawyers nor the judge could, in 1961, find any American case in point. No doubt, however, institutional medicine long before had decided that those in need of it were entitled to emergency treatment in hospital wards. This right to treatment was established in the inner orders of medical institutions, varying somewhat in content and detail from one hospital to another. Those who designed these inner orders of association had acted to effectuate a public aspiration long before the Delaware court vindicated the right to emergency treatment. That right is probably as effective and valuable in neighboring Pennsylvania, where the government has not yet vindicated it, as in Delaware, where it has.

My second medical illustration poses a problem involving, perhaps, an injustice existing in the inner orders of hospitals and calling for reform of those inner orders. Trained nursing is a medical service which is, I believe, in short supply. Suppose nurses often work at their craft only when they feel like it, that a significantly large number of nurses are unwilling to take cases on week-ends or holidays. Suppose that scarce private nursing is made available to well-to-do patients not needing it so much as poor patients. If these are the facts, do not professional societies of nurses, doctors, and hospitals have a responsibility to discover them and remold the inner orders of nursing care? I put this as a question because I do not know either the facts or the proper conclusion to attach to them. But I do know that, unless private associations create justice, our society will become increasingly unjust. I do not mean, of course, that all unjust inner orders of association can and should be reformed by private individuals. Private power, however, is not always utterly private; it some-

[40] *Wilmington General Hospital* v. *Manlove,* 174 A. 2d (1961) 135.

times is tolerated only because of the likelihood that those who wield it are both willing and able to advance some of the public's aspirations. When this promise fails, the resulting vacuum is likely to be filled by government; when such failures are common and intolerable, the government tends to expand to totalitarianism.

All who try (whether as private persons or public officials) to create justice as I have defined it need something more than technical knowledge and good will; they should have, in addition, some knowledge of the public's aspirations and a desire to further them. Those philosophers who attempt to build value systems out of consequences tend to suppress this point. Take, for instance, the social philosophy of John Stuart Mill.

The font of justice for Mill is man's capacity to apprehend the community of interest between himself and society; man's inborn inclination for self-defense therefore tends to expand to include the defense of society.[41] So those who resist a personal injustice tend to base each of their claims on some rule benefiting society.[42] A just cause attracts the strong emotional support of strangers because of the likelihood that social benefits will result from its advancement.[43] Claims of lesser social moment are looked on as desirable merely because they seem expedient.

Mill, however, notes that predilections on important topics can vary widely.

> There are [says Mill] some who say it is unjust to punish anyone for the sake of example to others; that punishment is just only when intended for the good of the sufferer himself. Others maintain the extreme reverse, contending that to punish persons who have attained years of discretion for their own benefit is despotism and injustice, since if the matter at issue is solely their own good no one has the right to control their own judgment of it; but they may be justly punished to prevent evil to others, this being the exercise of the legitimate right of self-defense. Mr. Owen, again, affirms that it is unjust to punish at all; for the criminal did not make his own character; his education and the circumstances around him have made him a criminal, and for these he is not responsible.[44]

---

[41] Mill, *Utilitarianism, op. cit.*, p. 63; *Great Philosophers*, p. 374.
[42] Mill, *op. cit.*, pp. 64–65; *Great Philosophers*, p. 375.
[43] Mill, *op. cit.*, p. 66; *Great Philosophers*, p. 375.
[44] Mill, *op. cit.*, pp. 68–69; *Great Philosophers*, p. 376.

Mill's method for choosing between such alternatives is utilitarian; by finding out how much happiness and pain each alternative will produce, we can select the alternative that will most advance men's welfare and equality.[45] If Mill, then, were omniscient, he would know which alternative would be the most just. Were he a legislator,[46] he would know which alternative would be the most just theory on which to base the penal code. Were he a judge or a member of a pardon board, he would know which alternative was the most just theory for dispensing clemency. Were he a director of a fraternal order of police, he would know which alternative should guide him in developing those inner orders of his fraternity that would favor the advancement of criminal justice. The important point is that Mill would, he believed, know justice by knowing what the public *ought* to want; what the public actually aspired to would be unimportant, except insofar as its stupidity impeded bright leaders from giving the public what it should have. Herein, it seems to me, Mill (who is one of my idols) is wrong.

The creation of justice is not properly left in the hands of those who act as principals, rather than agents. Lawmakers should play neither God nor philosopher-king. They serve the cause of justice only when they seek to realize, not their own, but the public's aspirations. An agent will often try to calculate his principal's attitude by asking himself what he would want if he himself were the principal. A lawmaker's job often can and must be creative—first, because the public aspires to new and more justice, which must be creatively understood and imaginatively implemented; and, second, because an understanding of the inchoate public aspirations often calls for creative insight and ingenuity.

Some public aspirations are not, however, for justice but are, for example, hopes for greater beauty or more truth. Insofar as these objectives involve the development of talent and the dissemination of its product, problems in distributive justice may be posed. But neither the artist nor the scientist can act as an agent. Unless an artist acts as a principal, he will be a panderer, not a creator. Unless a scientist acts as a principal, he will allow the

[45] Of course, not all utilitarians are as eager to promote equality as was Mill.
[46] Which, incidentally, he was.

predilections of others to absorb his energies and distort what he sees. Of course, both art and science arise from society and hope to communicate with society; both have institutional aspects. The creator of justice, however, not only must be a product of society, but must concern himself with discovering, understanding, and realizing, insofar as he can, the public's aspirations, and not his own. In no other way will justice, as such, be intentionally created.

Of course, both public and private aspirations are sometimes accidentally realized. Lucky coincidences can make men wealthy, rich, and (in minor ways) wise. The perfection of the cotton-picker (which, of course, was achieved by men not primarily concerned with injustice) smashed the unjust cotton economy of the Deep South. But accidents are also likely to produce misery, war, and irreversible injustice. Only through law (widely defined), law perfected by agents of the public intending to advance its aspirations, is there great likelihood of sustained growth of justice for men.

10

JUSTICE AS IDEAL AND IDEOLOGY

IREDELL JENKINS

I

It is a familiar charge against all theories of justice—as indeed against all forms of legal and political idealism—that the terms in which they are couched are either too general to offer guidance in concrete cases or too specific to be accepted as universal and absolute. All such theories, it is claimed, are caught in a dilemma on one or the other of whose horns they must eventually be impaled. If they try to maintain their position as truly neutral and objective principles, valid under all conditions and categorical for all decisions, then they must be expressed in formulas that are so abstract and imprecise as to be practically useless. If they try to define in detail the ideal conditions that they mean to realize and to embody themselves in exact norms and rules that will promote this realization, then they inevitably become partisan political creeds, based on preference and expedience as much as reason and so provincial rather than catholic in their relevance. The history of the theory of justice is in large measure the effort to turn the thrust of this corrosive either/or.

It is the gist of this charge that the concept of justice does not have and cannot be given sufficient intrinsic structure and content to control the logical inferences and the practical directives that are drawn from it. If this criticism could not be turned, it would evidently be lethal. The purpose of any concept—and of the laws, principles, and theories that are composed of systematic arrangements of concepts—is to enhance understanding and illuminate action. That is, concepts are tools through which we are enabled to explain, predict, and control the course of events. If a concept is to serve this function, the minimal condition it must satisfy is that its meaning—whether primarily descriptive, prescriptive, or normative—be precise and communicable. If this condition is not met, we cannot know accurately what the concept asserts as fact, depicts as ideal, or expounds as a rule of action. It is exactly this failure that the either/or discussed above attributes to the concept of justice. It is held that this concept is so ambiguous, so vague and variable in meaning, that it is useless as a rational tool.

The notion of justice, in its various employments, obviously has a threefold bearing: it designates a sentiment or motivating force that supposedly plays an effective role in human conduct; it pretends to describe an ideal state of affairs; and it lays down rules intended to promote the realization of this ideal. It fails, it is charged, in all three of these tasks, and always for the same reason —because its content is ambiguous and its structure amorphous. The sentiment it posits is so loose and complex that we cannot analyze its causes and effects, much less take steps to cultivate and guide it. The ideal it depicts is a counsel of general perfection, with all details left undefined. The rules it sets forth must be interpreted and filled out for every actual decision, but no provision is made to control this application.

These criticisms issue in the broad conclusion that the concept of justice has neither theoretical nor technological value, that it lacks both explanatory and pragmatic power. That is, it does not, out of its intrinsic content and structure, generate a body of doctrine that serves to amplify and apply it. It is a sterile concept, in the sense that nothing definite follows from it. Rather, it stands as an empty and formless receptacle that must receive its shape and substance from elsewhere and is ready to take on the lineaments of any doctrine proposed to it. Consequently, it is held, justice is continually degenerating toward either a congeries of merely honorific precepts or toward a series of competing action programs. Finally, these two retrogressive movements hasten their tragic climax by mutually supporting each other. Action programs supply to the precepts of justice the content that their ambiguity requires; these precepts, in their turn, lend to action programs the aura of ideality that they need to win the allegiance of men.

It must be admitted, I think, that there is a large measure of historical truth in these charges. In its appearances in legal-political speculation and debate, justice has often worn the guise of either vacuous generality or partisan specificity. The justice that philosophy and jurisprudence urge on us as the guide and rule of life has the habit of dissolving, when challenged to decision, into pious truisms and logical tautologies. The Eternal Justice to which political manifestoes ask us to dedicate our resources of mind and spirit soon puts on the clothes of a sectarian ideology that wants only the blank check of our emotional commitment.

The concept of justice has suffered under both these mistreatments: it has been debased by uncritical minds and betrayed by unscrupulous wills. There is nothing unusual in this fate. Sins beyond counting have been perpetrated and protected under the names of liberty, equality, patriotism, democracy, morality, the will of God, due process of law, the public interest, and other such convenient verbal shields. We have even come to accept it as an unfortunate but unavoidable fact that most of the ideas that figure prominently in the direction of our individual and group lives are to a high degree friable and volatile; they tend to crumble if we press them too hard or to undergo metamorphosis if we scrutinize them too closely. Furthermore, exactly this fate often befalls the concepts of the natural sciences, which we tend to regard as having a content so fully determinate and so objectively grounded that it renders them inviolate. Such concepts as evolution, relativity, Heisenbergian indeterminism, the second law of thermodynamics, and many others have been similarly exploited by those who wanted to use them either to explain everything or to justify a *parti pris.*

But, however sound and relevant these criticisms of the concept of justice may be, they still are not all the story. Despite its acknowledged vicissitudes, this concept has unquestionably exerted a positive and continuing influence on the movement of civilization. The facts of human nature and history, when read impartially, seem to indicate that there is a sense of justice that is widely shared among men, a sense of what is reasonable and equitable, what is right and fair; a sense that perhaps expresses itself most generally in the demand that there be a balance between desert and reward. Like all such "senses" or "sentiments" —like hope and fear, love and hate, pity and contempt—that of justice is aroused by our encounters with actual occasions; it occurs as part of our response to certain sorts of acts, events, and situations that confront us in life. In its immediate occurrence, this sense is apt to speak quite clearly and unequivocally, which is not to say, of course, that it is necessarily "right" or even "consistent," in any objective meaning of the terms. Even as a subjective occurrence, this sense is often confused or overcome by competing sentiments aroused by the same occasion.

As in similar cases, they are exactly these deficiencies in the sense of justice that lead thought to try to isolate and define the intrinsic characteristics of the situations that are its proper object. What is it about situations that arouses in us the sense that they are just or unjust? As is again usual in such cases, it is justice in the adjectival form—as a quality or property of acts, outcomes, and conditions—that first attracts attention. Thinkers seek to determine what constitutes a just man, a just decision or action, a just rule, a just society. From this, it is only a step to a higher level of abstraction, where justice is regarded as an independent essence, serving both to inform and evaluate concrete cases. With this step, probably taken as early as the Pythagoreans and certainly by Socrates, the theory of justice is in full bloom.

Thought is thus forced onward to deal with justice at the conceptual level because it is only in this way that the obscurities of the earlier, primitive levels can be fully clarified. To trust solely to the sense of justice is to deal with every case on its own terms, with no appeal to general rules and standards; this is "justice at the palace gate," and its deficiencies are matters of record, though this should not lead us to overlook its merits. If we seek to repair these difficulties by treating justice in purely adjectival terms, as a predicate or property of certain subjects, we gain only temporary relief.

We can now formulate a great many distinct definitions, rules, standards, and procedures that pick out a series of images of "the just" in various contexts. But these depictions are discrete and local. They are unsystematic and thus often overlap and conflict. There is no adequate provision for their criticism and correction—save by return to the fount of the sense of justice—so they tend to become static and dogmatic. Finally, their reference is chiefly to present reform of past abuses, so they have relatively little directive power. It is in the effort to make good the defects of these two levels that thought seeks to elaborate the concept of justice as a general substantive ideal. At this level, justice is established as the fundamental constitutive idea of social organization and the ultimate regulative idea of legal and political action.

Throughout these developments, two facts stand out clearly. First, the idea of justice, in all three of the guises just discussed, has played an important role in the growth of social, political, and legal institutions; it has given to group life an element of sensitivity, stability, and ideality that were essential to progress. But, second, efforts to extend and refine the sense of justice, to improve the apparatus through which it is administered, and to expound the goals that it envisages have been only partially successful; the data and doctrines at issue here are themselves quite recalcitrant to analysis, and competing forces have impeded the realization of the ideal of justice. These facts are perfectly familiar, in their general occurrence as well as in this specific case. Man's efforts to understand and control the world around him have always encountered impediments; ideas have power, but this power is neither unlimited nor unchallenged. This characteristic of the enterprise of inquiry is usually regarded as normal and viable. But there are occasions when the fact of failure seems to assume gigantic proportions and to exert a paralyzing effect on inquiry. These moments, when thought seeks to escape its frustrations by making of them a necessity or even a virtue, are familiar episodes in intellectual history. We have a rich vocabulary to describe them, depending on the context in which they occur and the ambit they sweep: agnosticism, anarchy, skepticism, amoralism, emotivism, antirationalism, dogmatism, nihilism, failure of nerve or of faith—all these terms and many others identify different species of this genus.

This state of mind is a widespread feature of contemporary treatments of the problem and concept of justice. In its extreme form, the attitude finds expression through the either/or considered at the beginning of this paper. On the whole, a more moderate view has prevailed; but even this has tended to be suspicious of justice conceived as a general substantive ideal pretending to give a definitive account of the values and structure of the good society. Even where it is acknowledged that justice is a meaningful and important concept, there is a strong inclination to deal with it at a lower level of abstraction. This means that studies of justice have usually gone in one of two directions—first, toward an examination of the sense of justice–injustice, of the manner in which this functions, the demands that it makes, and the role that it plays in social life; second, toward an investigation of the legal and political apparatus through which justice is done. Here, attention centers on the rules, standards, and procedures necessary to procure just outcomes. In short, the contemporary approach to the problems and issues of justice has been largely either psychological or operational, rather than metaphysical and moral.

Probably the most careful and thorough studies of the first kind mentioned above are those of Edmond J. Cahn.[1] But the same general emphasis is found more or less prominently in the work of Krabbe, Stammler, Del Vecchio, and Rommen; it also appears, though less centrally, in the doctrines of such disparate thinkers as Duguit and Geny. This point of view is a good deal more familiar on the Continent than in England or the United States. On the other hand, the procedural or operational approach to justice has for some time been the staple of Anglo-American jurisprudence. The formalism of Austin and Kelsen and their schools; legal realism; the sociological jurisprudence of Ehrlich and the jurisprudence of interests of Pound (as well as the closely corresponding work of Jhering, Phillip Heck, and others in Germany); the analytical investigations of such scholars as H.L.A. Hart and Glanville Williams—all these, in their often radically

[1] *The Sense of Injustice* (1949); *The Moral Decision* (1956).

different ways, seek to further the cause of justice by clarifying and improving its administration.

Each of these approaches to the problem of justice is legitimate and valuable—indeed, indispensable. But I think that, even taken in conjunction, they still constitute an incomplete attack on the problem. In their very natures they leave unsettled what must always be the central issue, namely, the final values on which the society is grounded, the ideal ends it seeks to promote, the conditions it means to realize. To the extent that this issue is left vague and tentative, the entire quest for justice is unguided. As we have seen, the sense of justice speaks unequivocally and compellingly in particular cases; but its disclosures are neither generalized nor systematic, so they cannot offer the coherent direction that purposive action requires. In a word, the sense of justice is largely retrospective and corrective; the deficiencies it identifies can be finally repaired only by a body of doctrine that is prospective and creative. The procedural or operational approach suffers in a similar way; it must necessarily accept from elsewhere the substance, or contents, of justice, that is, the values that it is to recognize and the conditions that it seeks to further. Procedural justice is concerned with developing an apparatus that will serve as a fair and impartial means to the attainment of ends that it does not itself determine. This approach runs the risk of equating justice with efficiency or utility.

I think that both the strength and the incompleteness of these methods of dealing with justice are brought out very clearly in Prof. Clarence Morris's most interesting paper, "Law, Justice, and the Public's Aspirations." Morris initiates his argument with this provisional definition: "justice is a translation of some of the public's aspirations into programs of action: this translation is creative, but its author can intend justice only if he intends to act as the public's agent."

This definition clearly seems to state an interpretation of justice that is a combination of the psychological and procedural methods just discussed. This doctrine, if I understand it correctly, holds that justice can be adequately conceived in purely intuitive and operational terms, without reference to an objective substantive content. On these terms, law is prior to justice and creates this latter by effecting a transition from aspiration to accomplishment. That is, justice is both made and measured by the success of law in actualizing the ends to which its public aspires. This doctrine is strongly pointed in a passage urging that one of the crucial legal problems we face is that of "developing methods, training, and knowledge to acquaint lawmakers with public aspirations" in order that judges and legislators may be properly "responsive to community values." Finally, the position that justice is created by society and law and has no objective status or character is given its most emphatic expression in the final paragraphs of the paper, where the creator of justice is sharply contrasted with the artist and the scientist. These latter pursue a beauty and a truth that are independent of the public's hopes and opinions; the artist's creation of beauty and the scientist's discovery of truth must be altogether free of any reference to what the public likes or believes, or the outcome will be a mere pandering. As opposed to these specialists, the creator of justice is "not enfranchised to play God or philosopher-king," but must abjure his own interests and opinions and seek only to "implement the public's aspirations"; he must, that is, become the product and servant of society, the voice through which this speaks.

There is no question that such an interpretation of justice has real value as both a check and a guide to legal action. Morris draws much illumination from it in his examination of what the pursuit of justice requires of those engaged in legislation, adjudication, and private negotiation. But I doubt whether this doctrine can be sustained as a sufficient account, for there seem to be too many occasions when law can neither find its ends and values clearly declared by the public nor generate them out of its own processes. Law must, rather, search for justice beyond both of these and then use this discovery first to define the correct social and human values and then to control its own outcomes.

Further, it seems to me that there are several crucial passages in Morris's paper that exhibit a clear confrontation with this fact. Thus, he speaks of "each party to a legal transaction" as naturally "interested in getting justice for himself" and "rarely . . . concerned with justice for strangers." He cites the need for "statutes protecting consumers against unjust transactions," and he urges that private organizations must be interested in more than "justice for their own members." He notes that a transaction often creates justice for one party to it and injustice for the other because of the disparate skills of their lawyers in protecting their interests. Finally, and most importantly, Morris recognizes and insists that the public's aspirations are often inchoate, unsettled, unreasonable, or disputed among various segments of this public.

All of this points, I think, to three conclusions. First, it seems to be clearly implied that the public's aspirations—or at least those of some segments of the public—can themselves be unjust. But, on the definition given, this is impossible. Second, a substantive meaning, and one quite prior to any legal considerations, is here being introduced into what started as a purely procedural definition. If justice is stringently defined as "a translation of the public's aspirations into programs of action," then the phrases quoted above are extremely difficult to construe. In these phrases, it appears that justice is being defined in terms of fairness, equity, concern, interest, and altruism. Third, even when justice is regarded as actualization of the public's aspirations, it often happens that law must itself define these aspirations and cannot simply take them from the public. That is, law must shape aspirations, not merely actualize them. Law, then, looks to an antecedent idea and a prospective ideal of justice for guidance in order that the ends it serves and the means it employs may themselves be just.

In sum, it seems to me that we have a forceful illustration of both the short-term fruitfulness and the ultimate incompleteness of the pragmatic method. This method relies on the assumptions that the proper and desirable goals of social action are self-evident and that the only problem confronting thought is that of devising effective means to secure these ends. But a moment's consideration should make it clear that such a pragmatism can work only under rather special conditions, namely, when the contrast between the actual and the ideal is both generally compelling and specifically precise. When this is not the case—and it rarely is—reliance on exclusively intuitive and procedural techniques breaks down, for then there are no "clear and present" ends in view for these to seize and realize.

The impetus to this way of dealing with the problem of justice is clear enough and has been discussed above: it is the strong need to make good the imprecision and ambiguity that have so often characterized the concept of justice when treated as a substantive ideal. These schools seek to accomplish this by treating justice as a series of local, concrete, and specific cases, rather than as a general, abstract, and universally relevant concept. But, if the above argument is sound, such intuitive-procedural approaches can only postpone this central problem of justice; they cannot solve it or eliminate it. Sooner or later, implicitly or explicitly, the concept of justice must be given an intrinsic meaning and an objective reference that can control the private intuitions and the public procedures of men.

The recognition that this is a compelling demand appears to me as the factor animating two other principal chapters of the present volume—those of Prof. Carl Friedrich and Prof. John Rawls. Rawls states his purpose and principles in these terms:

> An essential part of the political form of a constitutional democracy is provision for certain fundamental liberties. . . . There are, of course, various kinds of arguments which may be used to support the institutional forms embodying these constitutional liberties. . . . I should like to examine those arguments which derive from the concept of justice alone.
>
> . . . [W]hat distinguishes these arguments from those which invoke other moral concepts and, in particular, from those which invoke the concept of social utility? I shall try to show that the concept of justice provides conclusive arguments for these liberties. . . .
>
> The concept of justice which I shall use may be stated, for the moment, in the form of two principles: first, each person participating in an institution or affected by it has an equal right to the most extensive liberty compatible with a like liberty for all; and, second, inequalities as defined by the institutional structure or fostered by it are arbitrary unless it is reasonable to expect that they will work out to everyone's advantage and provided that the positions and offices to which they attach or from which they may be gained are open to all.

After a close analysis and development of these two principles and a careful consideration of possible objections to them, Rawls concludes:

> The peculiar feature of the concept of justice is that it treats each person as an equal sovereign, as it were, and requires a unanimous acknowledgement from a certain original position of equal liberty. . . .

> The concept of justice is distinct from that of social utility in that justice takes the plurality of persons as fundamental, . . . [and] The plurality of persons must construct among themselves the principles in accordance with which they are to decide between institutions, . . .

Friedrich makes his purpose equally explicit, and his motivation even more so. These are stated as follows:

> After excluding some of the great traditional issues surrounding "the just" as a quality of acts, rules, and persons, more especially whether justice is a relative or absolute value or what it is in and by itself and, more specifically, what kind of excellence or virtue it is in persons, I concentrate on that aspect of political situations and acts which is very widely observed and inherent in most of them: the comparative evaluation of persons according to the prevailing values of a political community.

Friedrich devotes the major part of his paper to a fresh and most illuminating account of the conditions that must be satisfied if this process of "comparative evaluation" is to be just. His conclusions are:

> That some values are prevalent and that persons will be differentiated according to such values seem indisputable. Such comparisons can only be "in accord" with the prevailing values if the facts upon which they are based are not untrue, if the relation between facts and values is not arbitrary, and if the norms derived from such comparisons are not impossible. The criteria not untrue, not arbitrary, and not impossible are, in other words, derivatives of the inherent meaning of the quality of "just" as defined. A political act is just, therefore, if it is based on a balanced evaluation of the persons it affects, comparing (and classifying) them upon the ground of values prevalent in the political community concerned. I show, finally, that such a view of justice as a quality of political acts (including rules) mediates the tension betwen power and authority and provides a deeper understanding of the legitimacy of rulers and their acts.

Both these treatments clearly give to the concept of justice an intrinsic and independent meaning and so secure it against the vagaries of the sense of justice and the indifferentism of instrumental justice. They accomplish this by defining justice in terms of certain inherent "principles" or "criteria." But the crucial point to be noted here is that these principles and criteria are still procedural, not substantive. That is, justice is a predicate that attaches to "a way of doing things," rather than to "that which is done." Or, to put it differently, justice is now regarded as an objective regulative idea of legal and political affairs, but still not as a constitutive idea. Justice judges acts, but not outcomes.

It may well be the case—as I take it Morris, Rawls, and Friedrich would all hold—that this is as far as one can safely go toward determining the positive character of justice and the just. Beyond this point, it can be argued, emotion is substituted for reason and preference for demonstration. But at least it would be admitted, I think, that a further step is a possibility in theory and a challenge in fact. This step is, of course, that of a substantive elucidation of justice that would issue in a precise and systematic account of the functions that a political-legal order must serve, the conditions it must promote, and the values it must achieve if it is to fulfill its objectives. Such an analysis would show, in short, what it is to "do justice" as well as to "do justly."

The character of this challenge, as well as the dangers it entails, are brought out by Friedrich with typical force and cogency. In a passage immediately following that quoted above, he says:

> By contrast, justice, when defined in terms of the highest good, as has been done by philosophers, political and legal, from Plato to the present day, constitutes a specific application of the general principle of comparative evaluation; it resembles in its specificity the selection of some particular religious and national value system. Such stipulative definition of justice is not excluded by my analysis, but should be seen as the act of personal preference which it is, in most instances. Only a reasoned elaboration of such a preference in terms of the demonstrable practical consequences for any given political order constitutes scientific knowledge.

These penetrating remarks require only one appendix: the insistence that this further step to a conception of justice as a substantive principle defining the ultimate ends and values of the community is absolutely necessary and indispensable. As I have just argued, no society can subsist indefinitely on an exclusively intuitive and pragmatic diet; there inevitably comes a time when it must formulate, explicitly and systematically, both its goals and its program. It makes little difference whether the covering name for these is justice, the public interest, the general welfare, the common good, progress, democracy, communism, or the historic nexus. The important point is to recognize that this step must be taken if a society is to act coherently and purposively.

The crucial problem that confronts all societies, then, is how to make this step as secure as possible when it is taken. What is required, in Friedrich's terminology, is that our conception of justice and our formulation of the just society be based on "scientific knowledge" and not mere "personal preference." I want now to offer certain suggestions regarding the manner in which this problem can most fruitfully be approached. The question to which I propose a tentative answer is this: How can we best assure that our ideas of justice and the just will have a content that is objective and cosmopolitan, rather than subjective and parochial?

II

The most effective way to deal with this question, I think, is by a genetic and functional approach. If we were to ask that mythical creature, the man in the street, for a quick, unprepared definition of "justice," the answer we would almost surely get would be roughly this: "justice is what law ought to be." This same idea is expressed in such professional adages as "the ministry of justice," "justice under the law," and many others. For both common sense and sophisticated thought, the most elemental meaning embedded in the concept of justice is that of the perfect accomplishment of the tasks of law. It is this general and spontaneous preconception that has served as the point of departure for most reflections on the nature of justice. Furthermore, it seems safe to say that the primary object of these reflections has been the phrase, "perfect accomplishment"; thought has been fascinated by the vision of the completely just social, political, and legal order. But inquiries that revolve around the ideal of justice cannot be adequately controlled or verified, since this ideal is not open to direct inspection, so the doctrines in which they issue tend to become utopian.

What I am suggesting as a correction to this situation is that attention should be centered on the tasks committed to law. It is the usual habit of thought to assume that these tasks are self-evidently compelling and clear, that we know, both systematically and in detail, the nature of the problem to which justice is the solution. It is this attitude that I would challenge and change. The evidence of history strongly indicates that many of our failures of justice arise because we do not have a satisfactory idea of its demands, with the result that our preparations fail and we are continually having to devise *ad hoc* measures to deal with unanticipated consequences. It would seem advisable to reach a clear view of the beginnings of the quest for justice before we try to decipher its ends. An inquiry into these matters can disclose quite exactly and systematically the essential tasks of the law, that is, the tasks whose consummation would be justice. I propose to seek the essential meaning of justice in the problems for which it represents a final solution, the inadequacies whose removal it envisages, the challenges to which it is the response, the purposes whose achievement it embodies. In short, I suggest that the actual origins of the quest for justice offer the best evidence for its ideal outcomes.

The structure of the argument here advanced can be summarized in two propositions: (1) justice is the completion of law; (2) law is a principle of order. The basic evidence and analysis in support of this argument have been presented in earlier papers.[2] I shall merely recapitulate the body of doctrine developed in those papers in order to apply it to the problems here under consideration.

We can start with the second proposition, which is the more basic. I have, in the articles just referred to, cited numerous and varied authorities to support the claim that this interpretation of the essential nature of law is shared by workers in all fields. In whatever context the concept of "law" is employed, it seems always to be defined by reference to the concept of "order." In this proposition, there are two terms that require explication: "order" and "is a principle of."

In most discussions in which the concept of order occurs, it is treated as though its meaning were primitive and self-evident, too simple to either require or permit definition; so it is usually exemplified rather than analyzed. But the ostensive meaning that the term carries is clear and familiar. The concept of order em-

[2] Iredell Jenkins, "The Matrix of Positive Law," *Natural Law Forum*, VI (1961), 1–50; "The Modes of Law," in Irwin C. Lieb, ed., *Experience, Existence, and the Good* (1961), pp. 192–212.

bodies pure discovery of pattern and regularity, of stability and continuity, in our surroundings. It refers to the web of relations that we find connecting discrete objects and occurrences. Order indicates similarities among things and uniformities of sequence among events. To say that "order holds" is to say that we are in the presence of distinct entities that follow established courses and hang together as a whole, so as to compose a systematic structure. "Disorder" conveys the opposite of all this; it means that the entities we encounter are amorphous, the structures they form are vague, the relationships among them are unstable, and the course of events is erratic. This seems to be the general meaning we have in mind whenever we use the terms "order" and "disorder," whether we are referring to a person's private life, a marital relationship, a human community, the decoration of a room, the conduct of government, or airline schedules. It should, however, be noted now, since the point will become important later, that there can be legitimate disagreements regarding exactly which arrangements constitute the proper or desirable order in any given case.

If we overcome the prejudice of self-evidence and subject this familiar meaning to analysis, I think it is apparent that the concept of order entails reference to four basic elements: a plurality of distinct entities that exhibit stable group characteristics; the organization of these into a series of higher-order entities; activities engaged in by these entities and energy exchanged among them; and all of this taking place in a regular and coherent manner. I shall identify these items respectively as "the many," "the one," "process," and "pattern," and I shall refer to them collectively as the dimensions, or elements, of order. These are the constituents and conditions that order denotes. Order appears to be a pervasive characteristic of reality; whichever region of our surroundings we examine, we find this to be at once a manifold, a universe, an arena of change, and a structured system. In the human context, these elements become individual human beings, living in a complex of groups, engaging in various pursuits, and standing in certain relationships to one another. These are, then, the basic factors with which law deals; they are, to put it so, the elements out of which law must compose justice.

We can turn now to the second key term mentioned above.

What do we mean when we say that law "is a principle of" order? This is a subtle question, an adequate answer to which must be quite complex; [3] so the ensuing discussion will be perhaps dangerously oversimplified. Accepting this risk and for our present purposes, a brief answer can be given: positive human law is "a principle of order" in the sense that it is an instrument through which men seek to secure and promote order against the threats and inroads of disorder. In the human context, order appears as a goal as well as a fact; it is something to be created as much as something given. Concomitantly, law is a principle that not merely reflects an order that it inherits, but must also define and guarantee an order that could not exist without it.

The basic distinction here is that of laws as descriptive or prescriptive of the objects and events to which they refer. I do not think that this distinction is so sharp and radical as it is often held to be, but it is at least a convenient starting point. With regard to most of the contexts of nature, when we say that "law is a principle of order," we mean this in only a descriptive sense; what we call "laws of nature" or "scientific laws," we interpret as reporting and elucidating an order that is primordial and preestablished. We do not think of these laws as in any way helping to create or maintain the order that they describe. That is, we tend to regard "the order of nature" as independent of the laws that formulate this order; these laws are carriers of information, not instruments of intervention.

It should, however, be remarked that common opinions on this matter are probably considerably distorted by the fact that they derive primarily from a consideration of the theoretical, or pure, sciences: here, laws do function very largely as reports and summaries of what has been found to be the case. When we shift attention to the technological or applied sciences, the situation changes importantly. In these endeavors, we do use laws as instruments of intervention; that is, we employ the power they give us to create "more" order or a "better" order than that we find. Our efforts in the areas of health, plant- and animal-breeding, the development of new materials, weather control, and many others are examples of behavior that bears interesting similarities to that which we seek to accomplish through legal and political action.

[3] I have discussed the issues in detail in the articles cited above, Note 2.

But this situation does change significantly, if not radically, in the human context. Here, when it is said that "positive law is a principle of order," much more is meant than that positive law describes an order that is already there. Of course, we do mean this; anthropologists and legal historians have emphasized the extent to which early law was merely the making explicit of habit and custom, and the sociologists of law have abundantly taught us that a great deal of contemporary law reflects established practices and tendencies. Furthermore, when a mature legal system is securely embedded in its society, it does to a high degree describe the usual courses of happenings, outcomes of events, and relations of persons in the various areas of life with which it deals; it is only because of this "factual" aspect of law that we can use it to predict and plan. However, all this still does not exhaust the relationship in which positive law stands to the human context. When we say that such law is a principle of order, we mean that it has the additional task of defining and securing a regime of order—a certain concatenation of the many, the one, process, and pattern—that does not yet exist but is held to be desirable. Positive law serves not only the functions of reflecting and conserving an antecedent order, but also those of depicting and realizing a prospective order. If we are to conceive positive law adequately, we must think of it as a creative agent that works between the poles of the actual and the ideal, what is and what ought to be.

It is precisely this incompleteness and openness of the human milieu that solicits the concept of justice. The fact that human affairs can be arranged in various ways, that human efforts can work toward any of several outcomes, that the conditions of human life can be differently disposed—these facts force man to choose among alternatives and to marshal his forces for the way that is chosen. This decision and dedication constitute, in bare essence, the quest for justice. The point here can perhaps be put most forcefully in the seeming paradox that disorder is the root from which justice springs. We often think of disorder as inherently dangerous and undesirable, since it represents a disruption of the regularity and stability, the coherence and continuity, that we count on so heavily in our surroundings. This is, of course, true. But it is equally true—and important—that disorder represents change, variation, indeterminateness, and hence the possibility for improvement and progress. And we count equally on these factors. As far as life in general is concerned, the primitive occurrence of disorder is in the form of genetic mutations and chromosomal recombinations. These are disruptions of established systems, and the greater number of them are either lethal or deleterious. But it is nevertheless through the material they furnish, acted on by natural selection and other agencies, that the whole movement of life has taken place.

The same remarks hold true of the infinitely more complex types of disorder that characterize the human environment. The ideas, forces, and events that we associate with Socrates, Christ, Copernicus, Rousseau, Darwin, democracy, communism, the industrial revolution, impressionism—all of these were in one way or another disruptive of an established order; but we do not on that account dismiss them as altogether "bad." Disorder is indeed a danger and a threat. But it is also an opportunity and a challenge; it offers man a situation that is full of possibility and promise. The problem that man confronts, as he assumes direction of his life, is that of preserving the "order" that is the necessary matrix of the human enterprise while at the same time exploiting the advantages that "disorder" opens to him. In this effort, man supplements natural selection with intelligence. For survival based upon force, he substitutes justice based on law. That is, law is envisaged as providing the solution that disorder requires and so as consummating order with justice.

In the literature, one frequently encounters the notion of a fundamental contrast between order and justice.[4] There appears to be a widely, if vaguely, held opinion that order—in the sense of security, stability, certainty, peace, harmony, efficiency—is the indispensable condition of social life; hence, the primary task of law and government is to ensure order, and they must not allow considerations of justice to obtrude too much on this effort. Then, later, if and when conditions permit and society can afford it, justice becomes a legitimate concern. Under this view, order and

[4] See, for instance, Radbruch, *Legal Philosophy,* trans. Wilk (1950), p. 118; Alf Ross, *On Law and Justice* (1959), pp. 281ff.; Kelsen, *General Theory of Law and State* (1949), pp. 3–15. The issue is well discussed in Max Rheinstein, "What Should Be the Relation of Morals to Law," *Journal of Public Law,* 1 (1953), 287.

justice are sharply separate ideas, they derive from differing considerations, indicate distinct goals, and propose divergent courses. My argument points to quite another conclusion, as is evident from the premises on which it is based. If justice is the completion of law, and law is a principle of order, then it follows that justice is the completion of order. There is continuity between these concepts and between the conditions they denote.

Conceived in these terms, justice is the form of the order that man seeks to create through law. The materials with which law deals in this effort are, of course, those of the elements of order—individual men living in a complex of groups, engaged in various pursuits, and intricately interrelated. But what of the form that law should strive to realize in these elements, the form that would constitute justice, the ideal outcome of its efforts? As I suggested earlier, the place to look for an answer to this question is with the tasks that are committed to law, that is, with the situation that gives rise to law, the problems it is called upon to solve, the functions it has to serve. We must first grasp the beginnings of law before we can understand its ends.

When we adopt this approach, we at once encounter two salient facts: that positive law is both a human and a historical phenomenon. These facts are so simple and familiar that we are prone to dismiss them as truistic. But when we take them seriously and scrutinize them closely, they make significant disclosures. The facts teach us that changes of a crucial sort are initiated at the human level; that they grow and spread gradually through the human context; that in doing so they produce the novel conditions, challenges, and opportunities that define the fundamental tasks of law; and, finally, that from these emerge both the concept of justice as the ideal form of social order and the institution of positive law as an instrument for the realization of this form. Consequently, the proper focus of inquiry is on the source, the character, and the outcome of these changes.

We can start with the obvious matter of fact that different segments of reality—different regions of nature—exhibit distinctive characteristics. Our recognition of this fact finds similar expression in our differentiation of the realms of the inorganic, the organic, the vital, the psychic, the social, and so forth. It is the well-documented teaching of the theory of evolution that the changes that mark these realms have developed gradually as successive phases of a single coherent process. There remains the problem of identifying the general course and the principal stages of this movement, with particular reference to the situation in which it issues at the human level.

As a solution to this problem, I have argued that the process of becoming as a whole passes through three main stages of development, which I designate necessity, possibility, and purposiveness. As this process unfolds, significant changes occur in each of the four elements that together compose the order that holds in any region of nature: that is, in the characteristics of individual entities; in the fields, systems, wholes in which these exist; in the processes and activities in which they take part; and in the kinds of relationship that run among them. That such changes have in fact occurred is the meaning of evolution. The hypothesis just suggested is merely an attempt to discern the grand design of this process.

Before expanding this hypothesis, two remarks are in order. First, the categories of necessity, possibility, and purposiveness are here employed in a strictly descriptive sense, not an explanatory one. They summarize the essential features of varying types of situation that occur in various regions of nature; they do not posit any esoteric forces that produce these situations. That is, these terms designate regimes, or states of affairs. To speak of the regime of necessity is simply to identify a certain set of conditions that hold among the elements or dimensions of order—many, one, process, pattern—at a certain level of development; possibility and purposiveness designate other such sets of conditions. Second, these regimes never occur in a pure state, but are always compresent and commingled throughout nature. But the sets of characteristics they denote are present in differing proportions in different regions; as there is progression from the dominance of necessity toward that of purposiveness, important changes occur. These points will become clearer as I trace in more concrete terms the features of each of these regimes and the process that moves through them.

The regime of necessity, which is most clearly exemplified in physical and chemical phenomena, exhibits the following general characteristics. The outstanding feature of the many is the close similarity of things of the same kind. When the structures of things are relatively simple and their powers correspondingly limited, their range of variation is slight. The distinctive individual nature of an entity is far outweighed by its specific or class character; so the uniqueness of things makes little difference, and similarity approximates identity. Concomitantly, individual things are largely subordinated to the milieux of their existence: the one dominates the many, the whole its parts. Entities have their status and function defined for and imposed on them by the field, system, or environment in which they occur. Things have little power over their surroundings and little influence on their life arrangements, with the result that their self-assertion is severely limited. Under these conditions, the processes in which things take part fall largely under the formula of "action–reaction." The behavior of things is a function of external forces and their own inherent characteristics, so things have little direction over the energies they release. Individual initiative and spontaneity have small scope in the face of the chain of events, so separate entities cannot intervene effectively. Finally, the pattern of relations that holds under such regimes is extremely rigid. An antecedent system of connections seizes things as they come into existence and holds them fast throughout their careers, defining their relations to other things and the courses they are to follow. Things have slight power to establish their separateness, to make individual plans, or to enter into private arrangements with other things.

The regime of necessity, as defined by these four conditions of similarity, subordination, action–reaction, and rigidity, nowhere holds absolutely and without qualification. But there are the prevailing characteristics of the situation that is exemplified in by far the greater part of reality, and they play a large and significant role even in the human context. Necessity is the substratum of all existence; without the persistence and recurrence, the stability and coordination, that it guarantees, things would become isolated and events erratic. This is as true at the human level as at any other. But there are also other conditions that characterize the dimensions of order throughout reality, though often inconspicuously. These gradually become more prominent and influential in certain regions, especially that of man. As this occurs, the regime of necessity is modified and supplemented—though emphatically not superseded—by the regime of possibility. This transition can be traced through the significant changes that now occur in each of the elements of order.

As regards the many, the essential outcome of possibility is differentiation. As the higher forms of life—notably man—develop complex structures and specialized functions and become capable of a wider range of activity, the room for variation increases, and individual differences become important. Within the limits of a shared human nature and situation, there is opportunity for large distinctions of capacity, temperament, and interest. In sum, man's endowment is extraordinarily plastic; his powers are generalized, permitting various developments, and these powers do not mature spontaneously, but must be trained.

Concurrently, in the dimension of the one, subordination is transformed toward participation. Things remain ineluctably parts of wholes—elements in fields, systems, environments, groups—which continue to exert a strong pressure on them. But, as entities increase in power and effectiveness, they attain a larger measure of independence and so are able to exercise a reciprocal influence on their surroundings. This is already apparent in man's control of his physical environment. It becomes far more complex and important in the relationships that individual men sustain with the social groups to which they belong. This relationship is subtle and ambivalent. Men regard their groups as both vehicles to further their personal interests and common undertakings that have a claim on their allegiance and service. To participate is at once to share in decisions and accept them, to receive from the group and contribute to it.

In the dimension of process, possibility issues in self-determination. As the capabilities of things increase, they are able to enter more effectively as independent agents in the causal process. Men can store energy in the present and direct its use in the future; they can select the transactions they mean to carry on; they can plan and persevere. The nexus of action–reaction is loosened, alternatives open, and men can intervene in the course of events. The individual is able to buffer, if not dominate, the pressure of circumstances and so to determine for himself what he is to do and be. The uniqueness and distinctness of things now make a real difference.

Finally, the outcome of possibility in the dimension of pattern is a large increase in flexibility. All things are ushered with existence into a system of relations that is antecedent to them. But, as we approach the human context, this system becomes open, fluid, and only generally defined instead of being closed, rigid, and minutely determined. The broad structure of the social order is established and transmitted through time, but it leaves men discretion as to the positions they are to occupy, the functions they are to perform, and the goals they are to pursue. Men are now able to plan their own lives; and, perhaps even more important, they are able to enter into private agreements, the terms of which they themselves can define, modify, and terminate.

As these new conditions spread through any region of reality, the regime of possibility is installed therein, supplementing the regime of necessity and modifying it in the ways just described. The distinguishing feature of the human context is precisely the high degree to which these conditions are realized there. It is this which discriminates man from all other creatures, confronting him with a challenge and conferring on him an opportunity that are altogether unique. The outcome of this process is the emergence of individual men as differentiated and self-determining participants in flexible social groups. Change and novelty now interrupt the nexus of persistence and recurrence; initiative supplements inertia; contingencies occur in the course of events, permitting alternatives and so requiring decisions. This situation is obviously fraught with both advantages and dangers—it opens the way to further radical, diverse, and rapid developments, but it also threatens confusion and incoherence. If we look at this outcome from one point of view, we describe it in terms of freedom, opportunity, and progress; if we look at it from another point of view, we describe it in terms of disorder, uncertainty, and insecurity. Both perspectives are necessary to a sound appraisal.

The crux of this development can be epitomized by saying that possibility inaugurates a state of affairs that is to a marked degree incomplete and tentative. Such a situation is unstable and unoriented; unless soon supplemented, it must revert to the regime of necessity or issue in the reign of sheer chance. Possibility requires that a proper use be made of it, that its advantages be exploited and its dangers averted. It challenges man to give it a content, a course, and a direction. Man responds to this challenge by installing in the human context the further regime of purposiveness. When what transpires in the present is not rigidly determined by past events and surrounding circumstances, it must be defined by reference to the future. Creatures so placed must intervene deliberately in the chain of happenings in order that they may lead to certain outcomes rather than to others. Man exercises this power of purposiveness to a high degree, using it to choose among possibilities and then to prepare and actualize them.

Positive law is one of the principal instruments that man employs in this effort, though it is by no means the only one, since it shares this role with such diverse institutions as education, religion, morality, science, technology, and economics. I suggested earlier that the basic problem man confronts is that of preserving the order that is the matrix of his undertaking while at the same time exploiting the advantages that disorder offers him. The preceding analysis should permit us to define this problem more precisely, for the "order" and "disorder" in question are those that man inherits from the commingling of the regimes of necessity and possibility. This is the situation with which law must deal in each of the dimensions of the human context—the many, the one, process, and pattern.

We can now state more exactly the essential tasks that are committed to law, the "perfect accomplishment" of which would constitute justice. Law must effect a reconciliation of similarity and differentiation, of subordination and participation, of action–reaction and self-determination, and of rigidity and flexibility. In each case, it is required to preserve the benefits of each of these regimes, to overcome its shortcomings, and to fuse the two coherently. Law begins to take shape as an institution, and justice emerges as a distinct conceptual ideal with man's awareness and acceptance of these tasks. Since law and justice are agents of purposiveness, their character can best be exhibited by an investigation of this new regime, which is intended to complete and consummate what the earlier regimes of necessity and possibility leave only potential. I now want to examine, briefly but synoptically, the task that law confronts and the end that justice envisages in each of these four major aspects of man's undertaking.

In the dimension of the many, this task and end find expression in the concept of cultivation. There are certain basic human similarities of nature and function, of need and desert, that must be guaranteed; and there are real differences in the talents, capacities, and interests of individual men. Cultivation must respect and further both of these. The plasticity that was noted above as such an outstanding human trait has two vital consequences; it means that every man has varied potentialities pointing to various realizations and that which of these is to be realized and to what degree are issues that depend at least as much on nurture as on nature. If differentiations are not properly trained and disciplined, they tend to relapse into mediocrity or to shatter into relativism and heterogeneity. Cultivation must pass on a tradition and produce a coherent population while preserving the integrity of individuals. In this effort, it often degenerates toward indoctrination or indifferentism. But the task is inescapable, for a mature and civilized human being is far more a work of art than a natural product.

The completion that purposiveness seeks in the dimension of the one is that of the creation and maintainence of authority. Men, in their exercise of participation, often turn this to their own ends; in so doing, they exploit public resources, run counter to one another, and waste their efforts in friction. To check these abuses and counter these divisive tendencies, the human group organizes itself as an effective entity. Authority employs planned cooperation and force to supplement spontaneous mutuality and persuasion. They are levers through which the group seeks to regulate and coordinate individual careers, distribute the benefits and burdens of group life, and distill general purposes out of separate interests. This effort is never more than partially successful. Authority is often debased by those who hold it, evaded by those who live under it, and confounded by the complexities it faces. Authority is power that is concentrated in some and acknowledged by all. These are the basic conditions that must be met if it is to serve effectively. If, in addition, it is to serve justice, it must also be legitimate and limited.

The outcome that purposiveness requires in the dimension of process is embodied in the concept of responsibility. Insofar as men exercise self-determination, they give to the course of events a content and consequences it would not otherwise have had. What they do has repercussions and makes a difference in what is to be. This being the case, it is incumbent on men to anticipate the results of their actions, to be concerned for their quality, and to act with a due regard for others. As men become creative agents, they need also to be responsible creatures. Men do not always assume this burden willingly or discharge it intelligently. To repair these deficiencies, it becomes necessary to define the limits of permissiveness within which men can act and to impose penalties when they exceed them. That is, responsibility is translated into the legal concepts of rights and duties, liberties and liabilities. Practical considerations require this. But it should be remembered that it is at best a buttress, and not a substitute, for the sense of responsibility itself, which motivates men before the event both to care and to take care about the differences they make.

Finally, in the dimension of pattern, purposiveness manifests itself as the quest for continuity. Since men are finite creatures and the world's resources are limited, individuals must coordinate their efforts if the energies and materials available are to be effectively utilized. Flexibility has the great advantages of promoting initiative, enterprise, and ingenuity. But it also threatens to dissolve or disrupt the relations that constitute the social order. The separate and joint undertakings in which men engage require an organized and stable milieu which will assure that established arrangements are maintained, obligations enforced, and results secured. If this is not done, the course of social life becomes erratic and arbitrary, with the result that engagements are interrupted, plans are nullified, and efforts are frustrated. The task of continuity is to both respect and integrate the separate careers of men, preventing alike their isolation from and their submergence in the total group enterprise.

III

If we summarize the results of the preceding analysis, we can reach a comprehensive view of the origins of law and of the outcome that it seeks in the name of justice. The regime of necessity constitutes the substratum, the fabric and framework, of human existence—men who share a common and continuing nature, whose reactions and behavior follow set courses, who are sensitive to their fellows and responsive to group pressure, and whose roles and functions are defined by a pervasive web of relationships. The regime of possibility ushers in the conditions that are peculiarly distinctive of the human situation—highly differentiated individuals with a large power of self-determination who participate actively in group decisions and affairs and whose private and joint undertakings require a flexible social milieu. Finally, the regime of purposiveness announces man's recognition, whether vague or clear, tentative or decisive, of the tasks with which these conditions challenge him—the cultivation of human potentialities, the inculcation and acceptance of responsibility, the establishment and control of authority, and the assurance of continuity within society. These are the tasks of law and the ends of justice.

I suggested earlier that justice is the form of the order that man seeks to create through law. This form itself is composed around the four poles of cultivation, authority, responsibility, and continuity. The contents of these aspects of justice are closely controlled by the antecedent circumstances that give rise to them, that is, by the problems to which they are the envisaged solutions. It is this complex of conditions that defines justice as a substantive concept constitutive of the good society and regulative of legal and political institutions. The quest for justice is the quest for a state of affairs where these four conditions are perfectly realized.

We come now to a final and crucial question. Is the theory of justice that emerges from this analysis able to turn the thrust of the either/or that was posed at the start of this essay? Does it yield any principles that, on the one hand, can make good their claim to be neutral and objective and, on the other hand, are sufficiently exact and systematic to generate and control practical directives?

In sum, can this doctrine chart a passage between the extremes of vacuous idealism and partisan ideology?

I would like to believe that the answer to this question is "yes." But I would equally want to insist that it is a qualified "yes." I think that this analysis does yield a comprehensive and reliable understanding of the basic conditions that must be met and the essential values that must be furthered by any social and legal order that is to qualify as just. But it is perfectly evident that this analysis does not and cannot yield a detailed picture of the "good society" to which all actual societies should conform; a determination of what constitutes the "best" or "most perfect" social and legal order in any particular case cannot be logically derived solely from this doctrine, but also depends on other considerations. This is to say that any such determination is a decision, not a deduction. Justice as here conceived is an ideal in the sense that it pretends to be objectively grounded and universally relevant. That is, it claims to enunciate goals and principles that hold true for all men at all times. But it is admittedly an ideal that requires to be filled out by an ideology before it can be implemented. These two aspects need brief examination.

Much of the confusion surrounding this matter arises from misunderstanding of what we can legitimately expect an ideal to be and to do. We tend to think of an ideal as a very definite and concrete model or a very precise standard, by reference to which we can make exact comparisons and evaluations of actual cases. But this is to ask both for what is far too much and for what is not, in the last analysis, very important. We cannot arrive at such ideals because we do not know enough about the future, or even about the present. We simply cannot say with any certainty what is the perfect fulfillment of tendencies and movements that are still incomplete. It is often impossible even to judge safely among the alternative outcomes that are presently available, for these may quite well be different without being "better" or "worse." Consider, for instance, the concept of "health," which is intrinsically a good deal simpler than that of "justice" and regarding which we have much more empirical and experimental evidence. No biologist or doctor would dream of delineating a full and final ideal of "health" or of setting up criteria by which we can determine exact degrees of "healthiness," as against a calibrated scale.

Health varies with the constitutions of men and with the uses they wish to make of it. The same is even more true in the case of justice.

Furthermore, as long as we hold that individual differences are legitimate and ultimate—as long as we acknowledge the regime of possibility—this kind of determination is not only futile but vicious. One of the prominent symptoms of the contemporary distemper is a terrible compulsion to measure. With reference to justice—as with respect to health, happiness, morality, beauty, and many other traits—it is of vital significance that we be able to distinguish between the licit and the illicit, the true and the false, the real and the illusory, the honest and the deceptive, the effective and the ineffective. But it is impossible and unimportant to arrange things on an exact scale of perfection as regards these traits, for there are too many differences that are legitimate and neutral. When we delude ourselves into thinking that we can attain this exactness and certainty in the subtle and recondite regions of human life, we are on our way to error, dogmatism, intolerance, and, finally, persecution. And these are clearly not functions that ideals are meant to serve.

What we can validly ask of an ideal is that it illuminate and guide our dealings with actuality, that is, with the actual things and situations that we encounter in life. An ideal can make a double contribution to this effort. First, it can, by its own completeness and coherence, alert us to the richness and complexity of reality; it can help us to a rounded and balanced consideration of things; it can prevent us from being blinded to some aspects of situations by the too-sharp intrusion of other aspects; and it can protect us against partiality and distraction. Here, ideals function much as conceptual models do for scientists. They synthesize the findings of many inquiries; they serve as compact expressions of complex situations; they point out expectations as we investigate actual cases; they expose facets and problems which without them we might overlook.

Second, ideals can animate and direct our efforts as they reach into the future. As I have just urged, they cannot depict beforehand the final and finished result that these efforts should seek. But they can give them a general destination and program. They can make us aware of the total consequences of courses where we would otherwise be engrossed in their immediate outcomes. They can indicate which paths are fruitful. They can mark out lines of development and progress, even though they cannot define perfection. They cannot reduce or promote the resolution of moral and social problems to logical deductions, but they can afford a full and clear view on which to base our decisions. In a word, ideals can both sharpen our insight into our surroundings and refine our vision of what we can do with these in the future.

Within these limits of reasonable expectation, I would hope that the present conception constitutes a legitimate and fruitful ideal. The analyses that it climaxes have not intended to depict any ultimate and utopian state of affairs where all human shortcomings and difficulties are repaired and man enters into an inheritance of perfection. Rather, they have sought only to decipher the general course of man's development, to elicit the opportunity and the challenge that are inherent in the human situation, and to extrapolate the future lines that must be followed if man is to achieve a yet higher fulfillment. This conception of justice maintains that cultivation, authority, responsibility, and continuity—as these terms have been systematically derived and analyzed—are at once the continuing tasks and the final goals of society. These tasks and goals have objective meaning and universal relevance because they are rooted in the conditions of man's being and well-being. This set of conditions functions as an ideal—a model or matrix—by reference to which we can reach a measured assessment of the ends we propose and the means we adopt in our social, political, and legal efforts. Above all, it serves to remind us of the complexity of this effort and to protect us against neglect of any of its facets. If a social and legal order deviates too much from the tasks and goals set by this ideal, then we may safely say that it is intrinsically distorted and incomplete. So we can condemn and abandon it or start at once to correct it.

This last point is especially important. The quest for justice, as here expounded, is evidently a complex undertaking. As in any such case, there is a strong temptation to simplify the problem, and the most obvious way to accomplish this is by reducing the terms involved in its solution. In the case of justice, there are two general ways in which this is apt to be done. The first is by restricting the quest for justice to only some of the dimensions of order, neglecting others. A legal and political system may concentrate its efforts on the tasks and goals that derive from one or two of the elements of many–one–process–pattern while ignoring or denying the claims of the other elements. For instance, it can be strongly argued that democracy, as it has developed especially in England and America, has largely restricted its efforts to the tasks of authority and continuity, that is, that it has been primarily a political and economic doctrine. Cultivation has been regarded as the province of education, and responsibility, as that of religion and morality. Furthermore, there has been popular insistence that these latter institutions must be independent of political influence.

The classical arguments in support of this position are sound, within limits: if society becomes too monolithic in structure and power is too much concentrated, familiar evils follow. But there is another side, for the authority and continuity that legal and political action seek to institute obviously require the support of citizens who are properly cultivated and responsive; if this material fails, the effort of government collapses. A good case can be made that this is exactly the problem that democracy now faces, most critically in the newly emergent nations but also even in the traditional strongholds of the democratic movement. Such a narrowing of effort is fed by the hope that, if only some of these problems can be overcome, then the rest will automatically be solved. If we can only assure cultivation *or* authority *or* responsibility *or* continuity, then the others must follow. But this hope is futile, for such a neglect creates a void that soon spreads and undermines the whole legal and political structure.

The other general mode of simplification is even more drastic and serious. It consists in refusing the challenge of purposiveness and seeking to dispose of the problems of life by a return to one or the other of the regimes of necessity or possibility. In the first case, an attempt is made to eliminate the occurrence of possibilities by a minute regulation of the human scene, which would be returned to the conditions of similarity, subordination, action–reaction, and rigidity. In a more familiar and concrete terminology, this state of affairs would enshrine social conformity, political absolutism, the minute regulation of both group and individual undertakings, and a rigid caste system. In a word, men would lose their private characters and independent careers and would be transformed into sheerly public entities, with status and function assigned to them. If the latter course is adopted, the attempt to define and direct the uses that men make of possibility is renounced. Differentiation, participation, self-determination, and flexibility are held to be absolute values, and men are left unhampered in their disposal of them.

Here, the emphasis would be placed on individual self-expression, political equality, personal freedom, and unrestricted competition (free contract and the open market). Under this regime (or lack of such) the very existence of the *respublica* is apt to be dissolved into a horde of separate and unrelated private strivings. Both these general modes of simplifying the problem of justice and the latter in both its specific guises are familiar features of legal and political life; only brief reflection on history and contemporary affairs will reveal innumerable instances of them. Of course, they rarely occur in the extreme and wholesale forms that I have described; they are themes, or abstract types, on which actual life plays a multitude of variations. The ideal of justice, as here conceived, dictates a categorical rejection of all such efforts at simplification and reduction, for it asserts that cultivation, authority, responsibility, and continuity are at once the heritage and the obligation of man. These are goals that man cannot reject and tasks that he cannot refuse without renouncing his own nature. This conception defines with at least some precision and coherence the conditions that any social order must satisfy and the values it must promote. To this extent, it embodies an ideal that is objectively grounded, systematically articulated, and universally relevant.

But this is still an ideal that requires further specification before it can be implemented, for it does not pretend to yield any detailed and final delineation of either the goals it posits or the tasks it imposes. These are matters that do not permit of any absolute and categorical predetermination that can claim to hold good for all peoples, times, and places. Justice is the ideal form of order. But it is a form that is itself flexible and will accept various contents. This means that the concepts of cultivation, authority, responsibility, and continuity designate goals and tasks that require more precise and concrete interpretation before they can function as guide-lines of legal and political action. These interpretations will vary, quite legitimately, along three major axes.

First, there will be differences in the exact meaning and content given these concepts. The conditions they envisage—the ends they depict—will not appear the same to all men everywhere. There are honest and reasonable differences of opinion as to what constitutes the proper fulfillment, the highest realization, of man's nature and by what process of cultivation this can best be promoted. The same is true of the question of how authority should be constituted, in whom it should be vested, to what extent it should be limited, and by what apparatus it should be exercised. And the case is similar for the other concepts at issue. In each of the dimensions of order, the goal sought is so complex that almost inevitably some of its aspects are going to have to be subordinated, if not sacrificed. Various peoples are going to make choices that differ without being better or worse. Of particular significance in this regard is the question of how the movement of purposiveness is to strike a balance between the regimes of necessity and possibility. As I pointed out earlier, the ideal resolution of this tension is that in which the benefits of each of these regimes are preserved, their shortcomings mitigated, and the two fused in a coherent manner. But we have clearly not achieved this synthesis in any of the dimensions of order, and we probably never will. On the other hand, I urged just above that any effort to return exclusively to either one of these earlier regimes is to be altogether rejected. But between these extremes of the ideal and the illicit there is a large area of permissiveness. If, in each of these dimensions, the conditions of necessity and possibility cannot be fused in a perfect synthesis, then they must somehow be compromised and conciliated. There is no single best way of doing this. The effort to mix liability and liberty in a proportion that will at least approximate responsibility is a continuing theme of political life. We are now thoroughly accustomed to attempts to achieve continuity by perpetually reblending the rigidity of a planned economy with the flexibility of free enterprise.

Both the theory and practice of cultivation (more familiarly, education) are rent by dissension between the adherents of a rigorous curriculum and the transmission of a coherent tradition, on the one hand, and those who advocate free self-development and the relativism of all values, on the other. The pressures of a complex and delicately balanced world are forcing all nations—particularly the newly established ones—to try to devise means by which the competing social and political aspirations of men can make themselves felt and yet can be controlled and coordinated, or, to state the matter differently, to find a way in which political authority can be kept both adequate to the tasks of government and sensitive to the will of the governed.

A second and less basic mode of variation arises from the relative importance attached to the goals and tasks that together compose justice. As was stressed above, any legal and political order that is to qualify as just must move in all four of these directions; but priority and effort may be very differently assigned among them, and in each case for reasons that are sound and with results that are satisfactory. Finally, there are legitimate differences in the means that are adopted for effecting these purposes. Even where there is close agreement on goals, the tasks of achieving them may be undertaken in quite different but equally justifiable ways.

Given the double complexity of the ideal of justice itself and of the actual circumstances in which it has to be realized, these differences are understandable and acceptable. As the physical, human, and cultural situations of societies change, these goals will impose themselves in differing terms and with varying degrees of urgency. The quest for justice does not take place under abstract and artificially simplified conditions, but amid the uncertain welter and flux of reality. The material within which the form of justice is to be realized is neither everywhere the same nor altogether plastic; it imposes demands, limits, and directions of its own. Superimposed on this basic source of variation are differences of human preference and judgment. The general goals of cultivation, authority, responsibility, and continuity will wear various specific guises and will appeal with differing intensities, depending on the temperaments of men, the traditions in which they have been raised, the deprivations that weigh on them, and the desires that urge them. When preference and circumstance have combined to move men in certain ways toward certain goals, judgment may still render differing verdicts as regards both the evaluation of ends and the selection of means.

Any legal system must be appropriate to the human and social order—to the particular concatenation of many, one, process, and pattern—that constitutes its actual environment. This necessity confronts the quest for justice at all times and places. But it imposes itself in an especially acute form whenever it is a question of trying to effect a drastic and rapid transformation either within a society or between societies. The critical occurrences of this problem at present concern, first, the states that have been newly created from former colonies and, second, the United Nations. The major difficulties that we encounter in both these cases are largely caused by our failure to distinguish sufficiently between ideal and ideology.

Each nation that is concerned with these issues has its own well-developed ideology, that is, its own interpretation of justice as the ideal form of order and its own political-legal apparatus designed to secure this order. Each such ideology has taken form gradually as the instrument of particular values and purposes faced with particular circumstances. Each nation then tries to deal with these quite new problems in the terms of its own ideology; it assumes that its values and purposes are common to all men at all times and that its apparatus is appropriate to all situations. In the case of the people newly come to independence, we assume that they give the same concrete meaning as we to such abstract concepts as liberty, equality, human rights, political responsibility, and so forth; and we assume that these can be secured to them if they will only adopt our own methods, such as parliamentary institutions, cabinet government, the party system, universal suffrage, constitutional provisions, court systems, and so forth. We do this in the face of the radical differences that exist in all of the dimensions of order between our two situations. Fortunately for us, the Communist bloc is equally inept. So the efforts of each power group are frustrated, and the new nations are left to make do as best they can with a welter of inappropriate contradictions. The matter is similar in the case of the United Nations. We treat this as though it operated on principles similar to those of our tripartite system of government, whereas the Communists deal with it as though it were constructed on the model of the party presidium.

Any such effort to export a legal system or to apply it out of context falls into what lawyers call the "vice of conceptualism"—

it treats concepts as though they could and should control facts. And this they cannot do, especially when the "facts" to be controlled—human beings—must interpret and acknowledge the concepts that are supposed to control them. For law depends on—and so must be adapted to—the human population with which it deals, the type of political organization that it administers, the interests and pursuits that concern men, and the way of life that men have already established among themselves and with their surroundings. These together constitute the actual matrix within which law is to function; they condition the ends that their law is to seek. Law is a principle of order, and justice is the completion of law; these are general and abstract statements, from which I have tried to derive an objective and universally relevant meaning of justice. But any particular legal and political system is the principle of a certain concrete and determinate order, and this requires an equally concrete and determinate completion. So justice, as the ideal form of order, must take on a similarly specific and local guise if it is to be effectively embodied in its actual order.

It is for all these reasons that any working idea of justice must always be an ideology as well as an ideal. If an ideal is to serve its proper functions of illuminating and guiding our encounters with life, it must be sharply articulated and comprehensive as to its structure, but open and flexible as to its content. If it lacks these formal characteristics, it becomes so ambiguous and amorphous that it is incapable of extending our insight and anticipation. If it lacks these material characteristics, it becomes so dogmatic and intolerant that it blinds us to all but a narrow range of fact and value. In the first case, it becomes an idol; in the second, a creed. In both cases it ceases to be and do what an ideal should.

This is to say that ideals are indispensable as directing and controlling agents in the conduct of life; but they are not by themselves adequate to this task. They are necessary but not sufficient causes. To function effectively, the general and abstract idea of justice must associate itself with a specific and concrete body of doctrine. That is, *the* ideal must be supplemented by *an* ideology. This is often regretted, on the ground that in this process the ideal loses its most significant features, namely, its objective reference and its universal relevance. But this is a mistaken view, for what happens here is gain rather than loss; the ideal, without in the least changing its intrinsic nature, assumes the guise of a definite and detailed interpretation of its own provisions. But this assumption is tentative and temporary, and herein lies the crux of the matter, for it is when we forget this that we fall into gross errors. When an ideal joins itself to an ideology, it surrenders its claim to objectivity and universality, for an ideology is the product of circumstance, preference, and judgment exercised on the goals and tasks that the ideal sets. Any ideology is subjective and local; it is the ideal tamed and caged. To treat this ideology as though it were absolute and categorical is to become doctrinaire in the most dogmatic and sterile sense.

To avoid this error, we need only remain aware of the distinction between ideal and ideology and of the transformation that we work in moving from one to the other. Then we can welcome rather than regret the multiplicity of ideologies, of interpretations of the ideal of justice. I gave prominent place at the beginning of this essay to the often-voiced charge that the concept of justice, being too ambiguous to generate any precise and fruitful meanings, continuously degenerates toward empty precepts on the one hand and partisan programs on the other. Further, according to this criticism, these retrogressive tendencies combine to produce a series of tragicomic denouements; partisanship gives content to precepts, and the latter justify partisan ends and actions. This certainly happens often enough, but there is nothing inevitable about it, precepts need not be empty, nor programs hypocritical. It is equally possible for precepts to define determinate goals and for programs to be effectively planned to achieve them, and, consequently, for the interplay of these two elements to be positive and constructive.

This is, in fact, the pattern of all legal and political movements that endure for any time and make any substantial contribution. Any such movement starts with a set of precepts that proclaims a certain vision of justice. This vision is at first cast in absolute and universal terms which give it the appearance of a simple evocation of the pure ideal of justice and so enhance its prestige and appeal. But the pretense is soon dropped, and these precepts are seen to enunciate a quite concrete and particular conception of order; that is, they give a definite meaning to the notions of cultivation, authority, responsibility, and continuity.

Such precepts constitute an ideology. They next embody themselves in an explicit social doctrine, a set of political institutions, and a legal apparatus.

These soon engender a detailed action program. The history of the movement consists of the interplay of these three factors. It is a process in and through which the implicit meanings of the ideology are elicited and elaborated; instruments are forged for the realization of these meanings and intentions; and, finally, they are made effective in society, and their total impact on human life is exposed. These three phases mutually illuminate and support one another. The ideology on which any such movement is based does much to determine its character, power, and reach. It must find or devise the proper instruments through which to express itself, whereas the test of actual consequences is the only way in which the ideology can prove and correct itself. This pattern can be clearly seen in case after case. Obvious, large-scale examples of it are the expansion of the political and legal meaning of the Constitution in this country; the history of the utilitarian movement of reform in England; the transition from Marxism through Leninism and Stalinism to the present situation in the U.S.S.R.; the abortive development of Fascism (or authoritarianism) in Italy and Germany, its continuance and transformation in Spain and Portugal, and its greater or lesser impact in several other places.

These movements are certainly not at all on a par as regards either the adequacy of their visions or the extent of their influence. But they all, in their various ways, represent so many experiments and explorations of the potentialities of human development. They can correct and supplement one another. We can even expect that they will gradually bracket their target; they will certainly never hit it, however, for the very good reason that it does not exist. The ideal as such is never embodied or realized. It remains always a sheer concept, defining the conditions of man's being and well-being, but not determining their content. This latter is for us to continually undo and redo, for variety and change require differing accommodations in the present, and they prepare a future that we cannot wholly anticipate. It is for this reason that justice must be both ideal and ideology.

11

THE SCHOLASTIC DISPUTE ON JUSTICE: AQUINAS VERSUS OCKHAM

DAVID GRANFIELD

I

A common starting point for the thirteenth- and fourteenth-century dispute over the nature of justice was the accepted definition: *reddere suum cuique,* to give to each his own. Thinkers, agreeing on its practical applicability, clashed over its theoretical justification. The operative word in the conflict was *suum,* since, for justice to have significance, it must be clear what belongs to a man, what he has rightfully, what his rights are. The word *suum* implies a whole *Rechtsphilosophie.* Here, Thomas Aquinas [1] and William of Ockham were in sharp disagreement.

The Dominican and the Franciscan both subscribed to the same moral code, the same general obligations of justice, but for fundamentally different reasons. Each believed in the transcend-

[1] *De perfectione vitae spiritualis, Opusculum Theologica,* ed. Spiazzi (1954), II, 153, No. 734, gives a glimpse of the spirit of Aquinas's life.

ent God, the one insisting more on His infinite wisdom, the other more on His almighty power. Philosophically, the split over the nature of law was this: Aquinas emphasized the primacy of the intellect; for him, law was an ordinance of reason; a right exists because it is just, *ius quia iustum.* Ockham emphasized the primacy of the will; for him, law was an arbitrary fiat; a right exists because it has been commanded, *ius quia iussum.* No actual dispute ever took place between these two men, for they were not contemporaries, but died seventy-five years apart. The radical conflict between Thomism and nominalism, in some ways still alive, necessitates the formulation of the fundamentals at stake in this battle—not of persons, but of ideas and, specifically, the idea of justice. This study is divided into two parts: first, an analysis of the notion of justice as found in Thomas; second, an analysis of the thinking of Ockham in its radical departure from the traditional Thomistic position.

II

An immediate point of contrast between the position of Aquinas and that of Ockham is the notion of justice in God. Ockham holds that all authority comes from God, whose law overrules all other laws; [2] yet, as we shall see, the power that makes the law is "absolute," the law, arbitrary. Thomas, too, sees God as the source of all legal authority, but there is a balance which, without setting limits to the infinite, more accurately reflects the perfections of God. Justice is both intellectual and volitional. "It must be said that justice, in respect to the regulating law, is in the reason or intellect; but in respect to the command, by which works are regulated according to law, it is in the will." [3]

The full beauty of this explanation is seen in its application to God. Thomas points out that things are not the measure and rule of God's intellect as they are of ours; rather, God's

[2] See Ockham, *Opus Nonaginta Dierum,* Chap. 88 (M. Goldast, *Monarchia S. Romani Imperii* [1614] II, 1146); *Dialogus,* Pars III, Tractatus II, Lib. II, Chap. IV (Goldast, II, 904).

[3] Thomas Aquinas, *Summa Theologiae* (Ottawa: Institute of Medieval Studies of Ottawa, 1941–1945), Pars I, Question 21, *ad* 1. Hereafter, it will be cited as *S.Th.*

intellect is the cause and measure of the things that are. "Therefore, the justice of God, which establishes an order in things conformable to the nature of His divine Wisdom, which is His Law, is fittingly named Truth." [4] Justice is distinguished from love: "The communication of perfections, absolutely considered pertains to goodness . . . , but inasmuch as these perfections are given to things by God according to their proportions, pertains to justice." [5] It is important to note the emphasis, in the above texts, on the sense of order, fitness, and proportion which are the result of the divine intelligence. God, who creates freely, does so in order that "what His Wisdom and Will have, and what His goodness manifests, may be fulfilled in things." [6] God is bound only because he freely binds himself, and this only in harmony with His eternal law, "for the whole community of the universe is governed by Divine reason." [7]

The relationship between the eternal law of God and the natural law is essential for a right understanding of the place of justice in Thomistic philosophy. Thomas contrasts the two in an important text:

> The human reason is not able to participate fully in the dictate of the divine reason, but (only) in its own way and imperfectly. And therefore, just as on the part of the speculative reason through natural participation in the divine reason, there is present in us the knowledge of certain common principles, but not the proper knowledge of every truth, as is contained in the divine wisdom; so also on the part of the practical reason, man naturally participates in the eternal law according to certain common principles, not however, according to particular directives of singulars, which, however, are contained in the eternal law.[8]

The eternal law orders all beings, actual and possible, to their proper ends. Not limited to general norms, it encompasses "particular directives of singulars." Man, in some way, shares in the eternal law. "The participation of the eternal law in the rational creature is properly called a law since a law is something pertaining to reason." [9] However, man's participation is imperfect,

[4] *S.Th.* I. 21. 2. c.
[5] *S.Th.* I. 21. 3. c.
[6] *S.Th.* I. 21. 1. *ad* 3.
[7] *S.Th.* I–II. 91. 1. c.
[8] *S.Th.* I–II. 91. 3. *ad* 1.
[9] *S.Th.* I–II. 91. 2. *ad* 3.

limited only to "certain common principles." But the natural law is not for this reason useless; it is a foundation on which to build a complete body of law. The structure of this work can be grasped by considering the first principle of the natural law. Thomas argues thus:

> Now as being is the first thing that falls under the apprehension simply, so good is the first thing that falls under the apprehension of the practical reason, which is directed toward action; since every agent acts for an end under the aspect of good. Consequently the first principle in the practical reason is one founded on the notion of good, viz., that good is that which all things seek after. Hence, this is the first precept of law, that good is to be done and evil is to be avoided. All other precepts of the natural law are based upon this; so that whatever the practical reason naturally apprehends as mans good (or evil) belongs to the precepts of the natural law as something to be done or avoided.[10]

T.E. Davitt uses the phrase "man-discovered-law" in preference to "natural law" to emphasize the necessary role that human reason plays and to indicate its nonauthoritarian character.[11] In the discovery of the guide-lines for legislation, man finds a guarantee that his "man-made law" will not be too much in conflict with reality, with the way things are. However stabilizing it may be, the natural law does not obviate the hard work of intelligent and conscientious lawmaking.

Natural law is insufficient for a really close approximation to the eternal law. It was insufficient even for God, who supplemented it by positive law, the divine laws he revealed, and the ecclesiastical laws he authorized his church to establish. Aquinas insists, however, that all human positive laws are derived from the natural law.[12] The word "derived" should be noted, for he does not mean deduced in an a priori fashion. Certain things are derived from the natural law by way of conclusions from premises. These are proportionately few. Most laws are purely positive law, that is, essentially a determination, a specification, a particularization of the natural law which reason makes, working on the facts of experience within the broad limits of the natural law.

This implementation of the natural law is seen in the work

---

[10] *S.Th.* I–II. 94. 2. c.
[11] T.E. Davitt, S.J., *The Elements of Law* (1959), Part II, pp. 95–143.
[12] *S.Th.* I–II. 95. 2. c.

that Thomas assigns to the four cardinal virtues whereby the virtuous state or individual chooses the right means to the right end. Prudence—with its three integral parts: observation, judgment, and execution—perfects the choice of the right means. The other three virtues concern themselves with ends. Temperance and fortitude look to the virtuous man himself. Phrasing their function in terms of the first principle—do good and avoid evil—we find that temperance achieves moderation in respect to good things, fortitude, in respect to evil things. Together, they keep a person from deviating from his proper end by restraining him from inordinate love of good things and inordinate fear of evil things. The virtue that looks directly to the end, or goal, is justice. Justice specifies the basic principle, "do good," by means of the general directive, "give to each his own." This precept, in turn, requires detailed implementation of what belongs to each person, the *suum* of the definition of justice: *reddere suum cuique.*[13]

Justice, then, presupposes a system of rights belonging to a human person as a creature of God.[14] The act of creation is necessary to the act of justice in that, through creation, a person is endowed by his creator with a special nature and dignity. Because of the relationship of man to his creator, certain human rights can be said to be inalienable. Josef Pieper writes:

> That something belongs to a man inalienably means this: the man who does not give a person what belongs to him, withholds it or deprives him of it, is really doing harm to himself; he is the one who actually loses something—indeed, in the most extreme case, he even destroys himself.[15]

Augustine phrased the same point graphically by saying that, to murder another, one must first pass the sword through one's own soul.

[13] Thomas also gives a fuller definition of justice: "Justitia est habitus secundum quem aliquis constanti et perpetua voluntate ius suum unicuique tribuit" (*S.Th.* II–II. 58. 1. c).

[14] See Thomas, *Summa Contra Gentiles* (1894), II, 28: "Then too, since the act of justice consists in rendering to each that which is his own, the act by which a thing becomes one's own property is prior to the act of justice, as we see in human affairs; a man's work entitles him to possess as his own that which his employer by an act of justice, pays to him. The act by which a person first acquires something of his own cannot, therefore be an act of justice. But, by the act of creation, a created thing first possesses something of its own."

[15] J. Pieper, *Justice,* pp. 18–19.

Thomas calls legal justice a general virtue and, in fact, foremost among the virtues, inasmuch as the common good transcends the good of an individual person.[16]

> Legal justice is said to be a general virtue, inasmuch, to wit, as it directs the acts of the other virtues to its own end, and this is to move all the other virtues by its command; for just as charity may be called a general virtue in so far as it directs the acts of all the virtues to the Divine Good, so too is legal justice, in so far as it directs the acts of all the virtues to the common good.[17]

Thus, in some way, temperance and fortitude are subordinated to justice, for "things referable to oneself are referable to another, especially in regard to the common good." [18] There is also another kind of justice, for, "besides legal justice, which directs man immediately to the common good, there is need for other virtues to direct him immediately in matters relating to particular good; and these virtues may be relative to himself [fortitude and temperance] or to another individual person [particular justice]." [19] Aquinas tells us that "whatever can be rectified by reason is the object of moral virtue." [20] But particular justice is not about the internal passions. "Since justice is directed to others, it is not about the entire object of moral virtue, but only about the external actions and things, under a certain special aspect of the object, in so far as one man is related to another through them." [21]

The distinction between the kinds of justice has been much discussed.[22] The basic division is between legal justice and particular justice, the latter being divided into commutative and distributive justice. The division is not a tripartite one, but bipartite with subalternation. Thomas writes:

> Private justice is directed to the private individual, who is compared to the community as a part to the whole. Now a twofold order may be considered in relation to a part. In the first place, there is the order of one part to another, to which corresponds the order of one private individual to another. This

[16] *S.Th.* II–II. 58. 12. c.
[17] *S.Th.* II–II. 58. 6. c.
[18] *S.Th.* II–II. 58. 5. *ad* 3.
[19] *S.Th.* II–II. 58. 7. c.
[20] *S.Th.* II–II. 58. 8. c.
[21] *Loc. cit.*
[22] G. Del Vecchio, *Justice*, ed. A.H. Campbell (1956), p. 35.

> order is directed by commutative justice, which is concerned about the mutual dealings between two persons. In the second place, there is the order of the whole towards the parts, to which corresponds the order of that which belongs to the community in relation to each single person. This order is directed by distributive justice, which distributes common goods proportionately. Hence there are two species of justice, distributive and commutative.[23]

Restitution is the act of commutative justice.[24] The imbalance engendered by injustice or indebtedness is remedied by the restoration of what is owed to another so that the equality of justice can be realized. Distributive justice, in preserving the relationship of the whole to the parts, of the state or ruler to the individual citizen, must give to each his fair and proportionate share of the common goods. "Equality is the general form of justice, wherein distributive justice and commutative justice agree; but in one we find equality of geometric proportion, whereas in the other we find equality of arithmetic proportion." [25] An interesting application highlights the difference between the two types of justice.

> When a man who has served the community is paid for his services, this is to be referred to commutative, not distributive justice: Because distributive justice considers the equality not between the thing received and the thing done, but between the thing received by one person and the thing received by another according to the respective conditions of those persons.[26]

The emphasis in this section on the notion of justice in Thomas Aquinas has been on its intellectual aspect, as contrasted to the voluntarism of William of Ockham. The proper role of the will in lawmaking is seen in Aquinas' solution of a dilemma. The objection was made that right (*ius*) is not fittingly divided into natural right and positive right. In the previous article, he had quoted approvingly Isidore's word, "Ius dictum est quia est justum." [27] Having shown that right is the object of justice, he is faced with this problem: "Divine right is not natural right, since it transcends human nature. In like manner,

[23] *S.Th.* II–II. 61. 1. c.
[24] *S.Th.* II–II. 62. 1. c.
[25] *S.Th.* II–II. 61. 2. *ad* 2.
[26] *S.Th.* II–II. 61. 4. *ad* 2.
[27] *S.Th.* II–II. 57. 1. *sed contra.*

neither is it positive right since it is based not on human but on divine authority." [28] After explaining how, in formulating positive law, the human will can, by common agreement, make a thing just if it is not contrary to natural justice but cannot make just something that is contrary to natural justice, Thomas applies, in his answer, the same distinction to God.

> The Divine right is that which is promulgated by God. Such things are partly those that are naturally just, yet their justice is hidden to man, and partly those made just by God's decree. Hence also divine right may be divided in respect to these two things, even as human right is. For the divine law commands certain things because they are good and forbids others because they are evil, while others are good because they are prescribed and others evil because they are forbidden.[29]

From the objection and its answer, we see further how deeply justice is rooted in right reason. Certain things are objectively good or evil. Willing by man or God does not change them. However, there is a large area of morally indifferent actions which can be forbidden or enjoined by human or divine authority; yet even here legislation must be reasonable in order to be just.

> Now laws are said to be just, both from the end, when, to wit, they are ordained to the common good; and from their author, that is to say when the law that is made does not exceed the power of the lawgiver; and from their form, when, to wit, burdens are laid on the subjects, according to an equality of proportion and with a view to the common good.[30]

Thomas is ruthless in his insistence that reason is an essential element of the law:

> Human law has the nature of law in so far as it partakes of right reason; and it is clear that, in this respect, it is derived from the eternal law. But in so far as it deviates from reason, it is called an unjust law, and has the nature not of law but of violence.[31]

Less than a century after Thomas, the awareness of reason's role had been lost in the minds of many. Social momentum car-

---

[28] *S.Th.* II–II. 57. 2. obj. 3.
[29] *S.Th.* II–II. 57. 2. *ad* 3.
[30] *S.Th.* I–II. 96. 4. c.
[31] *S.Th.* I–II. 93. 3. *ad* 2.

ried along the spirit of legal reasonableness, but the basic thought structure had been weakened. To appreciate this drastic revolution in ethical thought, it is necessary to see beside Thomistic jurisprudence the legal rationalization of William of Ockham.

III

Ockham's notion of justice, his "voluntarist ethics," was not simply an *ad hoc* solution to a polemical problem; it was rather an integral part of his philosophy, especially of his teaching on knowledge and on God. In these two areas, we find the source of his skepticism and authoritarianism. First of all, his epistemological position is one of radical empiricism buttressed by a thorough nominalism. He attributes certitude only to the immediate perception of existing things, to that direct experience which he calls *notitia intuitiva*. Yet even this intuitive knowledge is defective, for there is no guarantee that the direct perception grasps a reality that actually exists.

> It is a contradiction that there should be vision and yet the thing which is seen should not actually be or be capable of being. Therefore, it is a contradiction that a chimaera should be seen intuitively. But it is not a contradiction that that which is seen should actually be nothing outside the soul, provided that it can actually be or has been in reality.[32]

The implications of the notion of noncontradiction will be examined later; what is important here is the avowed unreliability of intuitive knowledge. This is not an isolated text; elsewhere he admits that he can see a star when none exists [33] and that he can be certain of seeing a stone, but not that it exists.[34]

The far-reaching consequences of his views on the doubt implicit in intuitive knowledge are shown by the statement: *Notitia abstractiva praesupponit intuitivam*.[35] But, for Ockham, the type of abstract knowledge called universals is suspect for another reason: universals have no reality. At best, they are vague images or pictures which group together many radically singular

---

[32] Ockham, *Quodlibeta Septem* (1491), VI, q. 6.
[33] *Ibid.*, I, q. 14.
[34] Ockham, I *Sent.* Prol., q. I, HH; ed. P. Boehner (1939), p. 29.
[35] *Quodl.* I. q. 14.

and unique individuals. He makes a very subtle distinction: "And so the genus is not common to many things through any sameness in them, but through the common nature (*communitatem*) of the *signum,* by which the same *signum* is common to many things signified." [36] Thomas, too, upholds the uniqueness of all beings, but he insists on a position of moderate realism concerning universals, based on the common essence shared by these singular beings. For Thomas, universals are formally in the mind, but fundamentally in things. Partly in thought, partly in things, universals make our thoughts realistic. Nominalism, however, rent asunder the two realms that moderate realism had joined together in lawful wedlock.[37] A divorce between legal thinking and the actual conditions of life is fatal to a sound jurisprudence, and yet there is present in Ockham's thought a doctrine even more lethal which hits at the heart of his legal philosophy.

Ockham's God is the problem center of his jurisprudence. It would not be accurate to speak here of Ockham's theodicy, for Leibniz used the term to indicate the science that justified God's ways to men. Ockham does not attempt to justify. It is as if he attributed to God the words of a woman in one of Juvenal's satires. She wanted her husband to crucify a slave for no reason. When questioned, her answer was: "Hoc volo, sic iubeo; sit pro ratione voluntas." [38] Nor could Ockham's teaching be called his natural theology, for his position is not a philosophical one arrived at by human intelligence, to be later supplemented by the faith which perfects nature. On the contrary, "Ockham's denial of natural proofs for any Christian proof begins exactly where the Credo starts." [39] He cannot defend his position philosophically against the philosophers who attacked him. He reaches his starting point by an existential leap or, to

---

[36] *Expos. aurea;* cited by De Wulf, *History of Medieval Philosophy* (3rd ed.; 1909), p. 423.

[37] See Étienne Gilson, *The Unity of Philosophical Experience* (1950), Chap. III, "The Road to Skepticism," in which he treats Ockham and his "psychologism," which he calls "the settled conviction that psychological relations between our ideas are a true picture of the real relations between things . . ." (p. 87).

[38] Juvenal *Satura* VI, 223.

[39] P. Boehner, "Ockham's 'Tractatus de Praedestinatione et de Praescientia Dei et de Futuris Contingentibus' and its Main Problems," *Proceedings of the American Catholic Philosophical Association,* XVI (1941), 182, n. 14.

phrase it more simply, by an act of belief in "the article of faith, 'I believe in God, the Father almighty,' which I understand thus that whatever does not include a manifest contradiction can be attributed to the divine power." [40] Note again the notion of noncontradiction which is crucial for Ockham's theory.

It should also be noted here, before Ockham's position is examined in more detail, that Aquinas, though primarily a theologian, insists on the power of the human mind to prove by natural reason the existence of an all-wise and all-powerful God. Once these "preambles to faith" have been arrived at, the acceptance of the revealed word of a God who can neither deceive nor be deceived becomes a reasonable act of faith, not a blind, unreasoning leap.

Ockham makes a fundamental distinction between what he calls God's *potentia ordinata* and his *potentia absoluta.* It is here that the notion of noncontradiction becomes operative. In a classic passage,[41] he explains that this distinction does not mean that in God there are two powers, for God is undivided. Nor does it mean that God sometimes acts absolutely, but not ordinately, for God cannot act inordinately. What is meant is that, when God acts according to the laws established by himself, he is acting with ordinate power. However, whatever does not involve a contradiction—whether or not God has ordained that he would do it, for God is able to do many things that he does not choose to do—God is able to do with absolute power. Pegis remarks: "It is, surely, a thin power that Ockham's God possesses, even if it be called omnipotence: the only world it can produce is a world of atomized facts surrounded by an unintelligible void." [42]

When Ockham makes a practical application of the function of the absolute power of God, he makes clear exactly what his notion of justice is.

> God does not sin whenever, as total cause, He performs the whole action that He now does with the sinner, as partial cause.

[40] *Quodl.* VI. q. VI.

[41] *Ibid.,* VI, q. 1, *circa primum.*

[42] Anton Pegis, "Concerning William of Ockham," *Traditio,* II, 478. The article which takes issue with P. Boehner's article "The Notitia Intuitiva of Non-Existents according to William Ockham" (*Traditio,* I [1943], 223–275), has the express intention "to point out that the traditional interpretation of William of Ockham as a nominalist and skeptic is correct" (p. 465).

> . . . For God cannot be bound to any action, and therefore *by the very fact that God wills something, it becomes just.* . . . Therefore, obligation makes a person a sinner or not a sinner. Whence if, as the total cause, God causes hatred of Himself in the will of someone else (as He now causes as partial cause), such a one would never sin. God would not win because He is obliged to nothing, nor would the other because the act was not in his power.[43]

This passage sheds light on the Ockhamistic relation between natural law and right reason. Superficially, Ockham seems in harmony with Aquinas. This is understandable, considering the influence of the earlier writer on the later one, but the underlying differences are vast. For example, Ockham writes: "No just positive law can be contrary to natural law." [44] The statement is sound, although there remains the further question: By what standards is a law called just or unjust? In the immediate explanation of his position, he seems far removed from voluntarism.

> And the reason for this is because there can be no law which is openly repugnant to superior law or to reason, whence any civil law whatsoever which is repugnant to divine law or to obvious reason is not law, and in the same manner the words of canon or civil law, in case they are repugnant to divine law, i.e., Holy Scripture or to right reason, are not to be observed.[45]

However, in his commentary on the *Sentences,* Ockham shows exactly what he means by right reason. "It can be said that every right will is conformed to right reason, but it is not always conformed to a prior right reason which shows the cause why the will ought to do this, but by the very fact that the divine will wills this, *right reason is called that which is willed.*" [46]

Therefore, the law established by the *potentia ordinata* is always subject to and easily supplanted by the arbitrary enactments of the *potentia absoluta.* L. Baudry writes: "The relations of things are as dependent on the divine will as the things themselves; everything in the universe becomes contingent." [47] Thus, the law enunciated from the relations that exist between things

---

[43] IV *Sent.* q. VIII–IX. E; quoted in Paul Vignaux, *Justification et prédestination au XIVe Siècle* (1934).

[44] *Dial.* I. VI. 100; Goldast, II, 629.

[45] *Ibid.,* p. 630.

[46] I *Sent.* d. XLI. q. I. A. *Quod sic primo;* K *ad primum principale.* Quoted in Vignaux, *op. cit.,* p. 138.

[47] L. Baudry, *Le Tractatus de principiis theologiae attribué à G.d'Occam* (1936), p. 38.

is contingent and unpredictable. Max Shepard too easily labels Ockham's position with Stammler's phrase, "natural law with a variable content." [48] The judgment is true to the extent that, as Copleston points out, "He [Ockham] evidentally [*sic*] considered that his predecessors had obscured the doctrine of divine omnipotence and liberty through their theories of immutable natural law." [49] But Ockham has done more than make natural law mutable and give it a variable content. He has, by his nominalism, destroyed the very possibility of a natural law. Without universal ideals, the natural law is actually unthinkable, for the mind cannot predicate general laws without basing them on a community of being which the mind formulates as universal ideas. Unless universal ideas are valid, there is no validity in the laws governing the various groups of beings.

More fundamentally, since the infinitely powerful God of Ockham is in no way limited by good or evil, by truth or error, the only restraint on the divine will is the principle of contradiction—God cannot do the impossible. Man is, therefore, unable to ascertain what the law is, because his reason has no access to the council chambers of a God whose law is an arbitrary dictate of the divine will, a will which is not bound to act in harmony with the beings it has created or the rules it has established for them.

This legal skepticism is based on both the debility of human reason and divine arbitrariness in a provisional universe. Aside from the certitudes that Ockham's faith afforded him, his view of reality is somewhat akin to that of Albert Camus. For Camus, the world did not make sense; it was absurd. For Ockham, the world need not make sense; it is arbitrary. For both, the underlying reasonableness of things did not appear. Ockham has a twofold source of uncertainty; not only are universals misleading images, but even direct intuitions guarantee only the possibility of existing beings.

Only what God reveals can be known with certainty. Thus, fideism substitutes for reason, and the philosophy of law built on this authoritarian foundation is a shifting structure of false generalities and ambiguous facts. Justice becomes exclusively

[48] Max Shepard, "William of Occam and the Higher Law," *The American Political Science Review*, XXVI (1932), 1015.

[49] F. Copleston, S.J., *A History of Philosophy* (1953), III, 109.

theological, based completely on faith, and in no way susceptible to philosophic justification or factual verification. Jettisoning philosophical proofs, Ockham is necessarily authoritarian. For him, justice cannot be attained through the seasoned judgments of the informed mind rooted in reality, but must be handed down from above as an authoritative precept, a despotic fiat of a God bound only by the law of noncontradiction.

IV

The history of ideas and human institutions shows the influence of these two conflicting theories of law. The *kirchlicher Positivismus* of Ockham,[50] has, in a way that would shock him, given rise to political absolutism and to an utter disregard of human rights. In a voluntarist world, Aquinas' principle that "all laws, in so far as they partake of right reason, are derived from the eternal law," [51] seems like naïve idealism. Such criticism would, at least, be logical, for, as Anton Pegis says, "Ockhamism is an ideal of a God who has power but not intelligence." [52] This revolt against reason, with manifestations in religion as well as politics, has brought to sad fulfillment a remark of Thomas: "Justice is destroyed in a twofold fashion: by the false prudence of the sage and by the violent act of the man who possesses power." [53] Ockham, sincere and subtle thinker though he was, has unwittingly justified the violence of the man of power. Justice has suffered a temporary defeat in which, according to A.P. d'Entrèves, "philosophers and theologians were more formidable foes than the professional lawyer." [54] And yet, that justice which is "fittingly named Truth," [55] can never really be destroyed; only men who recede from it can be destroyed. Thomas' role today is to show us the strength of the law of reason, to guide us in our own difficult task of making our human laws reasonable so that, with an awareness of human dignity and natural rights, we give to each his own.

---

[50] R. Seeberg, *Lehrbuch der Dogmengeschichte* (1930), III, 727–728.

[51] *S.Th.* I–II. 93. 3. c.

[52] *Op. cit.*, p. 479.

[53] *Expositio in Librum Beati Job, Omnia Opera* (1860), XIV, Cap. VIII, Lect. I.

[54] A.P. d'Entrèves, *Natural Law* (1951), p. 68.

[55] *S.Th.* I. 21. 3. c.

12

JUSTICE AS THE BASIS OF POLITICAL ORDER IN LOCKE

RICHARD H. COX

> And truly, if the preservation of all mankind, as much as in him lies, were everyone's persuasion, as indeed it is everyone's duty, and the true principle to regulate our religion, politics and morality, the world would be much quieter, and better natured than it is.

This statement from John Locke's *Some Thoughts Concerning Education* (§ 116) contains, I believe, a highly condensed version of his understanding of justice. The argument by which I hope to establish this point is divided into four parts. The first summarizes differing treatments of justice to be found in five of his works: *An Essay Concerning Human Understanding, Some Thoughts Concerning Education, The Reasonableness of Christianity, Two Treatises of Government,* and *A Letter Concerning Toleration.* The second proposes a hypothesis by which to account for and integrate the various treatments. The third shows the key role of the argument on property in the *Two Treatises of Government.* The fourth is a conclusion which brings us back to the original statement.

I

Two facts draw our attention at the very outset. First, Locke discusses the problem of justice in varying ways in various works. Second, not even the *Two Treatises of Government,* his major political writing, contains anything like an extended thematic treatment of justice [1]—only numerous references to and partial statements concerning it. These two facts are, I believe, aspects of the presentation of his teaching on justice, a presentation which must be understood as part of his general philosophical and political design.

The diversity of treatment of justice may be adequately represented by a summary of the relevant parts of five works. In the remarks which follow, I have deliberately placed the works in the indicated order the more fully to reveal the complex nature of Locke's intention.

An Essay Concerning Human Understanding. This most theoretical of Locke's writings is intended to clarify the principles and delimit the powers of the human understanding. Its references to justice are sparse and brief. In Book I, Locke refers to justice in the context of the question whether there are innate practical principles. In Book II, he speaks of the role of civil law, but does not specifically mention justice. In Book IV, in the context of an argument that morality is capable of demonstration, he uses the example of justice. Later in the same book there are references to justice as real knowledge and to just punishment.[2]

Locke does not in any way analyze the substance of justice; he is content to say that it is the practical principle "most men

[1] Compare the fact that Plato's *Republic* constitutes one long, explicit, thematic treatment of the question "What is justice?" I deliberately select the *Republic* here as my contrasting example in order to throw into relief the absence of such a discussion in Locke's works. Cf. Peter Laslett's introduction to his critical edition of Locke's *Treatises* (1960), p. 84.

[2] The exact locations are, in order, I. ii. 2, 9; II. xxviii. 9; IV. iii. 18, iv. 9, xvii. 4.

seem to agree in," and he equates it with respect for the life, liberties, and goods of others. As for its intellectual status as a principle, it cannot be innate, any more than can any speculative principle. Knowledge of it must, therefore, depend on sense experience and reflection, that is, on human activity.

Some Thoughts Concerning Education. In this work, Locke sets forth general principles for the physical, moral, and intellectual education of a gentleman. The treatment of justice is, once again, spare. Locke calls it the "great social virtue" and defines it only to the extent that he says that children "cannot well comprehend what injustice is till they understand property, and how particular persons come by it." He then concludes that the inculcation of an "ingenuous detestation" of injustice—a "shameful vice"—is the "true and genuine method to obviate this crime" (§ 110).

The Reasonableness of Christianity. The subject of this work, published some five years after the *Essay* and the *Treatises,* is "justification," in the theological sense of that which may justly earn a Christian salvation of his soul. It concentrates on what the Bible commands and promises concerning belief. The argument, reduced to its bare elements, is this. All Christians are under both the law of works and the law of faith. Under the first, to be just or to practice "righteousness" (the latter is Locke's own translation of the New Testament δικαιοσύνη) requires that the law of morality (the divine commandments) be strictly and unfailingly obeyed. But no man is capable of such strict observance. Thus, since no one is completely just, no one is entitled to salvation. It is here that the second law, the Christian law of faith, enters. By this second law,

> God justifies a man for believing, though by his works he be not just or righteous, i.e., though he came short of perfect obedience to the law of works. God alone does, or can, justify or make just those who by their works are not so: which he doth by counting their faith for righteousness, i.e., for a complete performance of the law.[3]

The crucial question, then, according to Locke, is *what* must be believed in order to act justly and to earn salvation. His an-

[3] *The Reasonableness of Christianity, Works* (2nd ed.; London; 1722), II, 479.

swer is: the belief that Jesus is the Messiah. There are, indeed, many other articles of Christian doctrine, but none so necessary, none so indispensable to divine "justification." And thus it is that men behave justly, so far as the Christian religion is concerned, by striving to obey the moral law and by believing in that great article of faith—Jesus is the Messiah.

Two Treatises of Government. Their purpose is to confute the false principles of Filmer and then to supply the "true original, extent and end of civil government." The *First Treatise* contains only two references to justice. The first (§ 42) provides a brief definition of justice and then juxtaposes it to charity. Justice, says Locke, "gives every Man a Title to the product of his honest Industry, and the fair acquisitions of his Ancestors descended to him." As for charity, it "gives every Man a Title to so much out of another's Plenty, as will keep him from extream want, where he has no means to subsist otherwise." [4] The second reference to justice (§ 165) simply says that the Levite, in the last three chapters of Judges, "appeals to the people for justice."

In the *Second Treatise,* references to justice—and, of course, injustice—are frequent, even though, as has been noted, there is no extended thematic treatment of it. An analysis of all the usages and contexts where the terms "justice" and "injustice" occur produces the following observations. First, there is only one further instance of the juxtaposition of justice and charity. This occurs in the chapter on the state of nature (§ 5), where Locke says that the "judicious" Hooker "derives the great Maxims of Justice and Charity" from the "Equality of Man by Nature." Second, there are several interrelated categories of reference for the term. One is the concept of justice as the execution of the law of nature, i.e., the putting into practice of the individual's indefeasible right to punish transgressors or to exact reparations. Parallel to this is the derivative governmental power to execute the laws of the civil society. In each of these cases, the emphasis is exclusively on punitive and restrictive actions; the object is the protection of men's property, i.e., their life, limbs, liberty, and possessions. A second category is that of "just property"

[4] Here and elsewhere direct quotations from the *Treatises* are from Laslett's edition.

(§ 46). A third is a "just precedency" given to certain men by "Age or Virtue" or in other ways. A fourth is the "justice" of parting with one's natural liberty in order to enter civil society; this even includes the justice of being punished by death for disobeying the orders of an army officer. The fifth category is the "justice of government," which is really an extension of the first category. The government's internal policy is to be guided by the rule *salus populi suprema lex,* which is "certainly so just and fundamental a Rule, that he, who sincerely follows it, cannot dangerously err" (§ 158). Its external policy is to be guided by the distinction of a just from an unjust war. The application of this rule with respect to men and possessions produces, in Chapter 16, the most frequent usage in the whole of the *Treatises* of the terms "just" and "unjust." Finally, there is the category of a "just" appeal to fundamental rights against a foreign, usurped, or tyrannical government.

A Letter Concerning Toleration. Locke here sets out to "distinguish exactly the business of civil government from that of religion, and to settle the *just* bounds that lie between the one and the other." [5] This distinction is nowhere in the *Treatises* made explicit; in that respect, the *Letter* goes well beyond the political treatise. But, on the other hand, the argument concerning civil government in the *Letter* is, though perfectly consistent with the argument of the *Treatises,* very much truncated. In that respect, the *Letter* does not go nearly so far as the *Treatises.*

As for the distinction, then, between civil government and religion: civil government is established by men "*only* for the procuring, preserving, and advancing their own civil interests," by which are meant "life, liberty, health, and indolency of body; and the possession of outward things, such as money, lands, houses, furniture, and the like." The magistrate's primary duty is to "secure unto all the people in general, and to every one of his subjects in particular, the *just* possession of these things belonging to this life." To carry out this duty effectively, the magistrate has exclusive direction of the "force and strength of all his subjects"; he who presumes to "violate the laws of public justice and equity," which are established only for the preservation of

[5] *A Letter Concerning Toleration,* ed. Patrick Romanell, p. 17. My italics.

men's "civil interests," may be "checked by the fear of punishment consisting of the deprivation or diminution of those civil interests or goods which otherwise he might and ought to enjoy." [6]

Religious society, in contrast to civil government, has as its end only the "public worship of God and, by means thereof, the acquisition of eternal life." Or, stated negatively, religious society has no power whatever over "the possession of civil and worldly goods" and no use whatever of force, which belongs "wholly to the civil magistrate." [7] But the reverse of this negative proposition is also true: civil government has no power whatever to extend its concerns or actions to the "salvation of souls." [8]

II

An analysis of the nature and context of all these treatments of justice reveals, it seems to me, an interesting and significant set of connections; those interconnections indicate, I believe, the over-all nature, but not the precise details, of Locke's design for justice.

I suggest that it is desirable to begin from a series of facts concerning the *Letter on Toleration* and then to consider its relation to the other works. The *Letter* was the first work Locke published. It contains the most general argument to be found anywhere in his writings on the distinction of earthly from heavenly things. He conceives of that distinction as a matter of justice; but he does not, in that work, provide an explicit, detailed analysis of the *basis* and *content* of either earthly or divine justice. However, if we reflect on the *Letter's* argument in its relation to the arguments of the other works, what appears is this: the *Letter* establishes the fundamental framework; the other works provide the detailed arguments concerning the basis and content of civil as opposed to divine justice, the nature and end of human as opposed to divine understanding, or the scope and purpose of private as opposed to civil education. In summary, the *Letter* contains the outlines of Locke's over-all design—to defend and pro-

[6] *Loc. cit.* My italics.
[7] *Ibid.*, pp. 22–23.
[8] *Ibid.*, pp. 17–20.

mote justice by the erection, and then the inculcation in men's minds, of the distinction between earthly and heavenly things. In that respect, his actions in writing, publishing, and, in the cases of the *Essay,* the *Letter,* and *Reasonableness,* vigorously defending his works against heated attacks would seem to constitute great acts of justice in themselves.

The *Letter Concerning Toleration* is, I believe, the most passionate of Locke's writings. That passion is a reflection of the fact that, from the time when he was a student at Oxford until the end of his life, Locke was profoundly concerned with the nature, the causes, and the possible amelioration of civil and religious conflict. As a young man, he had already formulated the ideas that the calamities and injustices of this world stemmed largely from the zeal, ambition, and ignorance of political and religious figures and that civil and religious liberty were necessary to check such vices.[9] That idea becomes, in the *Letter,* the basis of the then-bold principle of a radical distinction between the two spheres, a principle justified in the final analysis by the contention that "no peace and security, no, not so much as common friendship, can ever be established amongst men so long as this opinion prevails that dominion is founded in grace and that religion is to be propagated by force of arms." [10] Once this principle had been vigorously propounded in public, it was supplemented not only by lengthy, polemical rejoinders [11] to those numerous and hostile critics who attacked it, but by those other works which elaborated its consequences.

Consider, in this context, the nature and scope of the arguments in the *Essay* and the *Treatises,* both of which quickly followed the *Letter* into the world of public argument. The idea for the *Essay* took form when Locke was about forty. It originated in difficulties which arose in discussions about the "principles of morality and revealed religion." [12] The finished work, by determining the "limits" of "human understanding," also determines the extent to which men may and ought to be concerned

[9] *Essay,* ed. A.C. Fraser, pp. xvi–xxii; Maurice Cranston, *John Locke* (1957), Chaps. 5–11.

[10] *Letter,* p. 27.

[11] See *A Second Letter Concerning Toleration, A Third Letter for Toleration,* and *Part of a Fourth Letter for Toleration.*

[12] *Essay,* p. xvii; see also Cranston, *op. cit.,* pp. 140–142.

with certain kinds of questions, e.g., questions concerning "mysteries," which can only give rise to "disputes" because such matters exceed the bounds of that understanding.

This kind of determination, by laying such great emphasis on the scope and competence (even if limited) of the specifically human understanding and by revising the traditional connection of theology and reason,[13] produces three important practical effects. First, it reinforces, by theoretical arguments, the distinction of this-worldly and other-worldly things which is the core of the argument of the *Letter Concerning Toleration*. For example, it provides the basis for placing morality on an independent human foundation while permitting belief in the doctrines of salvation. Second, it strongly directs human attention, and then human faculties and energies, to those things which are of concern in this world: the "conveniences of life," the improvement of them, and the rules of conduct by which men are to be governed in respect to them.[14] Third, it clears the way (if only gradually) for "advancing the sciences" by turning "ingenious and industrious men" from the "rubbish" produced by vain and disputatious scholastic philosophy to the exploration of the world as it is; witness the praise Locke heaps on Boyle, Sydenham, Huygens, and the "incomparable Mr. Newton." [15]

But, for all this, the *Essay* does not provide truly substantive treatments of either civil or divine justice; they are dispersed, respectively, into the *Treatises* and *The Reasonableness of Christianity*. It will be necessary, presently, to turn to a more detailed analysis of the argument of the *Treatises*. But, in the present context of establishing the connection of that work to Locke's over-all design, it is sufficient to take note of the following points. The effect of the *First Treatise* is to demolish Filmer's version of the doctrine of the divine right of kings, thereby preparing the way for Locke's positive teaching. That positive teaching, in its turn, progressively reduces the dependence of principles of civil government on religious doctrines until, in the end, civil government is revealed as being grounded only on the desires and rights

---

[13] See John W. Yolton, *John Locke and the Way of Ideas* (1956), pp. 202–208.

[14] *Essay*, p. 29, § 5.

[15] *Ibid.*, p. 14.

of men, irrespective of such doctrine.[16] The positive teaching, therefore, carries out in detail the sketch of an argument concerning civil government contained in the *Letter Concerning Toleration;* it provides a detailed statement of the organization and ends of civil government. It does this by presenting, as a foundation, that which is only presupposed in the *Letter*—a knowledge of the true, *natural* origins and limits of a right to the things of this world (life, liberty, and possessions).

By its dissociation of the rules of civil government from religious doctrine, the teaching of the *Treatises* reinforces the rigid distinction already laid down in the *Letter*. It thereby conduces to both kinds of justice, first, by making the operation of civil government largely oblivious, insofar as explicit guiding principles are concerned, of religious doctrinal quarrels and, second, by tacitly permitting religious worship insofar as it does not challenge the civil rules.[17] Civil and divine justice thus come to occupy separate spheres, and the powerful reinforcement of that separation produced by the justification of men's coming rightfully to have "property" simply by reason of *natural* causes is a topic which deserves our attention presently.

Before turning to that, however, we must complete our analysis of the relation of the various works to the thesis of the *Letter Concerning Toleration* by briefly reconsidering the place of *The Reasonableness of Christianity* and *Thoughts on Education. The Reasonableness of Christianity* is the counterpart in the sphere of divine justice to the *Treatises* in the sphere of civil justice. It presents an interpretation of Christian doctrine explicitly intended to supply the chief principle by which men may expect, if they but believe that principle, to secure the salvation of their souls. But divine justice, as interpreted by Locke, is as exclusive of civil justice as civil justice is of divine. It is not only treated in a separate work, but is also separated by the fact that nowhere in either work does Locke refer to the desirability, let alone the

[16] I have argued this point at length elsewhere; I here simply summarize the conclusion of that argument. See *Locke on War and Peace* (1960), Chap. 2.

[17] It is to be noted, in this connection, that Locke nowhere in the *Treatises* explicitly refers to a "right to worship" or to "liberty of conscience" as being "every man's *natural* right," as he does in the *Letter*, p. 52. (My italics.) The *Treatises* thus seem to presuppose the first part of Locke's design.

necessity, of requiring the civil magistrate to enforce the belief even in that one article—Jesus is the Messiah. Thus, *The Reasonableness of Christianity* carries out the principle of the *Letter* that the soul's salvation is in the care of the person concerned. But it does so by a detailed argument for a narrowing of concern which is exactly parallel to the detailed argument for a narrowing of concern in the positive teaching of the *Treatises.* In the former work, the doctrines which it is *necessary* to believe are reduced to one. In the latter, the principles *necessary* to guide a properly ordered government are reduced to those which treat only of men's rights to the things of this world—their properties.

Indeed, as consideration of the *Thoughts on Education* in relation to the *Treatises* now reveals, the care of the soul almost disappears as such from the realm of civil government. In the *Second Treatise,* Locke maintains that parental power is only for the purpose of preserving, nourishing, and educating children until they come of age (§ 56). But this reference to education is nowhere in the *Treatise* expanded into a statement concerning the content of education, beyond the fact that it is to be directed to delivering children up to the freedom they possess by natural right. What is even more crucial, the government is nowhere said to have any concern with, let alone any right to be in charge of, the education of the young in matters which go beyond the stating of the ends of government. On the contrary, by its restriction to such powers as are contained in the original transfer of natural powers, the civil power "can have no other *end or measure,* when in the hands of the Magistrate, but to preserve the Members of that Society in their Lives, Liberties and Possessions" (II, § 171). It follows that a direct governmental concern for the virtues, moral and intellectual, characteristic of the schemes of good government propounded by Plato or Aristotle, is as rigorously excluded as is a concern for salvation of the soul. The concern for the virtues, in the classical sense of them, is thus transferred exclusively to the parents; the discussion of the inculcation of such virtues as men seem to Locke capable of is transferred to the *Thoughts Concerning Education.*

But that discussion—as distinguished, for example, from the elaborate analysis of the *nature* of the virtues in Aristotle's *Ethics* —is eminently practical and popular. Thus, when Locke categorizes the four aspects of a gentleman's education, he also indicates how close he stays to popular and therefore accepted meanings (§ 134):

> That which every Gentleman (that takes any care of his education) desires for his son, besides the estate he leaves him, is contained (I suppose) in these four things, virtue, wisdom, breeding and learning. I will not trouble myself whether these names do not some of them sometimes stand for the same thing, or really include one another. It serves my turn here to follow the popular use of these words; which, I presume, is clear enough to make me understood. . . .

Virtue itself, following this, is indeed spoken of in popular terms; it is said to consist of having a "true notion of God" and a "love and reverence of this Supreme Being," speaking the truth, and being "good-natured to others," since injustice generally springs from "too great love of ourselves, and too little of others" (§ 139). Knowledge of such virtue is to be obtained, first, from long practice directed by parents and teachers and only secondly from "discourses of morality." The discourses Locke recommends for this purpose are the Bible, Cicero's *De officiis,* and Pufendorf's *De officio hominis et civis.* . . . These are to be followed by either Grotius' *De jure belli et pacis* or Pufendorf's *De jure naturae et gentium.* . . . It is from these last two, says Locke, that the young gentleman will be "instructed in the natural rights of men, and the original and foundations of society, and the duties resulting from thence" (§ 186).[18]

To sum up: each work plays a part in the elaboration and inculcation of Locke's original thesis that no peace, security, or friendship—and certainly, therefore, no justice—can be established among men unless they know and respect the clear and rigid distinction between the things of this world and the things of the world to come. Conversely, the over-all effect which he seems to seek to achieve in his whole corpus is to lend support to justice by reducing concern for the other world and by encouraging and justifying concern for this world. He does this in three ways.

First, in all the works he presupposes, explicitly refers to, or

[18] It is fascinating to note that, in this context, where one might expect Locke to refer to his own *Treatises,* he is (modestly?) silent.

elaborately justifies the right to those things of this world which most men are willing to defend even by violence. He thereby encourages and justifies activity in support of the protection and acquisition of such things. Second, even though it is also true that he justifies a concern for the salvation of the soul, it is clear that the activity in support of that goal is to be excluded from the concern of civil society; that any religious practice repugnant to the principles of civil society is to be forbidden; and that the only civil principles to be positively inculcated by the magistrate are those which support the right to things of this world. Given the fact that men's desires impel them from the beginning to seek such things, the effect is to cause human concerns to converge on them. Finally, he encourages and justifies the direction of the human understanding toward the investigation of things both useful and profitable. This supports the general human inclination to be concerned with things of this world, and it directs those graced with theoretical inclinations away from vain and troublesome disputations about things of the other world (which may and often do culminate in bloody civil broils) toward matters which satisfy the inquisitive faculty and yet may contribute to the improvement of men's earthly condition.

III

Justice as the protection and encouragement of the right to the things of this world receives its most conclusive treatment in the *Two Treatises of Government,* for it is only in that work that Locke traces the right to property to its foundations by showing that it depends on nature, prior to and independently of civil society. The significance of such a foundation is that it insulates the right which is the basis of justice from the encroachments of either theological principle or civil convention. I will now illustrate this point by reference to certain aspects of the argument in the *Treatises.*

Let us start once again from the difficulty which arises, according to Locke, because of the confusion of earthly with heavenly things. The removal of that confusion depends most of all on the clear demarcation of the sphere of government from the sphere of religion. But it also depends, as we shall now see, on the institutionalization of the right to property in such a way as to make nature, not theological teachings, the guide to action. In the *Letter Concerning Toleration,* Locke had laid down the principle that "no private person has any right in any matter to prejudice another person in his civil enjoyments because he is of another church or religion." This principle is then supplemented, however, by the proposition that "we must not content ourselves with the narrow measures of *bare justice;* charity, bounty, and liberality must be added to it. This the Gospel enjoins, this reason directs, and that natural fellowship we are born into requires of us." [19]

Here, charity has the broad connotation of a duty to act in a Christian manner even toward those of another religion when it is a question of respecting their right to freedom of conscience. But it is striking that, in this context, Locke calls the honoring of "civil enjoyments"—by which, it will be recalled, is meant life, liberty, and possessions—the rules of *bare* justice. The significance of that restriction may now be more fully appreciated by considering the way in which Locke treats justice and charity in the *Treatises,* which is to say, in the context where justice is most comprehensively shown to depend upon the *natural* right to private property.

It will be recalled that Locke juxtaposes and briefly defines justice and charity in the *First Treatise.* In that context, it appears that charity is as much a right of those who are in need as justice is of those who possess. But, in the *Second Treatise,* the only further reference to charity is in the context of the statement that Hooker—but, note, not necessarily Locke—derives the "great maxims of justice and charity" from the "equality of men by nature" (§ 5).[20] When Locke finally comes to the thematic treatment of property in the *Second Treatise,* the emphasis ultimately is on the right to property and on the unequal right to possessions on the parts of those who are "industrious" and "rational" (§ 34). This positive statement, taken with the strictures against those who are "covetous" and the deep silence concerning charity, indicate the drift of the whole argument; it is away from a reliance

[19] *Letter,* p. 24. My italics.

[20] The maxims Hooker refers to are in the *Laws of Ecclesiastical Polity,* I. viii. 7. For a discussion of Locke's use of Hooker, see *Locke on War and Peace, op. cit.,* pp. 45–63.

on, and even away from a right to, charity and toward a reliance on human industry. We shall presently see the natural foundation of that transition when we consider the argument concerning the natural right of industriousness.

A second illustration of the movement, in Locke's design, toward a natural foundation for justice is the important place occupied by the notion of the state of nature in the *Treatises.* It is useful here, once again, to compare the *Treatises* to the *Letter.* In the *Letter,* Locke repeatedly speaks of men's right to their civil interests as well as a right to liberty of conscience. But, even though he occasionally refers to these rights as "natural," it remains in doubt what is meant by that term, how such a right is to be distinguished from a right of social origin, and why it is so important for the right to be understood as being natural. In the *Treatises,* however, these doubts are removed by the introduction of a thematic discussion of the state of nature, which is the state in which men first possess those rights which civil government is intended to protect.

The significance of this addition seems to me to be this: Locke's original thesis is that justice is imperiled by the confusion of civil and religious interests. Once having made this broad distinction, however, the problem remains whether justice may not be equally imperiled by a confusion of private rights and social rights. If, for example, it is thought that the right to material goods depends on the existence of government or that the amount of goods one may justly possess depends on principles established by government, it is then problematic whether the rights in question may truly be maintained against government. The effect of Locke's turning to the state of nature to establish natural rights is to render the question nonproblematic, at least in principle, by showing that the rights derive from natural necessity, independently of government.

A third illustration of Locke's conception is the rejection of the notion of a government of virtuous men in favor of a government bound by clear and simple rules concerning natural rights of property. The first alternative is referred to in several places in the *Treatises.* In one place, Locke goes so far as to speak of "goodness" and "virtue" as a kind of "natural authority" (II, § 94). In another place, he says that, where a man finds a "good and wise Ruler, he may not perhaps think it either necessary, or useful to set precise Bounds to his Power in all things" (§ 164). But the rule of good and wise men is highly problematic so far as its actualization and continuance are concerned. Even assuming that such men can be found and can then be persuaded to rule, the likelihood of always finding such men appears exceedingly remote. Furthermore, when good and wise rulers are succeeded by men of much less virtue, it is likely, in Locke's judgment, that the rights of the people will be in danger because there will then be neither conscious concern for nor effective institutional means to safeguard those rights (§§ 94, 159–168).

Finally, and more crucial than either of these points, Locke's argument rests on the premise that men are not free by *nature* to relinquish the care of their own preservation; nature impels each man, through the desires, to seek that which is the condition for the enjoyment of every other right. It is this principle which is ultimately the justification for his contention that nature does not subordinate or subject any man to another. But, since the guarantee of that first and most fundamental right is a natural function of the freedom to protect oneself as well as to secure and use the material goods necessary to that end, it follows that the protection of these natural rights must be the main object of government. The practical conclusion is that nature dictates that the governors be bound by clear and simple rules, for justice then depends, not on the chance appearance and rule of good and wise men, but on the constant operation of institutions which reflect the constant, natural operation of the necessity for property.

The preceding illustrations refer primarily to a natural and *equal* right to the things of this world as the foundation of earthly justice. But justice also includes, as Locke plainly argues, the right to possess the things of this world in *unequal* amounts (II, §§ 46–51). How he can ground both these rights in nature and therefore independently of government may be seen now from a more detailed analysis of the argument for private possessions.

The starting point is the irreducible fact of the natural distinctness of the human body. A man's body is his first right, as it is his first concern, because the operations of nature supply that body to him and to no one else (II, § 27). Nature also supplies the desires by which the body is guided to its preservation and well-being and the methods by which those desires may be carried out (I, §§ 39, 56, 86, 88). For example, over and above the necessity of physical protection against injury or destruction, the body constantly and naturally requires nourishment. Nature supplies the desire for and the physical processes by which nourishment takes place. But nourishment requires the ingestion and digestion of food, i.e., of substances distinct from the body. The action of making such substances part of the body is necessarily strictly private, just as the body itself is necessarily private (II, § 26). By making one and private that which is originally separate and common, a "possession" has been established. Yet it is simple, natural necessity which causes that to happen. Hence, it is simple, natural necessity which is the original basis of a right to the private possession of things other than the body (II, § 35).

The great difficulty, then, is this: each man must necessarily appropriate specific things; yet nature does not directly and unambiguously supply specific things in specific amounts to specific men in the same way that it supplies the body and the desires. However, a preliminary guide to allocation is the form of the primitive means and needs of men. The primitive means are the natural actions of the body, or labor. These being really but an extension of the body, they must belong to it. The primitive needs are the minimal amounts of things necessary to be "used" for bare subsistence. These needs being satisfied by relatively small amounts of things, that which belongs to a man is bound to be very meager.

This analysis of the problem yields the conclusion that natural justice requires all men to live always at the level of bare subsistence, achieved by repeated individual acts of appropriation of small amounts of every specific thing they need. Locke reaches this provisional conclusion only to reject it almost immediately by discovering a more complex and adequate basis for natural justice. What he does, in effect, is to argue from a beginning in an individual economy of bare subsistence to an end in a trade economy of plenty. The passage from the one to the other takes place always with respect to what natural justice requires, but depends also on what men may legitimately do to alter and improve their merely natural condition. Let us see how this takes place.

Consider, first, the argument concerning the desires. The first and strongest desire, as Locke explicitly says, is to be preserved (I, § 88). The second is to be nourished. But, over and above these desires, men possess the potentiality of desiring more than is barely needed (II, § 37). Whether that desire, as such, is just or unjust is never explicitly discussed. Instead, a judgment on it appears to depend on its effect in satisfying the *general* human need for useful things, as we shall see presently when we put it together with other parts of the argument.

Consider, second, the amount of labor a man may naturally expend. This has two aspects. First, he may naturally be capable, physically and mentally, of amassing many more material goods than are necessary for his bare subsistence. But, second, he may not naturally, by right, amass any more than will leave as much and as good in common for others nor any more than he can "use" before it "spoils."

On the other hand, labor is—as Locke never tires of saying—the real foundation of property and of value because it transforms the almost worthless things of unaided nature into things truly useful to men. The difficulty in a true subsistence, or natural, economy is then this: the actual expenditure of labor, and therefore the creation of value, is likely to remain far below the potentially available expenditure as long as the original, or natural, restrictions on the amassing of goods prevail. Yet it is precisely the creation of useful things which most effectively conduces to the satisfaction of man's basic desires and therefore to the realization of natural justice.

Locke's resolution of this difficulty and his justification of a trade economy of plenty depends on the making of certain distinctions which are still rooted in nature, but which go beyond the original natural restrictions on appropriation. First is the distinction of what is meant by the "use" of a thing. Second is the distinction of what constitutes "spoilage." In both cases, Locke—significantly, in view of the great importance of the right to nourishment—chooses examples which pertain to food. The initial meaning of the "use" of a thing is its consumption.

But Locke eventually adds that "use" may also mean "giving" perishable things to others, "bartering" for other but less perishable things, and "exchanging" for exceedingly durable things (II, § 46). In each case, of course, the transaction depends on consent, i.e., the mutual willingness of the transactors to *value* what the other has. The willingness to so value a thing is a reflection of a judgment that at some point in the process a certain equivalent amount of labor has been or may be obtained. The consequence is that the use of a thing in trade is as much justified as is its use in consumption, provided only that the traders let nothing spoil in their possession.

This side of the difficulty is then resolved by a natural distinction concerning spoilage. Some things, such as plums, will naturally last perhaps no more than a week. Other things, such as nuts, will naturally last perhaps a year. But still other things, such as gold and silver, will naturally last practically indefinitely. Once again, in each case, the transaction in the exchange of such things depends on consent. But, so long as that is given, the use of a thing to obtain durable goods in no way violates nature's intention, which is that nothing perish needlessly while in the possession of a man.

This conclusion provides the answer to two closely related questions already raised—whether men may justly desire more than is needed and whether they may justly expend more labor than is strictly necessary to amass the goods of bare subsistence. The answer is, in effect, that not only may they do so, but that in so doing they contribute to the good of mankind by increasing the general stock of goods which all men must have. Natural industriousness, impelled by the desire to have more than is needed, thus comes into its own as the driving force of the whole system. Justice no longer depends on the equal allocation of goods by individual labor, but on the general tendency of the system, through the division of labor, to utilize the unequal endowment of men by nature for the simultaneous benefit of those so endowed and the society at large. In a sense, this is the Lockeian replacement for the classical conception that unequal endowment in virtue is the natural principle of rule. But, precisely because the classical principle is of doubtful practical application, justice is of doubtful certainty. Conversely, since Locke's principle of the natural right of industriousness is more practical because less demanding, justice is more certain.

IV

A harsh critic of Locke's *Letter Concerning Toleration* said:

> It seems hard to conceive how the author of that letter should think to do any service to religion in general, or to the Christian religion, by recommending and persuading such a toleration. For how much soever it may tend to the advancement of trade and commerce, (which some seem to place above all other considerations) I see no reason, from any experiment that has been made, to expect that true religion would be a gainer by it; that it would be either the better preserved, the more widely propagated, or rendered any whit the more fruitful in the lives of its possessors by it.[21]

Locke returned barb for barb when he replied: ". . . if you do not know the author of the *Letter* places the advancement of trade above religion, your insinuation is very uncharitable."

It is not necessary for our purpose to decide whether that insinuation was indeed uncharitable. It is sufficient to note that Locke's argument for trade, which is based on the civil power's protection of the natural right of industriousness, is intended, as is the argument for tolerance, to conduce to the "preservation of all mankind." Trade supplements tolerance by providing a natural justification for the right to possess and a natural inducement to the production of the things of this world. It therefore tends to infuse private religious and moral principles with the quality of those publicly sanctioned practices which are the main care of civil government. Religion, politics, and morality being "regulated" by their "true principle," justice is served. Locke's design is as complete as a single man could make it.

[21] Quoted by Locke at the beginning of *A Second Letter Concerning Toleration, Works,* II, 259.

13

JUSTICE IN LOCKE'S PHILOSOPHY

RAYMOND POLIN

With modesty, with moderation, but with a firmness and steadfastness which, since it lasted for more than forty years, might justifiably be termed stubbornness, Locke devoted his life and work to the elaboration and defense of a just order among men. It could perhaps be said, and rightly, that the word "justice" rarely flowed from his pen. It is for this reason that certain readers who are more concerned with words than ideas have accused Locke's philosophy of lacking coherence. In Locke's eyes, the idea of justice, that is to say, the idea of a good and rational order, constituted the center of reference around which his metaphysical conception of the world, his theory of man, and his moral and political doctrines are coherently organized.[1]

[1] I shall permit myself to refer, once for all, to my recent book *La Politique morale de John Locke* (1960), where the interpretation of Locke's thought from which this article arises is put forth and defended. Chapter II, "L'Attitude morale de Locke," will be referred to in particular, as will Chapter VII, "De la justice dans la propriété, la distribution et l'échange des biens."

beings, as creatures endowed with understanding and reason which are clear in us constitute the foundation of this order and the principles of a demonstrative science of morality.[9]

To be sure, moral ideas are complex and subject to confusion to a much greater degree than are mathematical ideas. "The mind cannot easily retain those precise combinations of ideas so exactly and perfectly as is necessary in the examination of the habitudes and correspondences"[10] which compose them. We must apply ourselves, therefore, to the search for moral truths with the same method and the same detachment that we put into the search for mathematical truths. Thus should we be able to deduce evident propositions by necessary consequences, "the true measures of the just and injust."

If one were to read the text of Book IV of the *Essay concerning Human Understanding,* he would no longer consider raising the cry of incoherence or opposing the *Essay* of 1690 to the *Treatise of Civil Government* (also 1690) or to the *Essays on the Law of Nature* of 1664; he would not seek to put the rationalist critique of moral and political doctrines into question and oppose it to an empiricism which has been grossly oversimplified by a drowsy tradition which is little concerned with returning to the texts and a coherent interpretation of them. Actually, the law of nature, that is to say, the law of justice, is presented as early as 1664 as one of those ideas which is clear, but limited to the sphere of the practical, in which the idea of man and the idea of justice appear in their necessary relations to each other and as the model according to which the conduct of man can be regulated and his meaning comprehended.

The law of nature represents, in effect, for Locke, the principle and the foundation of justice and of all just order. A curious *lapsus calami,* which he may have copied from Grotius, shows this very symbolically. Citing Cicero in the eighth of the *Essays on the Law of Nature,* at the place where Cicero had written that, if Carneades was to be believed, *"nullam esse justitiam,"* Locke writes, *"nullam esse legem naturae."*[11] This indicates the

---

[9] *Essay.* IV. iii. § 18.

[10] *Essay.* IV. iii. §§ 19–20.

[11] *Essays on the Law of Nature,* ed. W. von Leyden (1954), VIII. 204, folio 105.

degree to which these two notions were interchangeable in Locke's mind. In the fifth *Essay,* he can, in effect, define justice: "justitia, eximis illa lex naturae et omnis societatis vinculum." [12]

NATURAL JUSTICE AND THE LAW OF NATURE

Let us not insist any longer on the way in which the idea of justice is known as the law of nature. Let us seek above all what it signifies, what its essential necessary structure is, or, as Locke says, what its real essence is.

The law of nature is the law of human nature, the expression in the form of law of an order which is essential to man and which he is under an obligation to bring about and maintain. The nature of man is not an empirical datum; it is an obligation. That is why it is expressed in the form of a law, a duty. Man is a datum of experience only in his capacities and faculties, that is, as a corporeal being capable of freedom and reason. His function is to exercise and develop his capacities in conformity to the law of his nature. The law of nature addresses itself, above all, to a being whose basic characteristic is freedom: ". . . we must consider what State all men are naturally in, and that is, a *State of perfect Freedom";* [13] it is with this statement that the *Second Treatise of Civil Government* begins. What is peculiar to man as a being capable of freedom is that he has as a function and an obligation the realization of his nature in conformity to the law of nature, "within the bounds of the Law of Nature," [14] that he always remains free to disavow and transgress. The nature of man is to act according to the law and through freedom. Our nature is given to us only by this law; to achieve our nature is to be just. Man's nature and justice are inseparable; the nature of man is to make himself just. Justice is the law of nature obeyed and the nature of man effectively realized in conformity to law.

But man is capable of achieving his nature according to a law of obligation (and not through the mechanical play of natural

---

[12] *Essays on the Law of Nature.* V. 168, folio 70.

[13] *Treatise of Civil Government, Locke's Two Treatises of Government,* ed. Laslett (1960), II. ii. § 4.

[14] *Loc. cit.*

determinations) only because he is "capable of law," [15] which presupposes that he is capable of reason. The law in its true significance is addressed to an agent who is free and intelligent, and it directs him in conformity to the true significance of his nature.

Reason, for Locke, is at once the existence in reality of an intelligible order among things; the discovery and interpretation of these facts and their significance by a reason which is none other than the capacity to explain and know this rational order; and the demonstration of the existence of a divine legislator who is perfectly wise and good, that is to say, perfectly rational. This amounts to saying that, for Locke, reason is essentially order among the realities of nature, a corresponding essential order among ideas, and an order willed by a rational God. It is also man's capacity to comprehend that order; to discover the meaning of it and the law; and to realize it, to conserve it, and to defend it among men.[16]

The law of nature is the law of reason, is reason itself.[17] It is the law of the order of nature which is such that, if the facts are adequately interpreted and the ideas are adequately reflected upon, they permit man to discover nature, since he is capable of reason. It is the reason within the facts, their order, the reason for the facts, and at the same time the natural revelation of that order in its divine and rational significance that the method of reason brings to light and demonstrates.

In the first place, the law of nature, the law of justice, teaches man to contemplate and understand in order that he may have reverence for the works of God, insofar as these works relate to him. In doing this, it commands each man to comprehend the law on its own grounds and recognize that neither moral and political life nor justice are possible for one who does not know that God exists. Locke's tolerance would never extend to atheists, who, in denying the basis of the law of nature, exclude themselves from all political society, and from all justice.[18]

In the second place, the law of nature commands man to preserve his person with all its essential attributes, since, ac-

---

[15] *Treatise.* II. vi. § 57.

[16] Cf. my *Politique morale de Locke, op. cit.,* pp. 116–118.

[17] *Treatise.* II. ii. § 6; vi. § 57.

[18] *Epistola de Tolerantia* (1961), pp. 18, 78.

cording to a formula that Locke revives time and time again, it is concerned with his life, his health, the integrity of his body, and his liberty or goods. All these goods are inseparable, and the human person can be discerned as well on the level of the freedoms which are essential to it as on the level of goods of which the person is owner. The terms of each description correspond to each other, or, better, they are equivalent.

It could be asked whether, for Locke, there are two sources of the right of gaining property and whether these two sources are even consistent. On the one hand, Locke agrees with the tradition that God has given the earth to all men in common.[19] On the other hand, each is owner of his person, his life, his health, and his goods—in virtue of the law of nature. But both principles are the expression of the will of God and of his rational will, since the mere idea of a just order implies that it has a meaning for man and that it has been made for him. The gift of the earth to all men in common defines this relation of natural agreement between the world and man and corresponds, at the same time, to the natural equality of men among themselves and to their equal freedom in the use of their possessions.

It is necessary to simply distinguish—moreover without incoherence or contradiction—between what men possess immediately (their persons, their bodies, their freedom, their ability to work) and that of which they acquire a just ownership by the mediation of their labors. It is known how, God having given the earth to all men in common, man acquires a right of ownership over all that property to which he joins what is naturally intrinsic to him, that is to say, "the *Labour* of his Body, and the *Work* of his Hands." [20] That is why men become proprietors of their works and even those things in nature to which they apply their labors and, above all, the land that they cultivate. Because the ability to work is intrinsic to the worker, no one may justly take possession of the goods with which he has been involved save the worker himself. They become the exclusive property of the worker. They cease to be the common goods of all men. The justification of the right to obtain and possess goods is derived directly from the law of nature. It expresses for every man the right

---

[19] *Treatise*. II. v. § 26.
[20] *Treatise*. II. v. § 27.

as well as the obligation to possess things not only in order to get along well but simply to exist.

But it is also the law of nature which limits the right of property to those things which a man can obtain by his own labors without spoiling, squandering, or destroying them to the detriment of others. All that to which his labors cannot be applied "is more than his share, and belongs to others." [21] The limits of just ownership are not fixed by considerations of size, but by considerations of the owner's ability to prevent the accumulated goods which compose the property from being wasted or destroyed to the detriment of others. This is at least what happens in the condition of abundance in the state of nature.

It is not astonishing, therefore, that there is, for Locke, no justice where there is no property.[22] It is an example of an essential relation characteristic of moral ideas. He confirmed this repeatedly [23] and thought that children, insofar as they are not mature enough to comprehend the idea of property, are incapable of knowing the meaning of just and unjust.[24] To say that men are naturally in *"a State of perfect Freedom* to order their actions and dispose of their Possessions and Persons as they think fit, within the bounds of the Law of Nature" [25] is to say that man is by nature "Master of himself, and *Proprietor of his Person* and the Actions or *Labour* of it." [26]

Man has freedom of property, and freedom is his property. This amounts to saying that there is no other freedom than that of property; that one cannot be free if he is not a proprietor; that freedom makes sense only in relation to the use of property; and, extending this, that freedom is itself property and that the ownership of his person and freedom are sufficient to make someone a proprietor. In defining property in a sense as wide as is necessary for the application of this concept to a right, Locke draws from it the analysis of an essential structure of rights as such and is protected from all Marxist-inspired critiques, which cannot oppose him on this point without confusion.

---

[21] *Treatise.* II. v. § 31.
[22] *Essay.* IV. iii. § 18.
[23] *Essays on the Law of Nature.* VII. 212, folio 116.
[24] *Some Thoughts Concerning Education.* § 110.
[25] *Treatise.* II. ii. § 4.
[26] *Treatise.* II. v. § 44.

Where there is a question of freedoms and property involved, there is equally a question of rights, powers, or customs held to be legitimate according to nature. But it is just as much a question of obligations. The law of nature, on the basis of which the rights of the human person are defined and which is the basis of these rights, is nonetheless above all a law, that is to say, a command, a rule which binds and obligates. What is primary is obligation, the obligation to preserve, that is to say, to mature, develop, achieve, and in consequence safeguard one's person and all freedoms and properties essential to it. The obligation to obey the law of nature is the obligation to realize one's nature in one's own humanity, to achieve and realize in oneself a human order. The rights of the person are those which permit the carrying out of these obligations and those which protect his works. Justice is primarily the realization of an order which has the law of nature, that is to say, reason, as a principle. It is then the defense of the integrity of this order. The negative aspect of justice ought not to conceal, as often happens, its positive aspect. The obligations or duties come first; the rights follow.

It is seen, for example, that, if freedom is a universal right to order one's actions and to dispose of one's person and goods as one sees fit, outside all control and totally independent of the will of any other man, then it is primarily an obligation to use one's freedom for the realization of one's nature as a man, in conformity to the law of nature. This right to freedom is primarily an obligation to free existence, an obligation to act freely according to the law. We are born free as we are born rational. Freedom is perfect in proportion to the degree to which it submits its power to the law of reason in the elaboration of a just order. This is why freedom, as well as life, is already for Locke an inalienable right. No one has the right not to use his freedom and his life. No one may legitimately renounce or alienate either of them. No one has the right to consent to renounce them. Any act contrary to these principles would be unjust. All contracts contrary to them would be null and void.

But we are touching here on a third command of the law of nature, the one which makes the natural social character of man explicit and which joins to the natural inclination which urges him toward others and to the rational consideration of the utility which he finds in living in society the obligation to live with other men in a situation of mutual aid and reciprocal agreement. As a rule of that existence in common, the law of nature imposes the natural equality of each to each, that is to say, the elementary and, since Aristotle, most traditional definition of justice. Men are by nature not only in a state of perfect freedom, but also in a state of equality which is the transformation to the concrete of that necessity of "reciprocal Power and Jurisdiction" to which nature binds us.[27]

Not only are men equal insofar as they are identical members of the same animal species—and in this sense their equality consists rather in an identity which is specific and present in virtue of their similarity—but they are equal because the law of nature, which makes them equal, free, and independent in relation to each other, makes them equal in a second way—by conferring on each of them the same power and the same right of jurisdiction, no one having as a gift of nature any more than any other. In this state of perfect equality, where no one is master, superior, or judge of any other man, each man has an equal right to accomplish all that he *can* accomplish to obey the law of nature. Without doubt, there are in fact great differences among the aptitudes and capabilities of individuals, and it is just that God has given the world "to the use of the Industrious and Rational . . . not to the Fancy or Covetousness of the Quarrelsome and Contentious." [28] "*Age* or *Virtue* may give Men a just Precedency." [29] Just inequalities in the distribution of goods will in fact follow; but, in the "first ages of the world," each man gains barely that which corresponds to his labors and to his needs. In the state of nature, natural equality does not exist any less perfectly because it is interpreted and recognized to flow from the law of nature; it is already an equality for the law, an equality of right. It is at least a moral equality.

In the state of nature, at least in that sort of state of nature that could be called theoretical, or one in principle, a natural justice reigns. Each man is invested with the obligation and the power to interpret the law of nature, to make it apply, eventually

---

[27] *Treatise*. II. ii. § 4.
[28] *Treatise*. II. v. § 34.
[29] *Treatise*. II. vi. § 54.

to defend it, and with it to defend the whole of humanity: "*every one has the Executive Power* of the Law of Nature." [30] That is why each man acquires a power over another, the power to make him respect the law of nature.[31] This implies the right to punish crimes committed against it and the right to obtain reparation.[32] In other words, the state of nature is the state in which—because each man is judge of violations of the law of nature, even of those which do not concern him—there is no superior authority who has the right to judge between men and the power to have his sentence carried out. "*Want of a common Judge with Authority puts all Men in a State of Nature.*" [33] Thus, as long as abundance prevails in these small peaceful groups or reason and virtue reign, natural justice can be exercised without difficulty.

But, as soon as vainglory, ambition, and the desire to acquire more and more possessions or to acquire them beyond the bounds of right—desires which have been sharpened by the rivalries to which penury gives birth—develop and ruin the efforts of the virtuous and rational, the conditions for the exercise of justice are profoundly transformed. As soon as a conflict or a disagreement on the interpretation of the law of nature arises, then, since each man is both judge and party to the dispute, he risks being carried away and corrupted by the weight of his own interests; he is inclined to partiality and injustice. ". . . 'Tis easily to be imagined, that he who was so unjust as to do his Brother an Injury, will scarce be so just as to condemn himself for it." [34] The exercise of all power that no rational consideration of the law of nature is any longer sufficient to hold in check falls naturally into excesses and abuses. In the absence of a common judge, "Force without Right . . . makes a State of War," into which the state of nature degenerates.[35] In that state of hostility and universal destruction where only force and violence reign, there is no longer a common law of reason, a law of nature, or a common judge. Everyone has

[30] *Treatise*. II. ii. § 13.
[31] *Treatise*. II. ii. § 8.
[32] *Treatise*. II. ii. § 11.
[33] *Treatise*. II. iii. § 19.
[34] *Treatise*. II. ii. § 13.
[35] *Treatise*. II. iii. § 19.

the right to put to death those who menace or attack him.[36] It is dubious whether the word "right" can still be used where the only remaining consideration is power. The idea of justice itself disappears.

CIVIL JUSTICE AND THE POLITICAL STATE

To escape partiality, violence, and arbitrariness and to re-establish and safeguard the security of person and property "for the Regulating and Preserving of Property" [37] is precisely to establish an order of things whose justice will be able to be universally defined and efficaciously defended and to which men take recourse in founding the political community, the civil regime. The order of justice, which concerns beings capable of reason and freedom, should not be the result of a simple mechanical game of natural determination. It is to be constantly established, maintained, and defended by force of reason and freedom. It is prescribed by the law of nature as an obligation. It is a duty: "Justice is established as a duty and will be the first and general rule of our Happiness." [38] He adds significantly: "Justice . . . being thus established, the rest will not be hard."

That which above all else characterizes the civil regime is that each of its members gives up his "Executive Power of the Law of Nature . . . to resign it to the publick," [39] that is to say, to legislative power and to the officials designated by it. Henceforth, these officials constitute a judge on earth, a judge common to all citizens who possesses the right to say what is right and the power to impose respect and to redress civil wrongs. The idea is to eliminate all private judgment and to take the community as the judge and arbiter: "The Community comes to be Umpire." [40] In effect, only the community as such, as legislative power—whose proper object is the general interest and the common good and which has no common measure, no parity of any sort with the citizens, who are all equal with respect to it—con-

[36] *Treatise.* II. iii. § 20.
[37] *Treatise.* II. i. § 3.
[38] Mss., Bodleian Library, Oxford, C 28, f141.
[39] *Treatise.* II. vii. § 89.
[40] *Treatise.* II. vii. § 87.

stitutes an impartial and disinterested judge, a judge who is consequently rational and just.

This impartial arbiter does not content himself with being the interpreter of the law of nature, though the law of reason continues to be the basis of all his decisions. The main characteristic of political power is, in effect, the "Right of Making Laws . . . for the Regulating and Preserving of Property" [41]—property, that is, in the sense of the freedom, the life, and the possessions of all those who comprise the community. This is a significant indication that the public power to which the powers of individuals entering the community are transferred is legislative power. The civil regime is thus the power to govern according to *"establish'd,* settled, known *Law,* received and allowed by common consent to be the standard of Right and Wrong." [42]

Although the law of nature is evident and intelligible to all rational beings, men, blinded by their interests as well as by their ignorance, may not be able to see that it is binding on them in any particular case. Consequently, it is necessary (and all the more if it is not written) that it be interpreted and applied to particular circumstances of time and place in terms as explicit and as little subject to criticism as possible under the form of the *"establish'd,* settled, known *Law"* [43] of which Locke speaks. Because of these laws, the common judge finds in practice that his task is regulated and facilitated. The existence of laws tends to eliminate arbitrariness—"the extemporary arbitrary decrees" —and irrationality. On the other hand (and Locke here takes his place between Aristotle and Rousseau, Kant or Hegel), these laws, which are common laws and which are the objects of a common consent, ought to be, in consequence of the obligation exercised by the law of nature which is their basis, the explication of the law of reason, the expression of reason itself, for justice is always rational. But Locke is not deceiving himself about this. The two principles which characterize that justice which the legislative power—that is to say, the supreme power in the state—is obliged to dispense in the civil order, since it received authority to do so,

---

[41] *Treatise.* II. i. § 3.
[42] *Treatise.* II. ix. § 124.
[43] *Loc. cit.*

are the existence of "promulgated standing laws" and the existence of "known authorized judges." [44]

The use of general laws and the presence of judges made impartial by their very position guarantees all citizens the civil and juridical equality which is the necessary form of justice in the state; each citizen has rights identical to those of all others insofar as he is a citizen, insofar as he is a proprietor. That this equality becomes law is sufficient to ensure the protection and maintenance of rights and property. It is certain that an equality of right, an equality which is abstract and formal, exists. This is to say that it is reconciled with a *de facto* inequality which is no longer limited, as in the state of nature, by the force of natural conditions. The *de facto* inequality is, on the contrary, multiplied, on the one hand, by the capacity gained by each person to occupy himself in acquiring things and his skill, which has become more effective in maintaining the possessions in a good state, and, on the other hand, by the invention of money, which constitutes a medium of unlimited accumulation. Since the value of money is an artificial convention to which men have consented, they have consented at the same time to "the disproportionate and unequal possession of the Earth" which the existence of money provokes.[45] There is no need of any contract; the consent is implied in the use of money.

This legitimate inequality may go quite far. It justifies enormous riches as well as great poverty, so long as it is a matter of inequality between proprietors, no matter how clear it may be that they are reduced exclusively to possession of their ability to work. At the limit, Locke would not hesitate to exclude from a proper human condition the "idle poor," the "idle beggars," the poor who owe their misery to their laziness and their vices and who are revealed by this to be degenerate beings. They are excluded from the human species by their irrationality and lack of sociability.

Inequality has no limits in the name of justice. In effect, it is justice which makes each man proprietor of the land that he can cultivate by his labors or of the goods that his labors produce.

---

[44] *Treatise.* II. xi. § 136.
[45] *Treatise.* II. v. § 50.

It is just that he can make the good results of his labors bear fruit or that he inherits the good results of the labors of his ancestors. But inequality has limits in the name of charity.[46] God has never left a single man at the mercy of other men, which would be tantamount to the right to let a man die of hunger at the pleasure of someone who might well be living in abundance. Charity gives each man a claim on that which other men have in superfluity, if there is no other way to survive except by sharing this superfluity. This is not a right which derives from justice. It is uniquely a claim to charity, to the duty of loving every man.

This view was made famous by Hooker, who tied it to the native equality of human creatures.[47] It is, however, charity which comes first, according to the original Latin text of the *Letter on Toleration* (and in spite of the contrary sense of the English translation): "The rule of justice ought to be added to the duties of benevolence and charity." [48] The Gospel commands it to us; reason recommends it to us. The love of neighbors which is present in us as creatures and the reason which is present in us as men recommend the duty of charity. It cannot oblige us, because charity is in the realm of faith. One believes in God because one is rational; this is the epistemological order of things. But one is rational because there is a God; this is the order of being, which is ontologically primary.

The direct appeal to the word of God and to the duty of charity preached by the Gospel does not come into conflict with the commands of the law of nature. All men being equal by nature and equally called upon to preserve their being by means of mutual aid which reason teaches them, it is reasonable that the richest share the surplus of their possessions with the poorer. This is simultaneously useful for the poor and prudent for the rich. The appeal to the love of one's neighbor derives from the condition of surplus. It serves as part of the basis of the rational achievement of the law of nature. It will even occur to Locke to see in it one of the sources of justice.[49]

Nonetheless, the account of these two sources of justification

---

[46] *Treatise*. II. v. §§ 41–43.
[47] *Treatise*. II. v. § 50.
[48] *Epistola de Tolerantia, op. cit.*, p. 24.
[49] *Treatise*. II. ii. § 5.

and the recourse to the second show clearly the important and delicate character of the problem posed. As strongly as Locke justifies the appropriation of possessions, he still imposes limits on the rights to property in the civil state, since the accumulation of possessions runs the risk of not having any limits intrinsic to it. He admits that the use of the right to property ought to be regulated; it is precisely for this essential goal that the exercise of political power is proposed.[50]

This is the function of laws and positive constitutions.[51] They have, in particular, the function of defining the methods of buying and selling goods, the methods of inheritance, and the methods of donation.[52] There is, however, room to take that declaration for what it is and to interpret it in the spirit of moderation which characterizes Locke's rational philosophy. It would be just as wrong to forget that he has considered this regulation and limitation legitimate as it would be to take the text as bringing to light a self-styled anti-individualistic and quasitotalitarian aspect of his doctrine.[53]

Thus, the direct appeal to God, which does not proceed by the intermediary of reason and the law of nature, "the common Rule and Measure, God hath given to Mankind," [54] is deferred as long as possible, whether this be until the laws are silent and the judge lacks this "common Rule and Measure" or until the nature of things excludes the presence of a judge. This is precisely what happens when a dispute arises in the state and puts into question the interpretation of "trusteeship" which links the government and the people. Locke does not hesitate to proclaim that it is just in certain cases for the people to resist their monarch and recover their freedom.[55] If it is a matter of a "breach of trust," of a breach of contract which brings into account some isolated individuals, then, although they always have the right to judge by themselves, although they can never be hindered in their despair

[50] *Treatise*. II. i. § 3.

[51] *Treatise*. II. v. § 50.

[52] *Treatise*. II. viii. § 120.

[53] Every systematically antiliberal, authoritarian, indeed, totalitarian interpretation of Locke goes contrary to the spirit and moreover to the letter of his work. Cf., or do not cf., Willmoore Kendall, *John Locke and the Doctrine of Majority Rule* (1960).

[54] *Treatise*. II. ii. § 11.

[55] *Treatise*. II. xvi. § 176.

from defending themselves against the abuse of power which strikes them, Locke does not counsel them to engage in an unequal struggle, for they would be assured of losing everything and perhaps of perishing. He thinks, therefore, that certain injustices are, if not inevitable, then at least without an effective remedy. Human justice is fragile, as are human beings themselves, and in this world their hands are weak against adversaries wielding power.

Without doubt, the law of nature and the authority that those who are governing received from the governed at the moment when the *pactum subjectionis* was established, the fundamental laws of the state which follow from this, and the obligation that the government has to act only through the laws and according to the laws together form the framework and principles of justice in the exercise of power.[56]

Locke's great worry is that the power of government should become an arbitrary power. That is why he takes very particular care in defining the conditions, the limits, and the legitimate ends of what he calls "Prerogative." He recognizes that there may be occurrences such that it is impossible to foresee or ascertain in advance what the "certain and unalterable Laws" will or will not sanction in the circumstances.[57] In general, he thinks that the exercise of power implies that the executive exercise a certain power of discretion, "the Legislators not being able to foresee, and provide, . . . for all, that may be useful for the Community." [58] The prerogative is a functional necessity of power. It is a matter of a right of necessity which is incumbent on those who govern, a right that can be recognized as theirs if it is seen that their task may be accomplished when the laws are silent or when it is necessary to adapt them to particular facts. The good of the people requires it. In Locke's eyes, justice can come about in this way; "*Salus Populi Suprema Lex* is certainly so just and fundamental a Rule that he, who sincerely follows it, cannot dangerously err." [59] But, in order that the prerogative

[56] We have express reservations about the violent critique by C.B. MacPherson in his recent book, *The Political Theory of Possessive Individualism (Hobbes to Locke)*. It is much too partisan, excessive, and it contains errors of interpretation too obvious to be convincing.

[57] *Treatise*. II. xiii. § 158.

[58] *Treatise*. II. xiv. § 159.

[59] *Treatise*. II. xiii. § 158.

may be a "just prerogative," in order that it justify itself, it must be manifestly "for the good of the people," all things considered. This is what at the same time defines and justifies it—"This Power to act according to discretion, for the publick good." [60]

Locke is perfectly conscious of the risk which is taken, for, after all, *"Prerogative is nothing but the Power of doing publick good without a Rule"*; [61] and we know that, for him, "Whosoever uses *force without Right,* as everyone does in Society, who does it without Law, puts himself into a *state of War."* [62] But he thinks that it is a risk that is inherent in any convention by which a limited number of citizens, those who govern, use public force. He thinks that this sort of convention is inevitable. Quite certainly, he knows that abuses can ensue and in consequence disagreements and bitter conflicts. But a moment always comes in the use of power when confidence must be firmly placed in man, however frail he may be, and in man's capacity to be rational. This is precisely the idea of "trusteeship," which is an authority and in consequence a trust. The moment for taking a risk always accompanies the use of force. This is the nature of the political.

If a conflict arises, it will bring the majority of the people into opposition to those who are governing. Who will judge the faithfulness of the government to its authority? Locke first responds: in this case, "there can be no *Judge on Earth."* [63] A kind of state of nature is established between those who govern and the governed, even if a constitution, a fundamental positive law, exists, since there is no judge, no "umpire," possible. The two groups of antagonists are simultaneously judges and parties to the dispute. Thus, nothing else remains, if enough is at stake, if it "is worth the Trouble and Cost of the Appeal," [64] except to "appeal to Heaven." A situation in which force dominates comes into effect as soon as the dispute arises. "In all States and Conditions the true remedy of *Force* without Authority is to oppose *Force* to it," [65] i.e., oppose a just force to an unjust force. *"God in Heaven is Judge."* [66] Invoking any kind of proof of God's

[60] *Treatise.* II. xiv. § 160.
[61] *Treatise.* II. xiv. § 166.
[62] *Treatise.* II. xix. § 232.
[63] *Treatise.* II. xiv. § 168.
[64] *Treatise.* II. xvi. § 176.
[65] *Treatise.* II. xiii. § 155.
[66] *Treatise.* II. xix. § 241.

judgment amounts to instituting a state of war.[67] Violence and injustice take over everywhere, even among those who have received the authority to create and maintain justice and among whom one might seek to defend himself or to obtain reparation. If there are no judges, then there is no recourse but to war,[68] the return to arbitrariness and violence, which leaves no room for justice. The law itself is no longer understood. Where there are no longer judges, there is no longer any justice.

This situation appears avoidable to Locke, because, since it is the people who, in a sort of *pactum subjectionis,* have entrusted their authority to the government, it is they who are the most qualified judges of it; "The People shall be Judge." [69] The people, as a body in which the source of supreme authority resides, are the true arbiters. They alone have no peer among men. This does not rule out the test of force if those who are governing refuse this solution. But it is in this way that the principle of a just order is defined and safeguarded, for, "The People have a Right to act as Supreme, and continue the Legislative in themselves, or erect a new Form, or under the old form place it in new hands, as they think good." [70] Right is born only of right; justice is born only of justice. With the institution of new laws and new judges, the conditions of justice are re-established.

JUSTICE AND THE *JUS GENTIUM*

We see that the fact that there is war figures as an obscure blemish in the Lockean theory of justice. War between individuals or war between states, the use of violence against right, the silence to which the laws of nature are reduced, or the absence of judges common to both parties eliminates all considerations of justice. Justice has a meaning before war begins or after it has ended, but never during the war itself.

It is quite striking to see that the reader of Hooker and Grotius has turned to account neither the "law of nations" of the one nor the *jus belli* or *jus gentium* of the other.[71] The only

[67] *Treatise.* II. xix. § 242.
[68] *Treatise.* II. iii. § 20.
[69] *Treatise.* II. xix. § 240.
[70] *Treatise.* II. xix. § 243.
[71] Richard Hooker, *Of the Laws of Ecclesiastical Polity.* I. x. §§ 12, 13.

chapter in which he treats international relations with any continuity, Chapter XVI of *The Second Treatise of Civil Government,* "Of Conquest," tells us only that war is born of the breakdown of right by violence—"'Tis the *unjust use of* force, then, that *puts Man into a state of War.*" [72]

Or, more precisely—according to a formula inherited from Hobbes—states or commonwealths are related to each other in a state of nature which is a state of latent war: ". . . the whole community is one Body in the State of Nature, in respect of all other States or Persons out of its community." [73] But it is a matter of a hostile state of nature of the Hobbesian type, because, not only does it not include a common judge, but Locke does not bother to define that to which the laws of nature would here correspond. Furthermore, everything happens as if there were no such laws. Any discontinuity not consented to, even in a situation which was in fact quite commonplace, would become, then, an act of war. The implicit right of nature for nations is the right to sustain themselves. But Locke seeks neither to explicate nor to amplify this point.[74] For him, the relations between nations properly take the form of the reign of force without right.

Locke does not seek to introduce the least respect for right into the conduct of war. If he speaks of wars as just or unjust, he defines these terms only in a verbal way: the just war is one waged by someone with right on his side; the unjust war is one waged against what is right. This can be seen more clearly only in particular cases in which the unjust war is one which involves the invasion of the territory of another and, perhaps, by extension, of all offensive wars or in just wars, which one wages in order to defend his own territory and his rights, even if he ends by invading the territory of the aggressor.

Locke's remarks do not bear on war itself, but only on its consequences and on the state of affairs which follows from the relationship of conqueror to conquered. For him, it is entirely a matter of limiting the consequences of a triumph of force, of preserving the natural rights of the conquered, and of permitting

[72] *Treatise.* II. xvi. § 181.

[73] *Treatise.* II. xii. § 145.

[74] The extrapolations of Richard H. Cox are full and perhaps weak (*Locke on War and Peace* [1960], pp. 123–130). They should be taken with a good deal of caution.

the law of nature, scorned in the war itself, to make itself understood and respected again. For Locke—and this is essential—the use of force does not have legitimate consequences for the justice of a political order or for its constitution, even if it in fact durably maintains a certain system of relations between the conqueror and the conquered. Justice is not born of violence; it cannot be born of it, even if it is triumphant and as enduring as could ever be wished.

If those who have waged an unjust war win the war, their victory will never constitute a state of right, inasmuch as the conquered will not give their free consent to the conquerors. Even if, for want of power, the conquered appeal vainly to heaven, they will never be legitimately subjugated; ". . . he that *Conquers in an unjust war, can thereby have no Title to the Subjection and Obedience of the Conquered.*"[75]

If those who have waged a just war win, then the rights of the conqueror will rarely be increased by the justice of their cause. Without doubt, he will have justly at his mercy those who have participated in the unjust enterprise of force against him, because they are rendered unworthy of the human condition and of life. Without doubt, he will have the right to impose indemnities for the losses which have been unjustly caused him. But he does not acquire any right over the conquered or over the children or the families of those who are responsible for his losses or even over their property beyond the just compensation that he can claim and only in an amount which will not put the survival of the defeated people or their children in danger.[76]

The reason is understood, and it is *this* that Locke sought to show; it is a fortiori evident that violent conquest can never, under these conditions, be the principle of a legitimate political sovereignty or the basis of a just order. Those who have made the counterclaim have quite wrongly confused the force of arms with the consent of the people—the order of arbitrary violence, which is the way of beasts, with the order of reason, which is the way of men.

In order to confirm this in other terms, let us say that justice, whether it concerns relations among nations or among indi-

[75] *Treatise*. II. xvi. § 176.
[76] *Treatise*. II. xvi. § 180.

viduals, comes only from itself. A sovereignty is legitimate, an order just, only if it is consented to and established in conformity to justice as revealed by the law of nature, which is the law of reason. The source of justice—and this is Locke's last word—is justice itself. Force changes nothing with respect to justice any more than it changes what is in conformity to reason.

Not even consent is sufficient to bring about justice. The just order is not just because it is founded on consent or even on contract. It is the contract itself which is founded on justice. It is only a way of implementing justice among men, who are imperfect. If, secondly, the just order of the state is defined by laws established in virtue of a contract of foundation, then the positive laws of the state would not be sufficient as the basis of right if they did not derive all their legitimacy from the law of nature itself, which is the principle of contract and of laws. In short, although the dominant idea of Lockean political theory is the idea of consent of assembled individuals, this is misleading, for people are rationally obligated to consent to that which is just because it is just. This is why, although justice concerns only free men, it does not depend on their free consent. It goes beyond it. It is the law in relation to which their freedom takes on meaning. It is the principle of a sensible order. It is the rationality within things and among men. Thus we discover Locke's premises at the same time that we discover the coherence of his thought, for this law of justice expresses, in its aspect as the law of nature, an eternal truth, a necessary meaning, even the idea of justice itself, which is the structure of reason, just as it is the obligatory order of things human.

14

JUSTICE AND CLASSICAL UTILITARIANISM

HUGO A. BEDAU

Utilitarianism is the theory that moral and political decisions are to be justified by their utility, their conduciveness to "the greatest good of the greatest number." The era of classical utilitarianism begins with David Hume's *A Treatise of Human Nature* (1739) and is dominated by the writings of the Benthamites, beginning with Jeremy Bentham's *A Fragment on Government* (1776) and ending with James Mill's *A Fragment on Mackintosh* (1835). Its epitome is John Stuart Mill's *Utilitarianism* (1861), and its fullest, most cautious statement is in Henry Sidgwick's *Methods of Ethics* (1874). Recent investigators of utilitarian theories of justice [1] have exposed various kinds of weak-

[1] See C.K. Allen, "Justice and Expediency," in Paul Sayre, ed., *Interpretations of Modern Legal Philosophies* (1947), pp. 15–28; Gregory Vlastos, "Justice," *Revue internationale de philosophie*, XI (1957), 324–343; and John Rawls, "Justice as Fairness," *Philosophical Review*, LXVII (1958), reprinted in

nesses on fundamental points, and the whole doctrine seems to be so unsatisfactory that there is at the present time no "thoroughgoing defense of an unrepenitantly [*sic*] utilitarian theory of justice." [2]

It is not my intention here to try to provide such a defense. Instead, I propose to examine the variations in the classical utilitarian theory of justice, especially among the Benthamites, and to trace out the vicissitudes of their attempts to show that the principle of utility is the foundation, in some sense or other, of the principles of justice and of whatever moral obligation there is to act justly. For present purposes, justice is to be understood not as the sum of all virtue nor as the principles of retribution, but as the principles which provide for fair distribution of benefits and burdens, privileges and immunities, whether in the form of legal or moral rules. Scholars have shown less interest in this subject than one might have expected of them, perhaps because the views on justice of the classic utilitarians seem so unsatisfactory that they do not deserve careful study and because, with few exceptions, the utilitarians left their opinions on the subject to be gleaned from a hundred scattered paragraphs and footnotes. Aside from gratifying the scholar's curiosity, this task commends itself to anyone who believes (as I do) that principles of justice make moral claims on persons independently of the moral claims of benevolence, serving the general good, or maximizing social welfare; [3] for it is classical utilitarianism, more than any other philosophy, which presents this viewpoint with its clearest alternative. I shall not try to defend this nonutilitarian conception of justice, nor shall I even state it very fully. Such clarity and plausibility as it can be given here will have to result by the way and in the course of my examination of the utilitarian theories. I think that the defects of those theories

---

Frederick Olafson, ed., *Justice and Social Policy* (1961), pp. 80–107. For some reason, the standard histories of English utilitarianism, by Leslie Stephen, Ernest Albee, Elie Halévy, and John Plamenatz, do not address themselves to this topic at all.

[2] Olafson, *op. cit.*, p. viii. But see R. Corkey, "Benevolence and Justice," *Philosophical Quarterly*, IX (1959), 152–163.

[3] No attempt is made in this paper to distinguish between the terms, "welfare," "felicity," "good," "utility"; I write here much as did the classical utilitarians, as though these terms were synonyms.

will sufficiently show the need for, and something of the nature of, this alternative conception of justice.

The easiest way to grasp the essentials of the classical utilitarian theories of justice is to begin with the central doctrine shared by the leading Benthamites—Bentham, James Mill, and John Austin—since all the other utilitarian theories (including Hume's, which preceded Bentham's by half a century) can be viewed as attempts to clarify its vaguenesses and overcome its weaknesses. It is also convenient to begin by considering not Bentham's nor Mill's but Austin's version of the theory—in the erroneous form advanced by some interpreters (I will not guess with what influence).

According to Austin, it has recently been said, "Justice is no criterion whatsoever for the evaluation of the law; it is a mere synonym for what is lawful." [4] This may be an echo of the opening remark in a passage in which Sir James Fitzjames Stephen, himself sympathetic to utilitarianism, wrote, "According to the view taken of law and morals by Bentham and his school, the proper meaning of injustice is partial application of the law." [5] The most that can be said for this interpretation (it was all, as we shall see, Stephen claimed for it) is that it is half of the truth.

Austin does say, "By the epithet *just,* we mean that a given object to which we apply the epithet, accords with a given law to which we refer it as to a test." [6] Bentham speaks of "injustice" and "partiality" in the same breath [7] and says that "rendering justice" consists in "taking that course in every case which coincides with the track marked out beforehand by the finger of the substantive law" [8] and that "the main end . . . of justice" is what he somewhat obscurely calls "the giving execution and

[4] F.E. Dowrick, *Justice According to the English Common Lawyers* (1961), pp. 178–179.

[5] James Fitzjames Stephen, "Bentham's 'Theory of Legislation,'" *Saturday Review* (1864), reprinted in his *Horae Sabbaticae* (1892), III, 215.

[6] John Austin, *The Province of Jurisprudence Determined* (1832), H.L.A. Hart, ed., p. 262, note.

[7] Jeremy Bentham, *The Principles of Morals and Legislation* (1789, 1823), p. 114.

[8] Bentham, *Principles of Judicial Procedure* (c.1820), in *Works,* John Bowring, ed. (1843), II, 20.

effect to the rule of action,"[9] i.e., enforcing the law. James Mill, too, asserts "Acts done in conformity with those rules ["that is, Laws . . . which men in society have found it essential for their mutual benefit" should be placed on "the powers of Individuals"] are called Just Acts."[10] These passages very nearly do amount to the theory that the meaning of justice is impartial application of the law.

It is also true that Austin—and J.S. Mill—accepted an etymology for the term "justice" which would derive it from the Latin *jubere,* and thus they connected the concept of justice with the concept of a command or an order.[11] This etymology is no longer accepted and does not appear in Hume or Sidgwick.[12] But since the Benthamites did advance an imperative theory of law and since they all probably accepted the above etymology, it may seem that they must have held that the only sense in which justice and its cognate expressions can be used is in a sense connecting the term to that which the law (impartially) commands.

Nevertheless, it is clear that every sense or meaning of justice which the Benthamites recognized is not limited by this etymology and that their theory of justice cannot be found in the passages thus far quoted from Austin, Bentham, and Mill. The true view is that the Benthamites seemed to defend a double conception of justice, of which we have thus far seen only the first and least distinctive half.

If the Benthamites believed that justice is no criterion whatsoever for the evaluation of the law, their views would have anticipated those of certain contemporary legal positivists who

---

[9] Bentham, *Justice and Codification Petitions* (1829), in *Works, op. cit.,* V, 445.

[10] James Mill, *Analysis of the Phenomena of the Human Mind* (1829, 1878), J.S. Mill, ed., II, 285.

[11] Austin, *Lectures on Jurisprudence* (1863, 1885), Robert Campbell, ed., I, 409, note 69; John Stuart Mill, "Utilitarianism," *Fraser's Magazine* (1861), reprinted in *The Philosophy of John Stuart Mill,* Marshall Cohen, ed. (1961), 376 f. According to John Grote, this etymology originated with another Benthamite, Horne Tooke (*An Examination of the Utilitarian Philosophy* (1870), J.B. Mayor, ed., p. 152, note 2).

[12] For example, Ernest Barker, *The Principles of Social and Political Theory* (1951), pp. 94, 102, 168.

do hold, "Justice is no guide for the legislator. . . . To assert that a law is unjust is . . . nothing but an emotional expression of an unfavorable reaction to the law." [13] But the utilitarian and the legal positivist, though they have some common historical ground, are by no means to be identified, least of all on this point.[14] Every Benthamite—indeed, every classical utilitarian, except, perhaps, Hume—made it clear that legal and moral rules can be appraised with respect to their justice or injustice. At a later point in the very passage quoted above, Austin asserts, "When a positive human rule is styled unjust, . . . *justice* is nearly equivalent to *general utility*." [15] Bentham, in his first book, comes to the defense of the Roman epigram, "Utility is the mother of Justice and Equity," because he thinks Grotius has unfairly attacked it.[16] In his most famous discussion of justice (like Austin's, a mere footnote to his text), Bentham observes, "The dictates of justice are nothing more than a part of the dictates of benevolence . . . justice, in the only sense in which it has a meaning, is an imaginary personage, feigned for the convenience of discourse, whose dictates are the dictates of utility, applied to certain cases." [17] Similarly, James Mill: the "rules of justice," he says, are among those general moral rules which classify "acts the good consequences of which are recognized as greatly overbalancing the bad." [18]

Thus, the Benthamite theory of justice has two distinct aspects. As Stephen put it:

> It implies, first, the impartial application of a law to particular cases which fall under it. . . . It implies, secondly, that the law so to be administered shall be for the general good, or at least shall

---

[13] Alf Ross, *On Law and Justice* (1953, 1959), pp. 274, 280.

[14] See H.L.A. Hart, "Positivism and the Separation of Law and Morals," *Harvard Law Review*, LXXI (1958), reprinted in Frederick Olafson, ed., *Society, Law, and Morality* (1961), pp. 445–446.

[15] Austin, *Province of Jurisprudence Determined, op. cit.*, p. 263, note; cf. his *Lectures on Jurisprudence, op. cit.*, I, 450.

[16] Bentham, *Limits of Jurisprudence Determined* (1780), C.W. Everett, ed., pp. 117f.

[17] Bentham, *The Principles of Morals and Legislation, op. cit.*, pp. 125–126, note. See also his *Theory of Legislation* (1802), C.K. Ogden, ed., p. 3; his *Deontology* (1834), *Works, op. cit.*, I, 117, 141, 152, 202; and his *Principles of Judicial Procedure, ibid.*, p. 21.

[18] *A Fragment on Mackintosh* (1835), pp. 165, 168–169.

> have been enacted by the legislature with an honest intention to promote the good of those whom it is intended to benefit.[19]

The theory has two aspects because the Benthamites looked at the demands of justice on conduct from two points of view. When they looked at conduct from the point of view of a judge with a case before him and a battery of rules to deal with it, they saw the obligation to be just as the duty to apply the appropriate rule and apply it impartially; but, when they looked at conduct from the point of view of a legislator attempting to formulate a rule to cover a whole class of similar cases, they saw the obligation to be just as the duty to adopt that rule which maximizes the general welfare.[20]

This double conception is the core of the Benthamite theory of justice and to a greater or lesser extent appears in every theory of justice in classical utilitarianism. Although this core doctrine does not imply everything Bentham, in particular, had to say about justice, most of what he did say can be analyzed in relation to this doctrine.[21] Likewise, the central difficulties in the Benthamite theory of justice all arise from its imprecision and its striking neglect of the idea of equality, as thus far stated.

It is not clear how one can make the Benthamite conception of justice precise except by distorting it. The form of expression sometimes used by the Benthamites, as in the passages quoted above,[22] suggests they mean to assert this doctrine. (1) Justice has two uses, senses, or meanings; in one, the etymologically

---

[19] *Liberty, Equality, Fraternity* (1873), p. 192. Although it is J.S. Mill's theory which Stephen is expounding, his statement more accurately describes Benthamism. In Stephen's essay, cited in Note 5 above, he also implies that justice, i.e., utility, is a test of legal or moral rules according to the Benthamites.

[20] Stephens, *loc. cit.*

[21] In particular, it has no relation to what Bentham on a few occasions referred to as our "love of justice"; see his *A Table of the Springs of Action* (1817), *Works, op. cit.*, I, 203, 210; and his *Rationale of Judicial Evidence* (1827), J.S. Mill, ed., V, 638f. Bentham makes it clear that this sentiment is simply the capacity to enjoy certain "pleasures of antipathy," prominent in which is the "pleasure of revenge." J.S. Mill professed to make little sense of this idea (see his essay, "Bentham" (1838), reprinted in *The Philosophy of John Stuart Mill,* pp. 26–27), but it seems to be identical with what he later called "the sentiment of justice" in "Utilitarianism."

[22] See also Bentham, *Theory of Legislation, op. cit.,* p. 3, and J.F. Stephen, *Liberty, Equality, Fraternity, op. cit.,* pp. 195–197.

prior, it signifies impartial application of the law; in the other, it signifies the maximal conduciveness of a legal or moral rule to the general welfare. If this is their view, they profess a naturalistic metaethics of justice in keeping with the well-known Benthamite naturalistic metaethics of value whereby justice is to be defined in terms of certain natural or empirical properties—the impartial and lawful properties of acts and the maximally felicific (or otherwise beneficial) properties of rules—and these and these only are the properties which the term connotes.

There is considerable history and usage to support the first half of such a definition, that which would connect justice with impartiality. But there is no reason anyone has ever produced, as far as I can determine, which commends the notion that there is another (indeed, the other) sense of justice in which the term bears a semantic relation to the property of maximal conduciveness to the general welfare. Partly for this reason and partly from other things the Benthamites wrote on the subject, I think it is at least doubtful whether they really wanted their conception of justice to be formulated so as to entail (1) above.

If, however, they did, it is not difficult to see that their theory is untenable. It simply is not true that in the English language the word "justice" has the meaning it would have to have if their theory is to be saved. Does anyone seriously believe that, if he heard someone say, "What he did conforms to the law, but he acted unjustly all the same" or "Whether or not the policy they propose is maximally useful to society, it is obviously unjust," he could make no sense of these remarks? This is not to deny the legitimacy with which Bentham attacked gaseous uses of the word "justice," in which the term is nothing but a deceptive way of pleading the speaker's private antipathies and sympathies.[23] It is to deny, however, that the Benthamites or others have shown that it is either a necessary or sufficient condition of talking sense (much less, of giving a sound moral appraisal) in terms of justice to mean nothing more than impartial conformity to law or maximal conduciveness to the general welfare. It is possible that the latter half of the Benthamite conception of

---

[23] See Bentham, *Theory of Legislation, op. cit.*, p. 280; *A Fragment on Government* (1776), *Works, op. cit.*, I, 269; and *Equity Dispatch Court Bill* (c. 1830), *ibid.*, III, 388.

justice was meant not as a descriptive, but as a persuasive, definition of justice, that is, as a semantic tactic in the campaign to make us all utilitarians. If so, the definition gains nothing in interest or plausibility.

More promising interpretations of the Benthamite conception of justice have no reference to what the word "justice" means, but refer instead to the characteristics which mark the path of justice itself. The most obvious formulation of such an interpretation is the non-semantic analogue to (1), as follows. (2) Any particular act is just if, and only if, it is an act required by an impartial application of the relevant legal (or moral) rule, and any particular legal (or moral) rule is just if, and only if, it is the maximally useful rule for a certain class of situations.

Aside from the fact that (2) implies that in any given instance there is only one relevant rule, whereas there are almost certainly many situations in which more than one rule is equally relevant, this version is incomplete in a crucial respect. Did the Benthamites really mean to imply that, in the case where some actual law or widely accepted moral rule does *not* seem to be the maximally useful rule for the class of circumstances it controls, nevertheless, the just thing to do is to apply that rule impartially? Did the Benthamites really mean to imply that, in the case where a legal or moral rule generally does seem to be the maximally useful one for a certain class of circumstances, although on *this* occasion breaking the rule seems even more useful, the obligation of justice is to obey the rule anyway? Or did they think that in such cases as these the path of justice for the utilitarian requires him to do the maximally useful act, even if he must break the rule? According to the Benthamites, what are the obligations of justice in such cases? No answer is given by their theory if it is formulated as in (2). Or did they blindly assume that neither of these possibilities could arise and that, if any given law is impartially applied where it is applicable and if utility is pursued when legal or moral rules are adopted, justice will invariably take care of itself?

In the light of this difficulty, which shows that some sharper distinction between the justice of acts and the justice of rules and the principle of utility is required, it is best to view (2) as a halfway house on the road to a better statement of the Benthamite theory, such as the following. (2a) Any particular legal or moral rule is just if, and only if, it is the maximally useful law or rule for a certain class of situations; any particular act is just if, and only if, either (i) it is the impartial application of such a rule, (ii) it is the impartial application of whatever rule in the legal system or moral code of the society in question is the relevant one, or (iii) it is the maximally useful act open to the agent in the circumstances.

This version of Benthamism is fairly precise, but its directive to conduct is utterly ambiguous and in many circumstances it is certain to be inconsistent. It is quite possible that there will be many situations in which, on this version of the theory, there will be three quite different acts open to an agent who is concerned to act justly, each of which is as just as the others though no two are compatible. This consequence ill suits the common assumption that the dictates of justice, however obscure and elusive they may be to determine with finality, cannot be both clear and severally inconsistent.

If, as I think, the Benthamite theory of justice must embrace this ambiguous theory, it must face the further fact that these ambiguities can be resolved only at a considerable price. None of the three available alternatives is satisfactory. If (2ai) is adopted, many impartial applications of a legal or moral rule must be judged to be unjust because so few of the rules actually applied are maximally useful when contrasted to those rules which could be applied. If (2aii) is preferred, then reform of the prevailing legal or moral rules in the name of justice cannot be undertaken, nor can the substance of these rules be appraised from the standpoint of their justice or injustice. But if (2aiii) is adopted, then the very idea of justice as involving the notion of impartial application of a legal or moral *rule* (in any ordinary sense of the term) seems to have disappeared.

Bentham himself never gives any evidence of contemplating the possibility that his theory is ambiguous and does not resolve, even in principle, the conflict of obligations which arises whenever a man must choose between applying a less than maximally useful legal or moral rule and breaking it in favor of trying to do what in the circumstances seems maximally useful to all concerned. Confronted with this dilemma, it is not clear what Bentham would advise. Both James Mill and Austin, however, seem to hint at how they would have resolved it. "The rules of justice," James Mill writes, "are a tissue, in which rules and exceptions are about equally numerous." [24] This is true, on his view, of all moral rules. As an example, he asserts that our duty to do "generous acts" is always subordinate to our duty to be just; [25] thus the moral rule, "Men ought to do generous acts," has the implicit rider, "Except when generosity conflicts with justice." But the whole drift of his analysis is toward the view that the moral rule, "Men ought to act justly," itself has the rider, "Except when acting justly conflicts with maximizing the general welfare." [26] For, if there are, as he says there are, exceptions to the rules of justice, they can originate only in the clash between justice and utility and the higher obligation arising from the latter. If this is James Mill's view, then all ordinary moral and legal rules are mere "rules of thumb" to be broken whenever the supreme obligation to serve the general welfare demands; James Mill thus resolves the ambiguities of (2a) into (2aiii) and emerges as a defender of what is now called "act" or "extreme" or "unrestricted" utilitarianism.[27] Austin's view, which probably resolves (2a) into (2aii), I shall discuss later in connection with Hume, from whom it probably was derived.

As for the concept of equality, the Benthamites never connect it directly with their conception of justice, nor do they connect it with impartiality. Equality figures only in relation to utility and then only because it is one of several factors usually involved in maximizing the general happiness.[28] Thus, Bentham writes, "The more remote from equality are the shares . . . the less is

---

[24] *A Fragment on Mackintosh, op. cit.*, p. 254.

[25] *Ibid.*, pp. 252–253, 256.

[26] See *ibid.*, p. 245, where Mill proposes a utilitarian justification of "base actions." A clearer account of the same idea has been lately offered by means of the distinction between right actions and actions rationally praiseworthy; see J.J.C. Smart, "Extreme and Restricted Utilitarianism," *Philosophical Quarterly*, VI (1956), 347, 353.

[27] For example, see John Rawls, "Two Concepts of Rules," *Philosophical Review*, LXIV (1955), reprinted in Olafson, *Society, Law, and Morality, op. cit.*, pp. 420–434; and Smart, *op. cit.*

[28] According to Henry Sidgwick, until after 1817 Bentham's democratic and egalitarian sympathies were severely constrained out of the fear that they would imperil the chances of favorable action on his grand Panopticon scheme. See his "Bentham and Benthamism in Politics and Ethics," *Fortnightly Review* (1877), reprinted in his *Miscellaneous Essays and Addresses* (1904), p. 158.

the sum of felicity produced by the sum of those shares." [29] This is clearly advanced as an empirical claim, for Bentham allows that it is a rebuttable presumption. His sole concession to egalitarianism is that the burden of proof is on anyone who thinks that inequalities do not lead to less than maximal felicity. But, if it should turn out (and who can say in advance that it never will?) that a certain law or policy seems likely to maximize general felicity at the expense of equality, the Benthamite cannot criticize such a law or policy in the name of justice. And, if he deliberately turns his back on those policies or laws which seem maximally useful even though they would work substantial inequality, if he does not even try them out for a while, he shows himself to be far less an empiricist than he has advertised himself to be. The equal distribution under law of benefits and burdens, privileges and immunities, irrespective of arbitrary distinctions of age, sex, race, color, education, intelligence, or social class, is not on very stable ground when it rests on nothing more than its presumed expediency in maximizing the general good.

This conceptual disconnection of equality from justice—and the merely empirical connection it bears to utility—is further shown by the attitude of the Benthamites to concrete social questions of the day. When Bentham proposes that slavery be abolished, he insists that gradual abolition is alone consistent with the slave owner's interest in the security of his property. He recommends that, under a program of gradual emancipation, the slaves to be freed first be chosen by lot, on the grounds that it is impartial and simpler to administer than trying to select as the first slaves to be freed those who are most worthy.[30] Thus, such equality of opportunity for freedom which Bentham extends to all slaves rests entirely on the superior administrative efficiency of selection by lot. That there is anything just in this method of selection, all other things being equal, and that this

[29] Bentham, *Leading Principles of a Constitutional Code* (1823), *Works, op. cit.,* II, 271; cf. *Theory of Legislation, op. cit.,* pp. 96 f., 108. On the Benthamite maxim, "Each to count for one, none for more than one," see Vlastos, *op. cit.,* p. 328, and Rawls, "Justice as Fairness," *op. cit.,* p. 99.

[30] Bentham, *Theory of Legislation, op. cit.,* p. 208. He says, "Equality ought not to be favored except in cases in which it does not interfere with security . . . ," p. 99; cf. pp. 119–120.

might be a morally relevant reason for choosing candidates in this fashion never seem to have occurred to Bentham. When James Mill considers the allocation of the right of suffrage in a society, he never really weighs the claim of all adult persons to equal voting rights, since he is convinced that universal suffrage (even universal manhood suffrage) is inexpedient.[31] Not even his son entirely threw off this yoke to his egalitarian sympathies, for his views on suffrage are hedged with the same expediential qualifications as his father's.[32] It may be that abolition of slavery all at once or universal suffrage are imprudent policies; it is even conceivable that persons might have sound moral reasons not to press for such revolutionary changes in certain political climates. But that such policies are not urged by the counsels of justice or that their justice can be denied by a showing of their inexpediency are conceivable only by someone on whom considerations of equality and of equal justice have made little impact.

As a consequence, I find it impossible to see in Benthamism, or, indeed, anywhere in classical utilitarianism before Sidgwick,[33] a recognition of that ideal of justice which holds that there are "equal claims all men can rightly make on the community simply because they are men." This ideal does not seem to rest on the kind of empirical grounds which ostensibly recommended equality to the Benthamites. It does not seem to be advanced in the name of effective management of human resources for the general welfare, as if justice were "a kind of efficiency." [34] If the Benthamites did contribute anything to our conception of justice, it may be the idea that a just society cannot be one which does not maximize the general welfare in the respects in which it could. Their idea, that the burden is on anyone who thinks the general welfare can be maximized when benefits and burdens are distributed according to the rules of law which prescribe gratuitously unequal distribution, is no small contribution. But it is marred by their readiness to override such claims of equality

---

[31] James Mill, *An Essay on Government* (1823), Currin Shields, ed., pp. 73, 89ff.

[32] J.S. Mill, *Considerations on Representative Government* (1861), A.D. Lindsay, ed., pp. 375, 381, 388.

[33] In contrast to Vlastos, *op. cit.*, p. 343; cf. p. 328.

[34] Rawls, "Justice as Fairness," *op. cit.*, p. 99.

by what they hold to be the higher claim of general utility.

The omission from the Benthamite theory of justice of any express reference to equality and of the failure even to consider whether equality does not recommend itself to us in the name of justice goes to the heart of a weakness in their whole conception of justice. In contrast to the Benthamites, I doubt whether justice ever relates to nothing but legal impartiality and maximizing utility. Even impartiality, which the Benthamites usually took for granted as one sense or reference of the word "justice," connects more closely with equality than it does with either law or utility. Moreover, the notion of equality, of share and share alike, of fairness, helps to bridge the gap between justice according to the law and justice of a law,[35] a gap the Benthamites never attempted to overcome. To take two familiar examples and them but briefly:

> (1) Neither law nor utility guides the parent in dividing some distributable good (e.g., food) among the members of his family insofar as the parent thinks of himself as making a just distribution. What guides his hand is the notion of equal shares, and this is how the division usually proceeds, except as it is influenced by rational grounds for inequality, such as differences in need, merit, performance, and prior agreement among the members of the family. Notice that not even these grounds for differential treatment have their source in any moral obligation to maximize the total welfare, much less in any obligation to apply some rule impartially. Their source is interior to the idea of justice itself, even the idea of equal justice.[36] (2) In situations where the circumstances and number of persons having a claim on the available necessities of life makes it highly probable that not all shall survive the ordeal (e.g., a boatload of castaways on the open sea, away from the shipping lanes, and with only a box of biscuits and a keg of water), the question of how to provide a just distribution of what is available to all is bound to suggest either a division of the goods into equal shares even if this results in portions which would not keep a sparrow alive or in a lottery in which all participate and where the winner(s) take(s) all (again, always barring just grounds for differential treatment). Neither of these

[35] I have borrowed this useful way of putting the distinction from H.L.A. Hart, *The Concept of Law* (1961), p. 7.

[36] The idea that the grounds for differential treatment are themselves justifiable within the framework of equal justice has been argued with great originality in Vlastos, "Justice and Equality," in Richard Brandt, ed., *Social Justice* (1962).

> solutions necessarily results in the most useful distribution as far as ensuring that the largest number survives or as far as maximizing the net satisfactions of the group. But there seems a clear separation between the question, "What is the most useful distribution (or, procedure for distribution)?" and the question, "What is the just distribution (or, procedure for distribution)?"

In such cases as (2), it is difficult if not impossible to determine (not in theory, perhaps, but in practice) the answer to the first question, but it is not difficult or impossible to determine the answer to the second one. And, where both answers can be determined, there is no great likelihood that they will be identical.

If anyone objects that in such cases as (1) and (2), or in all cases, the most useful distribution is the just distribution and that the justification of a just distribution is its superior utility, he has conceded that the meaning of "justice" and the criterion of a just distribution is not obtained from examining the utilities of possible distributions. His objection logically assumes that justice has already been placed on its own conceptual footing independent of the principle of utility. And, although his reason for adopting a just distribution is perhaps one which can always be brought forward by a utilitarian, at least, in the normal run of cases, it is difficult to see why the utility of just distributions should be the only reason for adopting them.

With this exposition of doctrine and difficulties in Benthamism behind us, it is a fairly simple task to appraise the variations which Hume, J.S. Mill, and Sidgwick give to the utilitarian theory of justice.

In Hume, one finds an attempt to analyze the concept of justice far superior to that found in the Benthamites. Yet, nowhere in his writings does Hume lavish on this subject the care he gave to the analysis of, for example, the metaphysical concepts of substance and necessity. What he does offer revolves around the "rules" or "laws of justice," which, with no little irony, he insists on calling "laws of nature" even though men have "invented" them.[37] These rules are laws of nature because they are in fact necessary to the maintenance of any society whatever; they are invented (or "artificial") because they are not naturally ex-

---

[37] David Hume, *A Treatise of Human Nature* (1739), in *Hume's Moral and Political Philosophy*, H.D. Aiken, ed. (1948), pp. 105; cf. pp. 55, 95.

pressed in human conduct and are embraced only after considerable experience and reflection in which their convenience in the long run becomes evident. What are these rules? They are three: the "stability of possession," "its transference by consent," and "the performance of promises." [38] As Sidgwick later observed, these are the sorts of rule which provides for the establishment of "order" in society. But it is not clear what relation social order bears to social justice. Granted that every society needs some rules embodying the principles of ownership, exchange, and contract, does not justice require that only certain ones among the various possible and workable rules be accepted? Hume does not even consider whether his rules of justice will provide for equal distribution of benefits and burdens, privileges and immunities, as far as what he calls "rules of justice" touch on these matters. Of course, the rules he cites could be specified so that they would provide for equal distributions if they were designed and applied by reflective and concerned persons, but there is no guarantee that they will be. Hume's primary concern on the issue of equality is to reject the egalitarian idea that the concept of justice requires "*perfect* equality" in the distribution of goods. He barely notices that "whenever we depart from . . . equality, we rob the poor of more satisfaction than we add to the rich." [39] At no point do equalitarian considerations play any part in his designation of the rules of justice as rules of *justice.*

Despite Hume's typical utilitarian treatment of the concept of equality and failure to come to grips with the concept of justice, what he had to say about the relation of justice to utility should have served his successors better than it did, for he was far clearer and cleverer than they on this score. The essence of his view is found in the statement, "A single act of justice is frequently contrary to the public interest." [40] Nevertheless, Hume thinks, the utilitarian has an obligation to do this inutile act, because "whatever may be the consequences of any single act of justice performed by a single person, yet the whole system

[38] *Ibid.,* p. 90.

[39] Hume, *An Inquiry Concerning the Principles of Morals* (1777), in *Hume's Moral and Political Philosophy, op. cit.,* p. 193.

[40] Hume, *A Treatise of Human Nature, op. cit.,* p. 65.

of actions concurred in by the whole society is infinitely advantageous to the whole and to every part. . . ." [41]

Not only does this view put out of the picture any suggestion that the meaning of justice is related to the property of maximizing the general welfare (a temptation to which the Benthamites, as we have seen, were all too susceptible), but it also firmly connects the concept of acting justly with acting according to rules and not according to the consequences of the act. Thus, the double conception of justice which the Benthamites held tends to disappear in Hume's theory, and there is no reference to appraising laws, policies, or moral rules in terms of their justice. Nevertheless, his doctrine of justice is fundamentally a utilitarian one, because it purports to establish the obligation to act justly through the beneficial consequences of obedience to and impartial application of legal and moral rules.

Much the same view is implied by Austin, for he denies that being a utilitarian implies appealing to the principle of utility to settle every question of conduct. Conduct, for Austin, is determined by moral and legal "rules, principles or maxims." These, to be sure, are to "be fashioned on utility"; but their proximity shows that our conduct is controlled by utility only indirectly.[42] The difference between Austin and Hume—and from the present perspective, it is considerable—is that Austin nowhere suggests that any of these "rules, principles or maxims" are peculiarly rules of justice, and he does not say that it is the requirements of justice which occasionally oblige us to forego opportunities to attempt to maximize utility by breaking a rule. If both Hume and Austin defend "rule" or "restricted" utilitarianism, only Hume professes a "rule" or "restricted" utilitarian theory of justice.

Hume's theory is not entirely clear and convincing, however. It is not clear when he speaks of hewing to the rule and eschewing the opportunity to maximize utility by breaking the rule, whether he has in mind only his three special "rules of justice" or whether he means all moral and legal rules. If the former,

---

[41] *Ibid.*, p. 66; cf. his *An Inquiry Concerning the Principles of Morals, op. cit.*, p. 277.

[42] Austin, *Province of Jurisprudence Determined, op. cit.*, p. 47.

his position is probably sound, unless the actual rules adopted by whatever society is in question are open to criticism on grounds of their substantial, structural inequalities, as is a system of ownership and transference of property designed to reinforce the most powerful vested interests at the expense of everyone else. But Hume may mean the latter; he may think that utilitarianism imposes impartial application and obedience of the law on everyone in the name of justice, no matter what legal or moral rule is in question and no matter what it prescribes. Such an emphasis on abiding by whatever the rule is, when coupled with a neglect of equalitarian considerations, has peculiar results. Thus, suppose a law is in force which prescribes for certain persons, on grounds of their color, religion, or sex, an education inferior to that afforded the rest of the population. Suppose an occasional exception to this law, managed by dissident administrators and teachers, whereby some of the former group are provided with educational opportunities equal to those provided for the latter. Such exceptions would be criticized on the version of Hume's theory currently being considered, not for their inutility (since the general observance of the law would probably continue if the exceptions were unpublicized and infrequent), but for their injustice. Yet it seems perverse to hold that exceptions to such a law are really unjust, when the injustice lies in such a law and in abiding by it. In this respect, Bentham was superior to Hume, for he did say that such built-in inequalities are usually to be rejected by a utilitarian because equality is almost always a condition of maximizing the general welfare. Hume noted this possibility in passing, but it evidently struck him as unimportant.

Hume's view also does not seem to account for one's duty to act justly except on the assumption that others will act justly. It is only when most persons obey the rules that any general benefit can result from a particular person's obedience to them. But it is only this general benefit that gives rise to the obligation that everyone on every occasion should obey them. Should a man find himself in a situation where it is unreasonable for him to believe that most people will act on the rule which he thinks is the relevant one, Hume's theory will not provide a reason that he should act on it.[43] This difficulty is not peculiar to Hume's theory of justice; it is common, in one form or another, to every purely utilitarian theory of justice. There is no basis for any-one's acting justly on a particular occasion (when "acting justly" means "applying impartially, or obeying, a legal or moral rule") which would have useful consequences were most people to act on it, unless most people are likely to act on it. To think other-wise is either to make a fetish of obeying rules or to import some non-utilitarian moral principle as the source of the obligation.[44] Is it unreasonable to ask of a theory of justice that it provide a reason for my acting justly in the absence of the likelihood that others will? I do not think so. But any utilitarian theory can derive a moral obligation to obey a rule only in a certain situation from what can reasonably be expected to be the con-sequences of what people will really do in such situations. It cannot derive this obligation merely from what could be ex-pected were people to obey this rule in such situations. This is not to deny that in the normal run of circumstances a utilitarian motive for acting justly can be forthcoming. What is argued is that one can without difficulty specify a class of circumstances in which there would be no obligation on purely utilitarian grounds to act justly. There are many cases where the only rea-son that someone will act justly is because he cares about seeing that justice is done. Neither Hume nor any other utilitarian, as far as I can tell, can allow that such behavior is rational and moral. Only a direct appeal to considerations of justice as an independent principle of conduct can provide this.

John Stuart Mill's and Henry Sidgwick's analyses of justice are distinguished in several respects which differ from, and are superior to those of their predecessors. First, no utilitarian be-fore Mill really tried to analyze our ordinary concept of justice, and no utilitarian except Sidgwick came near succeeding. Not surprisingly, once the attempt was made to analyze the concept, it turns out to be more complex than Hume and the Bentham-

[43] See Jonathan Harrison, "Utilitarianism, Universalization and Our Duty to be Just," *Proceedings of the Aristotelian Society* (1952–53), reprinted in Olafson, *Justice and Social Policy, op. cit.*, pp. 57–60.

[44] Thus, Harrison's revision of Hume's theory departs from utilitarianism in the direction of Kantianism; *ibid.*, p. 75.

ites realized. The interest which Mill and Sidgwick found in clarifying our common thoughts on justice for its own sake, with their utilitarian prepossessions falling to one side in the process, accounts in part for the superior permanent value in their theories. Second, Mill is the first utilitarian to propose that "equality" and "impartiality" are related and constitute "the highest abstract standard of social and distributive justice," [45] a view which Sidgwick takes over without any reservations. Third, Mill attempts to show that the direct appeal to the principle of utility, as far as it relates to deciding questions of justice, is limited to those occasions when there is a conflict among the rules of justice themselves. Thus, after reviewing four situations where he thinks these rules conflict and thus cannot dispose of the problem of choice, Mill advises, "From these confusions, there is no other mode of extrication than the utilitarian." [46] Much the same relation between justice and the principle of utility is advocated by Sidgwick, as when he says at one point, "I know of no method of determining a problem of this kind which is not either implicitly utilitarian, or arbitrarily dogmatic, and unsupported by Common Sense." [47] There is no doubt that at each of these three points, Mill's and Sidgwick's theories constitute a contribution to utilitarian theories of justice. Unfortunately, in Mill's case, each is vitiated by one error or another, whereas in Sidgwick's case, the utilitarianism of his position is constantly adulterated by non-utilitarian considerations of "Common Sense." Because of the detail and complexity of Mill's and Sidgwick's theories of justice, it is not possible to discuss here even these three points with the care they deserve. It will have to suffice to confine our attention to their views on the relation of equality and justice to utility.

In his "Utilitarianism," Mill holds the remarkable theory that equality and impartiality are "involved in the very meaning of Utility" and, as we saw above, that equality and impartiality are the two fundamental "standards" of justice. Remarkable, because he also claims, "Each person maintains that equality is

---

[45] J.S. Mill, "Utilitarianism," *op. cit.*, p. 395.

[46] *Ibid.*, p. 391.

[47] Sidgwick, *Methods of Ethics* (1874, 1893), in part reprinted in Olafson, *Justice and Social Policy*, p. 9; cf. pp. 30, 35.

the dictate of justice, except where he thinks that expediency requires inequality"[48] and "All persons are deemed to have a right to *equality* of treatment except when some recognized social expediency requires the reverse."[49] Logic leaves one free to affirm or deny that the idea of justice involves the idea of equality; it certainly leaves one free on the question whether the idea of utility involves the idea of equality; among utilitarians, only Mill and Sidgwick asserted the former, and only Mill the latter. Logic also leaves one free to assert that, although justice does involve the idea of equality, we are sometimes morally obligated to override justice (and thus equality) in the name of the general welfare or some other higher moral value. But logic utterly precludes anyone from asserting what Mill asserts: equality is the standard of justice, equality is involved in the "very meaning of Utility," and the claims of equality are sometimes subordinate to those of utility! This contradiction may not have been entirely lost on Mill, either. One cannot help noting that he maintains that equality bears a semantic relation to the principle of utility only in one passage, a passage bound fore and aft by paragraphs in which he clearly asserts that inequalities are sometimes required by the demands of maximizing utility. It is as if he really did not take seriously his novel idea of a semantic relation between equality and utility, even though he did not want to give up the connection between equality and justice which neither his father nor Bentham accepted. The same point of view dominates his thought in his last book, *The Subjection of Women.* The passionate conviction with which he protests the inequalities in the treatment of the sexes is rarely justified, and then only halfheartedly, by an appeal to the inutility of these inequalities. The primary justification for abolishing these inequalities, and the reason which seems to excite him, is "the advantage of having the most universal and pervading of all human relations regulated by justice instead of injustice."[50] Nor is this presented as simply another way of stating the utility

[48] P. 396.

[49] P. 375.

[50] Mill, *The Subjection of Women* (1869), chap. 4, para. 3. Herbert Spiegelberg has lately concluded (and I should have to agree) that in general ". . . Mill's utilitarian theory of justice does not fit the conception of justice which permeates his own social reform program." See his article, "'Accident

of the reform. Thus, it looks as if Mill really did think that equality is conceptually imbedded in the idea of justice and that his difficulties began only when he asked himself how this conviction can be justified on purely utilitarian grounds.

In Sidgwick, the relation between equality and justice emerges, if anything, with greater clarity than in J.S. Mill, and it is not blurred by Mill's utilitarian qualms. Also, the view that equality is one test of the justice of a law, both in its substance and in its application, and thus that equality and impartiality are related and involved in the idea of justice Sidgwick made clear once and for all.[51] Yet the fact remains that he is no clearer than Mill when the question arises, Why should a utilitarian hold such a view? Sidgwick asserts that "impartiality or the negation of arbitrary inequality," which justice requires both in the "establishment" and in the "administration" of laws, is a special case of the maxim, "It cannot be right to treat two persons differently if their cases are similar in all material circumstances." He immediately adds, "And Utilitarianism . . . admits this maxim no less than other systems of Ethics." [52] But he does not say on what ground it is admitted. Evidently it is not because of any semantic relation between equality and utility, as J.S. Mill proposed. Is it, then, the reason the Benthamites advanced, that in general the consequences of suppressing arbitrary inequalities are better than the consequences of not suppressing them? Or is it that, when the utilitarian admits this maxim, he accepts an independent moral principle of equality, impartiality, or fairness, with the result that the principle of utility no longer reigns supreme? [53] Sidgwick simply does not say, and we are left with the same unresolved question as in J.S. Mill.

The difficulties I have ascribed to all forms of classical utilitarianism fall into three main categories: (1) A failure to show what one ought to do in the name of justice when the justice of acts is determined by impartially applying a legal or moral

---

of Birth': A Non-Utilitarian Motif in Mill's Philosophy," *Journal of the History of Ideas,* XXII (1961), p. 492.

[51] Sidgwick, *op. cit.,* pp. 5–6, 21, 35.

[52] Sidgwick, *op. cit.,* pp. 30–31.

[53] The status of this and other ethical maxims in Sidgwick's moral philosophy are discussed by A.R. Lacey, "Sidgwick's Ethical Maxims," *Philosophy,* XXXIV (1959), 217–228.

rule and when the justice of rules is determined by their utility, in those cases whereby breaking the rule the agent can do a more useful act than by not breaking it. (2) A failure to prove that the principles of justice and the moral obligation to act justly are really rooted in nothing but utilitarian considerations. (3) A failure to analyze the concept of justice and in particular to show the relation of the idea of equality to this concept. These shortcomings are less apparent in Sidgwick's theory than in Hume's or J.S. Mill's, and they are most prominent in the utilitarianism of Bentham, James Mill, and Austin. Whether Sidgwick's theory masters them by giving up essential and traditional utilitarian assumptions and commitments, thereby showing the necessity in the end for at least a partly non-utilitarian theory of justice, is another question which I have not tried to discuss.

15

MARX AND DISTRIBUTIVE JUSTICE

ROBERT C. TUCKER

At the turn of the century it was a widely accepted view that Marxism, in distinction from most other socialist doctrines, was ethically empty. Such authorities of that time as Kautsky, Sombart, Croce, and Lenin were in broad agreement on this point. As they saw it, the various non-Marxian schools of socialist thought could be called "ethical socialism" since they tended to predicate socialism on the moral "ought." Marxism, on the other hand, ran in terms of causal relations. It had succeeded in showing the proletarian revolution and socialism to be the inevitable outcome of the developmental process or inner dialectic of modern capitalist society. Alone among modern socialist doctrines, therefore, it was "beyond ethics."

Granted that Marx was not a moral philosopher in the conventional sense and that his system was not an inquiry into the nature of the supreme good, still this line of argument no longer carries conviction. Marx and Engels did, of course, claim to have demonstrated that socialism was inevitable and were critical, even scornful, of socialists who based the theory of socialism upon a moral imperative. Yet this is no real proof of the ethical emptiness of Marxism. For a theory of history—and Marxism is basically that—may have a moral theme or content without its being presented on ethical grounds, and it may on this account view the historically inevitable as also morally desirable. The Marxist theory is unquestionably a case in point. From its standpoint the existing order is not only doomed by history, but deserves to die, and the coming proletarian revolution not only must, but also ought to, take place. Marx vividly expressed this idea in a speech in London in 1856. Referring to the revolutionary upheaval that he thought impending, he went on:

> To revenge the misdeeds of the ruling class, there existed in the Middle Ages, in Germany, a secret tribunal, called the *Vehmgericht*. If a red cross was seen marked on a house, people knew that its owner was doomed by the *Vehm*. All the houses of Europe are now marked with the mysterious red cross. History is the judge—its executioner, the proletarian.[1]

Marx here visualized the future revolution as an act of retributive justice against a civilization so criminal in character that it deserved nothing less than capital punishment. The symbolism is moralistic through and through. It expresses the judgment embedded in Marxism that there *ought* to be a world revolution. And though the passage stands out because of its striking imagery, it is otherwise typical of many to be found scattered through the later writings of Marx.

In some deep sense Marx was a moralist—a thinker whose thinking is decisively governed by a concern with values of good and evil. A moral theme somehow pervades his whole system of thought. This, at any rate, is a view that seems to have gained, or to be gaining, acceptance among Western students of Marxism. The problem is to determine the nature of this moral theme. Granted that Marxism morally affirms the historically inevitable, on what ground does it do so? Why, in Marx's view, ought there to be a world revolution? What is the basis of his value judgment to the effect that the present order is evil and that the

[1] Marx and Engels, *Selected Works* (1958), I, 360.

future communist order will be good? These are various formulations of one and the same basic question of the moral interpretation of Marxism.

One of the suggested solutions is the proposition that distributive justice was the value. According to this view, the Marxist condemnation of capitalist civilization expressed, at bottom, a protest against the injustice inherent in capitalism, and Marxism morally affirms the proletarian revolution because it will inaugurate a reign of justice in human society. Such is the interpretation of Marx and Marxism implied in the following statement by Harold J. Laski: "At bottom, the main passion by which he was moved was the passion for justice." [2] Laski was echoed by A.D. Lindsay, who said of Marx: "His fundamental passion is a passion for justice." [3] Another English interpreter of Marxism, E.H. Carr, has suggested that justice is the moral theme of Marx's principal work: "In *Capital,* published twenty years after the *Communist Manifesto,* Marx demonstrated for the first time that the victory of the proletariat would be the victory not only of brute force, but of abstract justice." [4] A similar interpretation is suggested by Sidney Hook, who writes: "The ethics of Marx did not merely express a demand for social justice but a specific *kind* of justice dependent upon the objective possibilities created by capitalism." [5] These are representative expressions of the point of view that takes the idea—or one of the ideas—of justice to be the moral key to Marxism.

There is no denying that much of what Marx and Engels wrote confers at least a superficial plausibility on such an interpretation. "Hitherto, every form of society has been based on the antagonism of oppressing and oppressed classes" runs the familiar statement of the *Communist Manifesto.* The drama of class struggle is a drama of oppression and resistance to oppression, and what if not injustice might lie at the core of this oppression? Does not the *Manifesto,* moreover, say that two of the first acts of the proletarian dictatorship should be the institution of a "heavy progressive or graduated income tax" and the

[2] *Karl Marx* (1933), p. 46.
[3] *Karl Marx's Capital: An Introductory Essay* (1947), p. 114.
[4] *Karl Marx: A Study in Fanaticism* (1934), p. 83.
[5] *From Hegel to Marx* (1961), p. 53.

"abolition of all right of inheritance"? Marx and Engels depict the capitalist society that they abhor as the scene of a great and growing inequality of wealth, where untold riches accumulate in the hands of a small and dwindling class of avaricious capitalist magnates while the masses of working people sink deeper and deeper into a black pit of poverty. Do they not, then, condemn capitalist society *because* of its inequalities? And finally, what is the capitalist "exploitation" of labor that Marxism talks about if it is not a relation in which the worker is robbed of what rightfully belongs to him? In all these ways Marxism invites a moral interpretation that sees distributive justice as its central issue.

On closer analysis, however, the writings of Marx and Engels not only fail to sustain such an interpretation, but also furnish conclusive evidence that it is untenable. The fundamental passion of the founders of Marxism was not a passion for justice. Their condemnation of capitalism was not predicated upon a protest against injustice, and they did not envisage the future communist society as a kingdom of justice. In general, they were opposed to the notion that socialism or communism turns principally on the matter of distribution. This is not to say that they were indifferent to working class poverty and the great inequality of wealth. Nor is it to deny that very many later followers of Marxism have seen in their teaching a gospel of social justice and have been attracted to it for this very reason; Marxism has meant many things to many Marxists, just as have other millennial movements to their followers. My point is simply that the common image of Marx as a prophet of social justice is a false one and that those who have seen distributive justice as the main moral issue of his Marxism have been mistaken. In what follows I shall present the evidence for this thesis under three headings: direct testimony from Marx and Engels bearing on the question, their analysis of capitalist exploitation of labor, and their picture of the post-revolutionary society.

I

Originating in the first third of the nineteenth century in the teachings of Saint-Simon and Fourier in France and Robert Owen in England, modern European socialism displayed from the start a distributive orientation, a concern with the problem of distribution in society. This did not necessarily mean that the principle of distributive justice was uppermost in the thinking of socialists. For Saint-Simon and many later socialists, for example, the moral basis of socialism was not the ideal of justice but rather the ideal of human brotherhood or love. This was given classic expression in the socialist formula enunciated by Louis Blanc: "From each according to his ability, to each according to his needs." It was not a formula for distributive justice or equity, since the needs of individuals may be in inverse proportion to their abilities and to their contribution to society, and in any case they will normally differ from person to person. What the formula expresses, therefore, is an ethic of brotherhood.

Among some socialist thinkers of the nineteenth century, however, the distributive orientation was linked with an ethic of justice. Foremost among these was Marx's French contemporary, Proudhon. Taking issue with the Saint-Simonians and others who predicated their socialism upon an ideal of brotherhood, he argued that the slogan, "From each according to his ability, to each according to his needs," was proper for a family but not realizable as the operative principle of a larger society. For him the ethical starting point was the dignity of the individual. Not love of others but respect for their dignity as persons was the proper basis of morality. And the formula for morality was justice, defined as mutual respect for human dignity. The key concept was "mutuality" or "reciprocity." This philosophy, to which Proudhon gave the name "Mutualism," underlay his plan to reorganize society as a *fédération mutualiste* composed of occupational groups functioning on cooperative principles under a system of reciprocal service. "Mutuality, reciprocity exists," he wrote, "when all the workers in an industry, instead of working for an entrepreneur who pays them and keeps their products, work for one another and thus collaborate in the making of a common product whose profits they share amongst themselves." [6]

Proudhon laid the theoretical foundations for Mutualism in his first major work, *What Is Property?* (1840), which enunciated the doctrine that "property is theft." By "property," it should be explained, Proudhon did not mean individual possession and use of goods, including producer goods; this he called simply

[6] Quoted in Martin Buber, *Paths in Utopia* (1949), pp. 29–30.

"possession" and did not regard as theft. "Property" meant quite specifically the right of the possessor of producer goods to employ wage workers and draw profit from their labor. This profit, consisting of a portion of the proceeds of labor that rightfully belonged to the laborer himself, was "theft." Anticipating Marx, Proudhon also called the relationship just described one of "exploitation of man by man, or bondage." [7] In *What Is Property?* his prescription for the social problem was to preserve the right of possession while abolishing the right of property in the special sense just defined. This was the idea behind his later program for reconstituting society as a federation of autonomous producer cooperatives within which and among which the principle of reciprocity of service, i.e., exchange of services on the basis of reciprocal equality, would be realized.

Proudhonism proved an influential current in European socialist thought. Especially important was Proudhon's idea that the wage worker under capitalism was being robbed of something that rightfully belonged to him or that profit was theft. The obvious programmatic implication for socialists was the demand that the worker receive the "undiminished proceeds of labor." This and other similar slogans, such as "a fair distribution of the proceeds of labor," became increasingly prominent as socialist movements in Europe associated themselves with trade unionism and practical working class politics. In Germany the slogan of fair distribution was vigorously promoted by the influential socialist thinker and politician Ferdinand Lassalle and his followers. Their influence was reflected, for example, in the Gotha program, a program for a united German workers party that was drafted in 1875 and is now best known through Marx's posthumously published critique in a set of marginal notes privately written for the edification of the party leaders. One of the draft program's clauses reads: "The emancipation of labor demands the promotion of the instruments of labor to the common property of society and the cooperative regulation of the total labor with a *fair distribution of the proceeds of labor.*" [8]

Marx's attack on this clause forms an appropriate introduction to a review of his position on distributive justice. He was

---

[7] *What Is Property?* (1902), p. 257.

[8] *Critique of the Gotha Program,* in Marx and Engels, *op. cit.* (1951), II, 19. My italics.

incensed at the very idea that the German workers party should demand a "fair distribution of the proceeds of labor" as part of its program. "What is a 'fair distribution'?" he inquires acidly. Do not the bourgeoisie claim that the present mode of distribution is the only "fair" one, and are they not right in their own frame of reference? Nor can socialists agree among themselves as to the meaning of "fair distribution": "Have not also the socialist sectarians the most varied notions about 'fair' distribution?" [9] Going on in the same vein for several paragraphs, Marx finally breaks into a tirade. He declares that such slogans as "fair distribution," "equal right," and "undiminished proceeds of labor," which might have had some meaning at one time, have now become "obsolete verbal rubbish" which it would be a "crime" to force upon the party again. The German party's hard-won realistic outlook should not be perverted by "ideological nonsense about right and other trash so common among the democrats and French socialists." [10]

Though unusually violent in language, this denunciation of the distributive orientation was otherwise representative of the position that Marx and Engels had been upholding for decades in both their private correspondence and their published writings. They showed contempt for socialists who attempted to ground a critique of capitalist society in the principle of justice. "It is really very superstitious of the fellow that he should still believe in the 'idea of justice,' absolute justice," wrote Engels in a letter to Marx of December 2, 1861, commenting on a new book by Lassalle.[11] Marx, ridiculing Proudhon for applying an ideal of justice to economic relations, inquired:

> Do we really know anything more about the "usurer," when we say that his actions conflict with "eternal justice," with "eternal equity," with "eternal mutuality," and with other "eternal verities"—than the Fathers of the Church knew when they said that the actions of the usurer conflicted with the "eternal grace," with the "eternal faith," with the "everlasting will of God"? [12]

These statements accurately reflect the Marxist viewpoint as it emerges from the texts themselves. The writings of Marx and

[9] *Ibid.*, p. 20.
[10] *Ibid.*, p. 23.
[11] Marx and Engels, *Selected Correspondence 1846–1895* (1942), p. 128.
[12] *Capital,* trans. Eden and Cedar Paul (1933), pp. 59–60.

Engels over a period of fifty years contain a torrent of testimony that the principle of distributive justice is alien to the mental world of Marxism.

Much of this testimony is provided by the polemic that Marx and Engels carried on for many years against Proudhon and his concept of socialism, which they classified under the heading of "Bourgeois or Conservative Socialism" in the *Communist Manifesto.* It is true that *What Is Property?* played a momentous part in the mental evolution of Marx during the formative period of his system in the early 1840's and that he always professed admiration for this book.[13] However, in 1847 he published *The Poverty of Philosophy,* in which he declared intellectual war on the whole approach to social and economic problems in "the equalitarian system of M. Proudhon." The war went on without letup. Twenty-five years later Engels was still waging it in his anti-Proudhonian pamphlet *The Housing Question,* one of the themes of which is the fatuousness of Proudhon's ideal of "eternal justice" in a society of equal exchange among individual producers each receiving the full value of his labor. Rejecting the very idea of "eternal justice," Engels here states that justice is "but the ideologized, glorified expression of the existing economic relations, now from their conservative, and now from their revolutionary angle." For the Greeks and Romans, slavery was just; for the bourgeoisie of 1789, feudalism was unjust. It all depends on time, place, and socioeconomic circumstance. And, even if one were to grant that expressions like "right," "wrong," and "justice" are usable in everyday life in view of the simplicity of the relations discussed, they have no place in any scientific investigation of economic relations. To go on talking about the idea of justice in relation to economic matters, as Proudhon does, is to create the same hopeless confusion as would be created, for instance, in modern chemistry if the terminology of the phlogiston theory were to be retained. "The confusion becomes still worse if one, like Proudhon, believes in this social phlogiston, 'justice.' . . ."[14]

---

[13] For a discussion of the role of Proudhon's book in the mental evolution of Marx, see my *Philosophy and Myth in Karl Marx* (1961), pp. 108ff.

[14] *The Housing Question,* in Marx and Engels, *Selected Works, op. cit.,* I, 624–625.

II

Does Marx consider the capitalist system unjust and condemn it on this ground? To many it has seemed so, especially in view of the central part that the concept of exploitation plays in his system. Marxism defines capitalism as a way of production founded on the exploitation of wage labor for the accumulation of capital. "Exploitation" is a term that carries a conventional connotation of injustice. One party, the exploiter, receives more than is rightfully due him, and the other, the exploited, receives less. This, as noted above, was the position taken by Proudhon, for whom the exploitation of wage labor for profit meant theft or legalized robbery whereby the working man was deprived of part of the proceeds of his labor. It seems plausible to assume that Marx, who developed his own position in part under the influence of Proudhon's *What Is Property?*, understands "exploitation" in the same or a very similar way. But examination of the Marxist writings shows this to be a false assumption.

In his specific analysis of capitalist society, Marx formulates the theory of exploitation more concretely as a theory of surplus value. He starts here from the postulate of classical political economy that the exchange value of any commodity depends upon the amount of labor, or labor time, incorporated in it, labor being taken by Marx as the sole agent creative of exchange value. He then goes on to argue that labor power—which itself becomes a commodity under capitalism—has the peculiar attribute of creating more new exchange value in a day's use than it itself, economically speaking, is worth. What it is worth—its own exchange value as a commodity—is equal to the amount of labor incorporated in it, i.e., the amount of labor required to produce enough means of subsistence to maintain the worker in a fit state to work and to reproduce his kind. Briefly, the value of the worker's labor power for a day, as determined by the general law of value in capitalist society, is a subsistence wage. However, in a full day's work for the capitalist, the labor power so purchased creates an amount of new exchange value greater than this. The discrepancy, greater or less depending on the length of the working day, is called by Marx "surplus value." He depicts capitalism as a system of exploitation of labor power for the amassing of surplus value ad infinitum. This exploitative relation of capital to labor is said to constitute the very essence of the capitalist mode of production, and the proletarian revolution is seen as having the mission of abolishing exploitation forever. As Engels expressed it, "This exploitation is the basic evil which the social revolution wants to abolish by abolishing the capitalist mode of production." [15]

The question at issue here is whether a concern for justice underlies this value judgment. The objection to the affirmative view is that it flies in the face of the most emphatic and unequivocal assertions by both Marx and Engels that their condemnation of capitalist exploitation has nothing whatever to do with justice and injustice. They explain in this connection that the exploitation of wage labor for the accumulation of capital cannot be described as unjust. On the contrary, it is perfectly just or equitable in accordance with the only applicable norms of justice—those operative in the existing mode of production and exchange. Since the subsistence wage represents the full value of the worker's labor power as a commodity, he is not being robbed or cheated or treated unjustly when he receives less than the full produce of his day's labor as recompense. The labor time during which he creates surplus value for the capitalist rightfully belongs to the capitalist as the purchaser of a day's labor power of the worker at full value. In Marx's own explicit statement in *Capital:*

> It is true that the daily maintenance of the labor power costs only half a day's labor, and that nevertheless the labor power can work for an entire working day, with the result that the value which its use creates during a working day is twice the value of a day's labor power. So much the better for the purchaser, but it is nowise an injustice (*Unrecht*) to the seller.[16]

Having purchased the labor power for a day at full value, the capitalist, in other words, has every right to appropriate all the

[15] *Ibid.*, p. 558.

[16] *Capital, op. cit.*, p. 188. The same point was later made by Engels in practically the same words: "The circumstance that the value which the use of it [i.e., the labor power] during one day creates is double its own value for a day is a piece of especially good luck for the buyer, but on the basis of the laws of exchange of commodities by no means an injustice to the seller" (*Herr Eugen Dühring's Revolution in Science,* 1947, p. 305).

value that the exercise of the labor power for a day creates. This leaves open, of course, the issue of the exact length of the working day, and here, according to Marx, there is simply no determining what is right and just. The capitalist is merely exercising his right when he attempts to prolong the working day further, and the worker is exercising his when he resists: "Here we encounter an antinomy in which right conflicts with right, both of these rights being hallowed by the law of exchange of commodities. When two rights come into conflict, force decides the issue." [17]

The Marxist conclusion is that the wages of the worker under capitalism are all that he has any right to and that the surplus value appropriated by the capitalist is no more than he has a right to. The capitalist mode of distribution, as determined by the law of exchange of commodities in capitalist society, is entirely fair, just, and equitable in capitalist terms. But is there no standard of justice superior to the one implicit in the capitalist "law of exchange of commodities"? No general criterion of right by reference to which the capitalist exploitation of labor, although just enough on capitalist principles, might be pronounced unjust per se? The answer given by Marx and Engels is clearly and definitely negative. "Right," according to Marx, "can never be higher than the economic structure of society and its cultural development thereby determined." [18] "Social justice or injustice," according to Engels, "is decided by one science alone—the science which deals with the material facts of production and exchange, the science of political economy." [19] In short, the only applicable norm of what is right and just is the one inherent in the existing economic system. To each mode of production, its own mode of distribution and its own form of equity, and it is meaningless to pass judgment on it from some other point of view. Thus, capitalism for Marx and Engels is evil but not inequitable. They do not accept Proudhon's interpretation of exploitation. They do not admit that profit derived from wage labor under the capitalist system is "theft." We may therefore conclude that the Marxist condemnation of capitalism is not predicated upon a belief that its mode of distribution is unjust.

---

[17] *Capital, op. cit.,* 234–235.

[18] *Critique of the Gotha Program,* in *Selected Works, op. cit.,* II, 23.

[19] Marx and Engels, *Kleine Ökonomische Schriften* (1955), p. 412.

Turning now to the third area of evidence—the Marxist view of the post-revolutionary future—the question is whether Marx and Engels show a distributive orientation in their thinking about socialism or communism and, more concretely, whether they envisage the future communist society as a realm of distributive justice. Although they left no detailed prospectus of communism as a social system, material pertinent to this question is to be found here and there in their writings. The best known statement is Marx's in the *Critique of the Gotha Program,* where he draws the distinction between the two phases of communist society—the short transitional phase (later called "socialism" in the Marxist literature and the "higher phase" beyond it.

It is noteworthy that this *locus classicus* of the Marxist view of communism occurs in the context of Marx's angry attack, examined above, on the concept of "fair distribution." Having asserted that capitalist distribution is the only fair distribution under the capitalist mode of production and that the "socialist sectarians" are anyhow unable to say what a "fair distribution" would mean to them, Marx goes on to argue that in principle "bourgeois right" will still prevail during the first phase of communist society. Though production for profit will presumably have stopped, exchange will still be based on commodity equivalents: so much labor time in one form (labor) will be exchanged for an equal amount of labor time in another form (consumption goods). Furthermore, says Marx, the application of this essentially bourgeois standard of equality will make the first phase of communist society a realm of inequality, since individuals are unequal in native endowment and in needs. Thus individuals will receive equal recompense for periods of labor in which one works harder and more efficiently than another, and individuals with equal pay will be in unequal circumstances owing to differences of family status, and so on.[20]

---

[20] *Critique of the Gotha Program, op. cit.,* pp. 20–22. Engels made the same point in a letter to Bebel in 1875: "The notion of socialist society as the realm of equality is a superficial French idea resting upon the old 'liberty, equality, fraternity'—an idea which was justified as a *stage of development* in its own time and place but which, like all the superficial ideas of the earlier socialist schools, should now be overcome, for they only produce confusion in people's heads and more precise forms of description have been found" (Marx and Engels, *Selected Correspondence, op. cit.,* p. 337).

So much for the lower phase; what about the "higher phase" or true communist society? Here at last, according to Marx, it will become possible to transcend the "narrow horizon of bourgeois right." People will receive according to their needs. At this point Marx quotes, for the first and only time in his writings, the old French socialist formula, "From each according to his ability, to each according to his needs." As pointed out earlier, this is not a formula for justice. Nevertheless, it does connect the idea of communism with a principle of distribution. It injects a distributive theme into the discussion of communism. All the more significant, therefore, is the fact that, having done this, Marx immediately returns with great vehemence to the anti-distributive main theme of his argument. Dismissing the notions of equal right and fair distribution as obsolete verbal rubbish which it would be an outright crime to foist upon the party, he goes on, "Quite apart from the analysis so far given, it was in general a mistake to make a fuss about so-called *distribution* and put the principal stress on it." It was characteristic of "vulgar socialism" to give a presentation of socialism as turning principally on distribution; "why retrogress again?" [21] From all this it should be abundantly clear that Marx does not envisage communism as a realm of distributive justice and that, although he does refer on this one occasion to the well-known formula on distribution according to needs, communism, in his conception of it, does not turn principally on distribution.

III

The issue implicit in Marx's repudiation of the distributive approach goes to the philosophical core of Marxism. His contention that socialism or communism should not be conceived in fundamentally distributive terms concealed and, in a negative way, revealed his own positive conviction, rooted in the basic thought pattern of Marxism, that socialism or communism should be conceived primarily in terms of *production*. If a distributive orientation was characteristic of most socialist doctrines in the nineteenth century, a production orientation

---

[21] *Critique of the Gotha Program, op. cit.*, pp. 23–24.

was characteristic of Marx's. By this I mean that the central concern of Marxian theory, morally as well as intellectually, is with the mode of production, with man's activities as a producer, and with the conditions under which he carries on these activities. The theme of man as a creative being who expresses his nature in productive activities, foremost among which is economic activity or the production of material objects, is fundamental to Marxism from beginning to end.

This production orientation belongs to Marx's philosophical inheritance as a thinker of Hegelian formation for whom the doctrine of communism was part and parcel of a comprehensive theory of world history. The proof of this is available in the now published *Economic and Philosophic Manuscripts of 1844*, in which the young Marx set down a first systematic sketch of Marxism in terms of concepts and categories derived mainly from foregoing German philosophy. Elaborating what he conceived to be the hidden or "esoteric" import of Hegel's dialectic of history, he here constructed his own conception of history as a process of self-development of the human species culminating in communism. According to it, the species, which is represented at any one time in the totality of living individuals, develops itself in productive activities that externalize and materialize its productive potentialities or powers. Industry, for example, represents a huge complex of already materialized productive powers of the species, the human collective's tools of production. World history is thus pictured as basically a history of production (*Produktionsgeschichte*) in the long course of which the whole world of produced material objects that environ man emerges as the collective handiwork of the species. It is in this world-building productive activity, according to Marx, that the species develops and realizes itself. This he takes to be the scientific or "materialistic" restatement of the Hegelian position, which projects the history of production "upside down" as a history of mental production on the part of the world spirit.[22]

[22] For a detailed analysis of this "original Marxism" both in its relation to foregoing German philosophy and to the mature Marxism of Marx's and Engels' later writings, see *Philosophy and Myth in Karl Marx, op. cit.* An English translation of the manuscripts of 1844 is now available in Erich Fromm, *Marx's Concept of Man.*

Still following Hegel's basic scheme, Marx holds that the history of production has, thus far, also been a history of alienation (*Entfremdungsgeschichte*). Up to now man has always been "alienated" from himself or divided against himself in his producing activity, for this activity has always been performed in the service of the greed for accumulation, the acquisitive urge. It has therefore taken on the character of "labor" or "alienated labor," by which Marx essentially means forced or compulsive productive activity. Humanity's way of escape from alienation lies in the seizure and socialization of the world of private property in a proletarian communist revolution. Beyond this lies freedom, the emancipation of human creativity from the acquisitive passion, the transformation of labor into creative leisure and artistic self-expression. Man, fully matured and through industry repossessed of his once alienated powers of production, can at last realize his nature as a free, conscious producer. Communism is thus envisaged by Marx as the end or goal of the world-historical process of human self-development; it is the stage of man's self-realization, of the transcendence of his historic alienation. In the Hegelian terms used by Marx in the manuscripts of 1844, communism is the reintegration of man with himself, corresponding to the ultimate stage of Hegel's *Phenomenology* at which spirit returns to itself out of its alienation and comes to be "at home with itself in its otherness."

This "original Marxism" of the manuscripts of 1844 was the foundation of mature Marxism as elaborated in *The German Ideology* (1846) and other later writings of Marx and Engels. The basic production orientation prevails throughout. Human history is expounded in historical materialism as fundamentally a history of production. There is a succession of epochs each characterized by a particular "mode of production," which in turn is conditioned by a given set of "means of production" (i.e., state of technology) and associated with a given set of "relations of production" (i.e., property relations). In mature Marxism, moreover, the self-alienation of humanity or division of the producer against himself becomes the hostile "division of labor" in production into man the owner and man the producer—it turns into the class war. So the communist revolution, still conceived as a world-wide proletarian seizure and socialization of private property, is now said to have the mission of abolishing the division of labor in society, meaning first the division of society itself into owning and producing classes.[23]

Communism itself is still envisaged in terms of a fundamental transformation—which will result in human self-realization—of the mode of production. The capitalist mode of production, associated with modern machine industry as the principal means of production, is defined by Marx as wage labor for the creation of surplus value. Mature Marxism holds that the communist revolution, by destroying the division of labor in society into capitalists and workers, will eliminate wage labor itself as a mode of production. In other words, it will eliminate production for profit, for accumulation of capital, as a way of carrying on the human life of production, although, as noted above, Marx foresees that the wage system in a new form will continue briefly in the transitional phase of proletarian dictatorship. However, the ensuing "higher phase" of communist society is to be marked by the total "emancipation of labor" from all historic forms of division of labor and from the bondage, torment, and misery involved in each. Liberated from both the social division of labor into owning and producing classes and also from division of labor in the conventional sense of occupational specialization (which Marx also sees as a hateful and enslaving thing), man will achieve self-realization as a free creative being devoting himself to a multitude of productive life activities for the sake of the aesthetic satisfaction they afford him. This is Marx's conception of communism. He alludes to it in the very passage of the *Critique of the Gotha Program* that contains the well-known reference to distribution according to needs. In the "higher phase," he says, the "enslaving subordination of the individual to the division of labor" will have ended, and labor will have become "not only a means of life but life's prime want." [24] This was the vital part of the passage for Marx.

All this lies in the background of Marx's opposition to the distributive orientation and the idea of justice. Regarding the problem from the point of view that has just been briefly sum-

[23] Marx and Engels, *The German Ideology* (1939), pp. 67, 69, 74.
[24] *Critique of the Gotha Program, op. cit.,* p. 23.

marized, he could not help but consider it crass, vulgar, superficial, and simply wrongheaded for a socialist to put the emphasis on the distributive aspect or espouse justice as a social ideal. For Marx the basic and burning issue was the life of production. What made capitalism evil and condemned it to death before the *Vehmgericht* of history was the anti-human character of wage labor itself as a way of leading the life of production. The crime for which the existing order deserved capital punishment by its executioner the proletarian was the dehumanization of man under a division of labor that transformed his productive activity into "labor torment," that reduced him in the factory to a mere fragment of a man bound to some minute, mindless operation endlessly repeated. And, by the same token, what made communism appear so desirable to Marx was the revolution of the mode of production and therewith in the state of man the producer, that, as he saw it, would inevitably result from the coming proletarian upheaval and abolition of private property on a world scale. Freed from his age-old imprisonment in the division of labor, which had reached its most intolerable extreme in the capitalist stage of history, man could and would finally become fully human. He would achieve self-fulfillment in his essential role as a producing animal. The new mode of production, marking the maturity of the race after the long painful development in history, would be akin to art. Naturally men would now have enough to eat and generally be released from material worries. But this was not the essential thing, for the main content of man's life was producing and not consuming.

Given this notion that the basic evil of the existing order resided in the mode of production, it naturally seemed senseless or worse to Marx for socialists to complain about inequities of distribution. First, the low rate of pay, the great disparity of reward between capitalist and worker, was but one of many symptoms of the situation that needed correcting. As such, however, it was inherent in a system of production that subordinated everything to the one overriding aim of accumulation of capital out of surplus value, hence nothing much could be done about it on this side of world revolution. Further, even if some small improvements in pay and working conditions—such as the ten-hour day in England—could be wrested from the capitalists, these represented palliatives rather than a real solution or the beginning of one. No mere rectification on the distributive side could make the evil mode of production tolerable. Moreover, to suggest the contrary, as was done by those socialists who called for "fair distribution of the proceeds of labor," was to run the risk of disorienting the proletarians, of sidetracking their spontaneous revolutionary strivings and tendencies into the pathways of piecemeal reform within the present order. Such slogans were calculated to sow in the workers' minds the illusion that their problems could be resolved and their suffering alleviated without a fundamental revolutionizing of the mode of production. From Marx's point of view, therefore, the distributive orientation ultimately pointed the way to treason to the revolutionary cause. His fears on this score were, of course, well grounded, as was shown by the later evolution of social democracy in Europe.

The ground of Marx's aversion to the idea of justice is now not far to seek. The idea of justice connotes a rightful balance in a situation where two or more parties or principles are in conflict. It typically involves an adjustment or settlement based on a delimitation of mutual claims. Now, for socialists to raise the cry of justice with reference to economic relations in capitalist society was to imply that a rightful balance might be struck or an adjustment reached in the conflict between capital and labor. It was to suggest the possibility of a negotiated peace or, at any rate, armistice in the warfare between capital and labor. This was anathema to Marx. As he saw it, there was no possibility of settling this conflict, no way of achieving a delimitation of mutual claims between these two antagonists. The civil war in modern society was a battle unto death. The only possible formula for peace was the total victory of labor and the total destruction of capital as a social force. To Marx's mind, therefore, socialists like Proudhon who preached social justice were misguided and dangerous men. They were misguided because they failed to see the irrelevance of the idea of justice to the social problem, the inconceivability of any adjustment of claims or settlement of the conflict in modern society short of a revolution of the mode of production. And they were dangerous because this inclined them to pursue (in the phraseology of a later age) a no-win policy in the class struggle instead of a policy of victory looking to the establishment of total peace in the classless society.

Marx's issue with Proudhon over the idea of justice may be seen, ultimately, as an issue over unity and conflict in human society. Proudhon was opposed in principle to a search for unity in society. He argued that contradiction, that is, conflict or antagonism, is the first law of the universe and that justice or mutuality is the principle of balance or equilibrium of antagonisms. Borrowing the Hegelian dialectical categories of thesis, antithesis, and synthesis, he defined justice as the reconciliation of opposing claims in a higher synthesis. This, for example, was his approach to economic problems in *The System of Economic Contradictions, or The Philosophy of Poverty,* to which Marx responded in 1847 with his scathing attack, *The Poverty of Philosophy,* and with repeated attacks in later years. And in these attacks Marx specifically assailed the dualistic or pluralistic idea at the base of Proudhon's philosophy of social justice.

"M. Proudhon," he says, "has of the dialectic of Hegel nothing but the language." He has only the "sacramental formula." [25] He has failed to comprehend the real meaning of the dialectical idea, which looks to the overcoming of all dualism, all contradiction. Proudhon, says Marx elsewhere apropos of the same point, is the true petty bourgeois. He is "composed of On The One Hand and On The Other Hand. . . . It is so in his morals, in everything. He is a living contradiction." Further, "one finds with him a *dualism* between life and ideas, soul and body, a dualism which recurs in many forms." [26] This is the nub of the issue. Proudhon's philosophy of justice is dualistic in essence. It assumes that antagonistic duality, situations of conflict between two parties or two principles, are inherent in life, especially in social life, and it looks to the establishment of equilibrium, to a delimitation of mutual claims. Marx, too, sees that human life is shot through with situations of conflict, with *Lebenskollisionen,* as he sometimes calls them. Unlike Proudhon, however, he regards this fact as profoundly abnormal, even

[25] Marx, *The Poverty of Philosophy* (n.d), pp. 115, 122.

[26] Marx and Engels, *Selected Correspondence, op. cit.,* pp. 17, 176.

intolerable, and his prescription, accordingly, is radically opposed to Proudhon's:

> In his desire to reconcile the contradictions, Monsieur Proudhon does not even ask himself if the basis of those contradictions must not itself be overthrown. . . . All he is looking for is a new formula by which to establish an equilibrium between these forces.[27]

To Proudhonian justice as equilibrium of antagonisms, Marx opposes revolution as abolition of antagonisms. He wants to overthrow the "basis of those contradictions," to uproot conflict at the source, to eliminate the conflict situation. His philosophy expresses a search for unity—for a world beyond all antagonisms and therefore beyond justice as equilibrium of them.

---

[27] *Ibid.*, p. 16.